D1572194

Critical Essays on

JOHN HAWKES

CRITICAL ESSAYS
ON
AMERICAN LITERATURE

James Nagel, General Editor
Northeastern University

Critical Essays on
JOHN HAWKES

edited by

STANLEY TRACHTENBERG

G. K. Hall & Co.
BOSTON, MASSACHUSETTS

Library of Congress Cataloging-in-Publication Data

Critical essays on John Hawkes / edited by Stanley Trachtenberg.
      p. cm.—(Critical essays on American literature)
   Includes bibliographical references and index.
   ISBN (invalid) 0-8057-7304-4 (alk. paper)
    1. Hawkes, John, 1925-   —Criticism and interpretation.
  I. Trachtenberg, Stanley. II. Series.
PS3558.A82Z63   1991
813'.54—dc20

                                      91-12129

The paper used in this publication meets the minimum requirements of
American National Standard for Information Sciences—Permanence of Paper
for Printed Library Materials, ANSI Z39.48-1984.

Printed and bound in the United States of America

For Stephen and Francine Trachtenberg

Contents

◆

INTERVIEW

ESSAYS

General Editor's Note

◆

This series seeks to anthologize the most important criticism on a wide variety of topics and writers in American literature. Our readers will find in various volumes not only a generous selection of reprinted articles and reviews but also original essays, bibliographies, manuscript sections, and other materials brought to public attention for the first time.

Critical Essays on John Hawkes is a comprehensive collection of essays on one of the most important modern writers in American literature. It contains a sizable gathering of early reviews as well as a broad selection of more modern scholarship. Among the authors of reprinted articles and reviews are Joan Didion, Thomas LeClair, Roger Sale, David W. Madden, Robert Scholes, and Albert J. Guerard. In addition to a substantial introduction by Stanley Trachtenberg there are four original essays commissioned specifically for publication in this volume, new studies by George P. E. Meese, Carol MacCurdy, Patrick O'Donnell, and Donald J. Greiner. We are confident that this book will make a permanent and significant contribution to the study of American literature.

JAMES NAGEL
Northeastern University

Publisher's Note

◆

Producing a volume that contains both newly commissioned and reprinted material presents the publisher with the challenge of balancing the desire to achieve stylistic consistency with the need to preserve the integrity of works first published elsewhere. In the Critical Essays series, essays commissioned especially for a particular volume are edited to be consistent with G. K. Hall's house style; reprinted essays appear in the style in which they were first published, with only typographical errors corrected. Consequently, shifts in style from one essay to another are the result of our efforts to be faithful to each text as it was originally published. In *Critical Essays on John Hawkes,* the possessive of *Hawkes*—with or without the additional *s*—appears as it did upon initial publication in the reprinted essays and appears with the *s* in essays original to this volume.

Acknowledgments

◆

I am grateful to Texas Christian University for granting me a leave during which I was able to complete this project, and to the staff of the Mary Couts Burnett Library and, in particular, Joyce Martindale of the Interlibrary Loan Department for their unfailing courtesy and help. For support of another kind, I am deeply beholden to Stephen and Francine Trachtenberg, to whom this book is dedicated.

STANLEY TRACHTENBERG

Introduction

◆

STANLEY TRACHTENBERG

For more than four decades John Hawkes has continued variously to startle, mystify, outrage, and challenge readers, chiefly in a body of lyrical, hallucinatory novels that reject the conventional elements of plot, character, and setting—Hawkes has called them "enemies" of the novel—while taking a darkly comic view of the human psyche. With no assurance of drawing upon some level of general agreement about Hawkes's place in American literature, to say nothing of agreement on his meaning, criticism has seldom been confined exclusively to analysis. With Hawkes, perhaps more than with any other contemporary figure, critics have felt the obligation to defend or attack not only the work under consideration but frequently the validity of Hawkes's approach to fiction—his conviction that art must risk going to extremes in resisting the at once repressive and exclusionary impulses of conventional morality. Perhaps as a consequence of this aesthetic vision, critics have felt compelled to defend or attack even the writer himself. Hawkes's uncompromising stand against the conventions of mimetic fiction has consistently resulted in the charge that his novels are not accessible and that he appears to take too much satisfaction in the darkness of the vision he presents. Even while acknowledging the brilliance of Hawkes's first novel, *The Cannibal*, reviewers complained of the difficulty its style presented. In a brief notice, the *New Yorker* critic described Hawkes's writing as "cold, brilliant, and cryptic," while Robert Gorham Davis in the *Partisan Review* observed that "Hawkes's vision is really so alien to our normal experience that the reader cannot grasp it readily."[1] The critic for the *New Statesman* noted that "For all his obscurities [Hawkes] uses language and imagery with such hypnotic power that if you can take him at all, you are engulfed to the point where plot and meaning seem almost immaterial."[2]

Although the difficulty of Hawkes's earlier work, while not entirely overcome, has given way over time to works generally felt to be more accessible, the initial acclaim, unusual for a writer just starting out, has never broadened into popular acceptance. Hawkes had already published four novels when Leslie Fiedler pointed out that he was probably "the least read novelist of substantial merit in the United States," and though Fiedler was surely overstating the case, Hawkes remarked more than fifteen years later that "there is probably a strange conspiracy, conscious or not, to keep my work from getting real public attention."[3]

Accessibility requires that readers are able to locate themselves in relation to the world of the narrator, which is to say to its fundamental assumptions about value. It requires as well that events be connected to one another; that they occur as a consequence of what has led up to them and in turn serve as the motive for what follows; that they take place in some recognizable sequence forward or back, or even side to side; and finally that they reflect the conditions or circumstances that make up an identifiable sense of place. Hawkes's fiction has seldom provided these reassurances.

If his fiction has frequently been regarded as inaccessible, however, Hawkes himself clearly has not been, and in a succession of interviews he has tirelessly attempted to explain just what it is he has tried to do in his novels and what he has not. Unlike many authors who would rather have their work felt than analyzed, Hawkes feels it is worthwhile to talk about fiction.

> I don't like those writers who *know* they are writers, who never talk about their work because it's beneath them. They leave all that to the dull critic. Well, I simply deplore that attitude. I think that once a fiction is done, you should try to keep apprehending it, to understand it. And it may change, I don't know. I by no means feel totally secure in my terms of what I've written. I want to explore it as much as other people, and I want to expose whatever I can that went into the process of writing it. I feel it's probably helpful, in some way or other. I am pleased to talk about fiction.[4]

He is also pleased to listen. In an early interview with John Enck that remains one of the most comprehensive statements of the author's intention, Hawkes remarked, "I happen not to share the contempt for literary or academic criticism which appears to be current now. . . . I won't pretend not to be affected by newspaper reviews—in this area I'm easily outraged and just as easily pleased—but despite some of the silences and some of the more imperceptive or hostile responses, I have the impression that reviewers and readers alike in America are becoming increasingly receptive to original work."[5]

Despite its dreamlike quality, Hawkes's writing is not as chaotic as the world he depicts. "My own writing process," he observes, "involves a constant effort to shape and control my materials as well as an effort to liberate fictional energy" (Enck, 148). The connections he provides are more pictorial than discursive; the linkages of image and symbol (horses and photography often serve here, as do colors) or of repetitive motif and thematic cluster often express the simultaneously liberating and destructive nature of sexuality. Yet despite the example set by many of the most prominent writers of the twentieth century, the modern reader continues to find himself unprepared for Hawkes's spatial forms.

Expressing his belief in "the absolute need to create from the imagination a totally new and necessary fictional landscape or visionary world," Hawkes suggests the qualities that make his fictional landscape: "As a writer I'm concerned with innovation in the novel, and obviously I'm committed to nightmare, violence, meaningful distortion, to the whole panorama of dislocation and desolation in human experience" (Enck, 142). Although Hawkes finds such qualities in both American and European literature, he identifies the beginnings of the fiction that most interests him in the "comic brutalities" of the early Spanish picaresque writers and later in the "comic appetite for invented calamities" of Ferdinand Céline (Enck, 141). Hawkes expands the list of writers with whom he feels the closest affinity to include the British picaresque novelist Thomas Nashe, Nathanael West, Flannery O'Connor, James Purdy, and Joseph Heller—writers in whom he sees a "quality of coldness, detachment, ruthless determination to face up to the enormities of ugliness and potential failure within ourselves and in the world around us, and to bring to this exposure a savage or saving comic spirit and the saving beauties of language" (Enck, 143–44). It is this comic approach along with the redemptive aspects of language that Hawkes thinks critics initially overlooked in favor of the grotesque and nightmarish qualities of his work. "Comic distortion," he insists, "tells us that anything is possible and hence expands the limits of our imaginations. Comic vision always suggests futurity, I think, always suggests a certain hope in the limitless energies of life itself" (Enck, 146).

Although comedy has been recognized as an important element in Hawkes's fiction, the main outlines of what would continue to be the central critical issues in Hawkes's writing deal more with the author's surrealistic technique and the psychological matter it projects. Hawkes has himself underscored the importance of this concern. "The writing of each fiction," he told Patrick O'Donnell, "is a taking of a psychic journey; the fictions, themselves, are a form of journey."[6] The journey, it turns out, is at least as much for revenge as for discovery—revenge, Hawkes acknowledges, for the deprivations and terrors of his own childhood and also, in a Jungian sense, of humanity's.[7] His novels are thus uniformly marked by violence and an often perverse sexuality that have made his work unpalatable to many. To take just one example, Joseph Epstein found the The Passion Artist at once horrifying and boring and described the writing as too "psychically claustral" to be erotic. Epstein felt the novel's loving preoccupation with the representation of sexual repression and the consequent exploitation of women that it ostensibly sought to expose resulted in an obscene book that could have been written only by an author "bred in an English department."[8]

Hawkes does not seek to exploit his subjects for the sake of shock alone, but he may see it as necessary to unsettle the reader's comfortable assumptions about life and the fictive strategies through which life is at its deepest levels engaged. "My work," Hawkes has insisted, "is an effort to expose the worst in us all, to cause us to face up to the enormities of our terrible potential for betrayal, disgrace, and criminal behavior. I think that it is necessary to destroy repression while showing at the same time that the imagination is unlimited."[9]

Not only acts of revenge, then, Hawkes's novels are also acts of rebellion, as Donald Greiner points out; in fact, his fictive forms can be seen to parallel the protest he makes against the repressive absurdities of conventional morality.[10] "I want my fiction to destroy conventional morality and conventional attitudes," he has claimed. "That's part of its purpose—to challenge us in every way possible in order to cause us to know ourselves better and to live with more compassion."[11]

Compassion is a theme that Hawkes continues to come back to. "We need to know what it is to feel compassion for the most vicious people," he told one interviewer. "That's why my fiction is poised, as it is, between the detestable and the sublime."[12] In another interview he defends himself as a "comic compassionate writer, one who considers the art of fiction is intended to extend the compassion of its reader and the reader's sexual and imaginative perceptions of himself."[13] Compassion alone, however, does not confer imaginative authority for Hawkes. Commenting sympathetically on the compassion and directness he finds in Carson McCullers, he distinguishes the humor in her treatment of the material of childhood fantasy from the more ruthless fictions of Flannery O'Connor, which similarly have been labeled gothic (Enck, 146–47).

Hawkes has been careful to discourage an equation between his life and his art, and between any mimetic representation of life and art. Commenting on what he describes as the essentially topical nature of the Beat writers' rebellious posture, for example, Hawkes finds no evidence of artistic upheaval. "I don't like soft, loose prose or fiction," he remarked, "which tries to cope too directly with life itself or is based indulgently on personal experience" (Enck, 144). The absence of mimetic or representational clues with which the reader can orient himself in the narrative is in part a reflection of Hawkes's insistence on the imaginative element in his fiction. "I don't like autobiographical fiction," he explained, "I don't write in order to use up my life as its source."[14] On the contrary he has insisted, "I want whatever I create out of words to be clearly an artifice."[15]

This stance has not resulted in metafiction. Neither Hawkes's narrative voices nor the characters whose adventures they describe ever suppose themselves to belong in some level of reality other than the one in which they exist, and though Hawkes's novels often explore the unreliability of narration and the relation of art to experience, such explorations are seldom the ostensible subject of the narrative. The difficulties his fiction presents, however, are not limited to stylistic or even structural displacements. Even the imagination is subject to the same uncompromising scrutiny Hawkes brings to more conventional attempts to repress it and the truths it reveals. Accordingly, his novels also reveal the price of imagination and rarely allow the reader a secure place from which to view events or a confident moral position from which to judge them. Focusing on *Charivari,* George Meese examines the rhetorical strategies that provide the basis for such judgment. Among those strategies, Meese identifies the use of an apparently sympathetic but actually condemning narrator. Through this device, he claims, Hawkes strives to generate in the reader a "reverse sympathy" with those excluded by conventional social standards. Though Hawkes succeeds in dramatizing the human impulse to create art through imagination, Meese concludes, the lack of moral options in his work makes questionable his commitment to a sympathetic view of the human predicament and leaves unresolved whether Hawkes's sensuous rhetoric serves larger issues or becomes an end in itself.[16]

In spite of this difficulty and what he calls the lack of human dimension in Hawkes's novels, Bruce Bawer complains that Hawkes is nonetheless regarded as a visionary writer, and that his reputation has been promoted exclusively by a "fan club" of academics who consistently bemoan the fact that Hawkes's work has not received the widespread acceptance it deserves.[17] But where Bawer sees in the development of Hawkes's fiction an increasingly prurient, even totalitarian vision that refuses to distinguish between virtue and evil, more responsible critics have found an alternative to the constraints of realism. Comprehensive full-length studies by Donald Greiner and Patrick O'Donnell offer unusually perceptive syntheses of Hawkes's work. In the absence of realistic devices, Greiner notes, Hawkes offers "unreliable narrators, created landscapes, lyrical language, a mixture of comedy and terror, and finally a parody of the novel form itself." O'Donnell sees Hawkes's approach to fiction as "detached, humorous, and ironic," and finds his true subject to be "the imagination and consciousness of the artist."[18]

In an early review that says a good deal about the period in which Hawkes first began to write, Wallace Markfield identified in The Cannibal a "sense of desolation as terrifying as anything in modern literature." Markfield also recognized that the ludicrous, macabre images in the novel serve only to intensify the reader's sense of horror, and he concluded that, though preoccupied with filth and decay, Hawkes succeeds in achieving the truth of his material through these distortions.[19]

More ambivalent, Vivian Mercier finds in The Cannibal a "strange mingling of realism and surrealism" that confronts some "comic-strip Germans" with "sharply visualized, though unreal, horrors." Mercier points out that this cartoon quality is echoed but improved in The Beetle Leg, a "comic-strip Western" whose vernacular style suggested "some of Al Capp's grotesque, wry humor." Comparing Hawkes's style to Faulkner's extended conversations, which depend on knowledge gained over time and on the listener's shared regional background, Mercier says the difficulty Hawkes's disconnected fictions present lie in their drawing upon a complex mythic understanding that resists interpretation on the literal level.[20]

It is the recognition of this shared sense of nightmare that Joan Didion observes in The Lime Twig, a novel whose hallucinatory quality she describes admiringly as "every waking wish carried to its logical extreme."[21] Also emphasizing the psychological aspects of Hawkes's novels, Claire Rosenfield attributes the response he has elicited from the public to the force with which he projects the terror of the hidden self. Through his subtle control of symbolism and his use of novelistic distortion, she maintains, Hawkes evokes the hallucinations of nightmare—the obsessive fantasies that readers can only obliquely recognize that they carry within themselves.[22]

In terms of fictional technique, critics have not always recognized the elaborately pictorial devices that Hawkes employs to structure his uncompromising posture. For Stanley Edgar Hyman, the decomposing world of Hawkes's nightmare vision lends a shapelessness to the fiction itself. In his retrospective assessment of Hawkes's early novels, Hyman finds spiritual as well as political fables and identifies affinities with Faulkner as well as Kafka, but he objects to what he sees as the fallacy of imitative form.[23] It is precisely this style, however, that Susan Sontag feels really *is* the story: After the publication of *Second Skin,* Sontag wrote that she considers Hawkes "one of the half dozen authors of the first rank in America today."[24]

Apart from its stylistic considerations, most critics have commented on the cheerfulness in *Second Skin* that breaks through for the first time in Hawkes's work, and Hawkes himself has remarked on the relative accessibility of this watershed novel, which he claims both approaches and parodies the conventional novel.

> I have always thought that my fictions, no matter how diabolical, were comic. I wanted to be very comic—but they have not been treated as comedy. They have been called 'black, obscene visions of the horror of life' and sometimes rejected as such, sometimes highly praised as such. In *Second Skin* I wanted to be sure, first, that the comedy would be unmistakable. Second, I wanted to use some of the fictional methods that I have become increasingly aware of—mainly the first-person narrator—so I used a first-person narrator who is a fifty-nine-year-old ex-naval Lieutenant, Junior Grade, a rather ineffectual man, who comes out of a world of suicide . . . undergoes all kinds of tribulations and violations and by the end of the novel, I think we do have, in effect, a survivor.[25]

Part of Hawkes's comedy in *Second Skin* is the result of his gentle mockery of the first-person narrator, Skipper, who has evolved from Hencher in *The Lime Twig* and who overcomes, through his stubborn insistence on the principle of love, the death that marks all of his relationships. If Skipper's affirmation is willed, constituting a triumph of the artificial over the natural, it indicates a refusal to accept victimization as definitive, especially victimization of the human by the naked and treacherous reality of nature.[26]

Neither humor nor affirmation are found by Roger Sale to be elements of *The Blood Oranges,* the first of a triad of novels Hawkes wrote in the 1970's devoted to the theme of sexuality and the liberating power of the erotic imagination in opposing prudery and social taboos. Commenting critically on the novelist's "nightmare vision," Sale finds the novel to be "the work of a contemptible imagination" for which people do not matter and in which the representation of cruelty and horror are not so much parodied or even simply depicted as unacknowledged and voyeuristically indulged.[27] Sale's review prompted a spirited response from writer Gilbert Sorrentino, who takes a generally negative view of criticism as a profession. For Sorrentino, it is precisely the artifice of the novel, that is to say the distance between the first-person narrator and the authorial judgment its excesses reveal, that provides the sort of critique Sale requires. Granting the possibility of distance, Sale replies that no judgment illuminates the meanness of the narrator in *Blood Oranges,* indicating his belief that such self-conscious deliberations about narrative stance, whether internal or critical, obscure the moral discoveries the novel must define.[28]

For Hawkes, however, such judgment is far from the point. Defending Cyril, the narrator in *The Blood Oranges,* who he insists is innocent of the dissolution with which the novel ends, Hawkes points to the absurd death of one of the characters who opposes Cyril's ambition. That accidental death was a means by which he attempted to trick the reader into believing a moral judgment had been made on the multiple relationships in the novel. "I had hoped most of all," Hawkes insists of *The Blood Oranges,* "to write this novel in the tradition of high comedy."[29] Explaining the exaggerations of perception in the novel as expressions of the narrator's comic imperfections, Hawkes claims, "My sympathies are all with Cyril. I don't see any way to argue that he is reprehensible. I do not think he is a manipulator. . . . It seems to me that he is a god of love, a kind of eros."[30]

In *Death, Sleep, and the Traveler,* the second novel in the triad, many of the same themes of sexual sharing, guilt, abandonment, and death recur, but here there is little question of Hawkes's return to nightmare. Writing in 1974, the same year the novel was published, Hawkes maintains that he is no longer interested in writing comic novels. "I'm wary now of the 'safety' inherent in the comic form," he explains. "From now on I want to come still closer to terror, which I think I'm doing in the short novel I'm trying to write at the moment."[31] For Celia Betsky the displacement of psychic actuality, which lent substance to the violence and horror pictured in Hawkes's earlier surrealistic writing, by the more realistic sexual wars described in *Death, Sleep, and the Traveler* results in the loss of much of the novel's significant truth about human nature. "Hawkes becomes so involved in thinking up dreams for his hero," she writes, "that he forgets to give anyone the life that inspires them."[32] Donald Greiner argues that for such fictive conviction, it is necessary to shift from the literal level of the narrator's exploration of orgasm and death to the fictive process by which that exploration is described.[33] The shifting perspectives of narrative consciousness allow the novel to support alternative interpretations— that the narrator Allert is insane and writing of his experiences from a mental institution is one, that his ocean voyage is real but his experiences are suicidal psychic distortions, another. In either case, the narrator's inability to understand that his preoccupation with self-gratification has led to the failure of his marriage and to the endless wandering to which he is condemned.

In *Travesty,* the last novel in the triology, this preoccupation has more fatal consequences for the narrator, Papa, who does consciously what Allert does unconsciously.[34] Tony Tanner acknowledges the multiple interpretations that *Travesty* invites and approvingly describes Hawkes as "perhaps the most 'disturbing' contemporary American writer." In *Travesty* he attributes that disturbance largely to the absence of any reliable indications of how the novel is to be read. As in the two other works in the trilogy, Tanner finds that this novel is "marked by that dark circuitous lyricism" and by "nameless landscapes each marked by that hallucinatory vividness that Hawkes so magically dilutes from geographical anonymity," and he concludes that *Travesty* is one of the author's most remarkable fictions.[35] Attempting to reconcile the opposing fictive polarities of "design and debris," Papa drives his automobile, carrying with him his daughter and her lover (who is also the lover of Papa's wife), into a stone wall. Thomas LeClair finds that Hawkes's attempt at "suicide as high art, the crafted event without a message" comes off as only the minor work of a major novelist, and that Papa is a travesty of Hawkes's earlier narrators, nevertheless the novel provides a welcome coda to the trilogy while allowing Hawkes to parody some of the more exaggerated elements of his own fiction.[36]

From the first-person narrators of the trilogy, Hawkes returns in *The Passion Artist* to a third-person account—that of a satyr-figure, Konrad Vost, whose willed innocence in the face of encounters with "cruel, vicious women" Karen Osborne regards as part of a "painful journey to liberation." Describing the novel as an erotic education that should become a classic, Osborne places it along with Djuna Barnes's *Nightwood* and the novels of D. H. Lawrence as a work that puts mythic materials into the service of a "powerful, organic irony" and that provides a "vision of an Eros reborn out of the chaos and destruction men and women have wreaked upon each other."[37] Valerie Brooks places Hawkes in the tradition of Kafka and Hesse, "with a propensity for the macabre that might make Edgar Allan Poe shudder." Brooks complains, however, that in *The Passion Artist* Hawkes's didactic if exquisite writing results in a novel without recognizable characters or emotions that leaves the reader with surreal, often sexual images that never take on substance.[38]

Stanley Trachtenberg identifies sexual liberation as the theme of *Virginie: Her Two Lives,* in which Hawkes's treatment marks something of a departure from his earlier fiction. The central figure is a precocious eleven-year-old whose journals—wide-ranging in time and space—limit the narrative to the way a child might see things. Accordingly, though the point of view allows Hawkes to employ techniques of disintegration—linking scenes by repetition rather than progression, by related imagery, recurring circumstances, and symmetrical patterning—the novel does not explore psychic processes, but rather the ways in which they are projected. The reader is not in the heroine's mind Trachtenberg maintains "but in her story."[39]

The central importance of storytelling is also recognized by most reviewers of *Adventures in the Alaskan Skin Trade,* Hawkes's next novel and one in which he attempts to distance the highly autobiographical elements by making the narrator a woman. The result may be seen to rework the father-daughter relationships Hawkes treated in *Second Skin* from the point of view of the daughter. Nonetheless Jack Beatty, at least in partial disparagement, says the novel refers to nothing outside itself. "Sound and rhythm, the music of writing, is what Mr. Hawkes is interested in here," Beatty concludes in his review, "not in plot, character, psychology, society, history or the cosmos." As a consequence he finds the novel, like its setting, Alaska itself, "cold, grand, and all but empty."[40] Terrence Rafferty also finds the novel's prose self-indulgent and the self-conscious narrative shapeless and slow-moving, but he was impressed by the adventurous spirit conveyed in the author's not always successful mimicry of the tall-tale tradition of the American novel, which, Rafferty maintains, strongly influenced Hawkes's literary generation.[41] In contrast, Bob Halliday, who describes the novel as "a real page-turner" says it is Hawkes's "most moving and accessible novel yet." Underneath its true subject—"the irrational reality that lies under the surface of things"—Halliday finds the novel to be a psychological study of "a disturbed father-daughter relationship" that ends with a liberation from guilt and the self-acceptance of the central character.[42]

Although in one reviewer's judgment *Adventures in the Alaskan Skin Trade* lacks the "startling revelation of depths [and] extraordinary images" found in Hawkes's best novels, critical opinion of the novel has been generally favorable.[43] Most agree that it is among Hawkes's most accessible novels. Robert Taylor regards it as his finest book since *Second Skin,* while Elliot Krieger was persuaded that the novel should finally give Hawkes the public recognition he deserves.[44] A thematic unity is identified by Rob Swigart, who sees the disappearance and death that serve as the focus of the narrative as metaphors, like Alaska, for "the challenging wilderness within." For Swigart, the solution to the mystery at the center of this high-spirited novel allows its heroine to deal with the loss of her father and to tell her own tall stories to gain a sense of self-awareness and an independent identity.[45]

Questions of representation figure prominently in *Whistlejacket,* which, Patrick McGrath notes, deals with the correspondence of photography and painting (one of the novel's central figures is a photographer, another a painter known for the amazing accuracy of his portraits of horses). While McGrath finds the destruction of the father's authority is projected in both the novel's formal discontinuities and its thematic revelations, it is the correspondence of painting and photography that frames the central "sexuality and nightmare violence" (revolving around Hawkes's familiar image of the horse), so that the novel is made to "address its own anatomy and architecture."[46] A less favorable view of what she terms the "fetishistic allure of art" is taken by Wendy Steiner, who observes that "there is not one novel by Hawkes that does not equate women and art as manipulated objects of observation." Although she finds the formula by now tired, what redeems it from pornography in *Whistlejacket* is the successful revolt against the male compulsion "to beat down the maddened fetish—woman or horse or art" and the aesthetic perception that allows Hawkes to penetrate the "prurience of interpretation."[47]

The postmodern concern for the "unreliability of signs and the uncertainty of seeing" becomes in Donald Greiner's reading of *Whistlejacket* a demonstration of the true artist's process of creation—a process of "first deconstructing and then reconstructing" an object, rather than the photographer's "striving for only accurate descriptions of surfaces." By exercising firm control of tone, sign, and language to undercut the narrative that relies on plot, Hawkes, Greiner points out, updates the technique he employed as early as in *The Cannibal* to merge fictional character and historical personage. Like the figure of George Stubbs, the painter-hero of *Whistlejacket,* Hawkes is thus able to reveal the exterior of his subject—the ambiguous multivocality of the narrative itself—from the inside out.[48]

In his pioneering study, Albert J. Guerard, in whose fiction writing classes at Harvard Hawkes wrote his first two novels, stresses Hawkes's stylistic control, particularly in the discrimination of the narrative voice, the fine modulations of tone, and the ironic use of syntactic displacement and pause. Hawkes's novels, Guerard feels, reveal a progression from "murky, groping, brilliant, eccentric expression to deliberate rhetorical manipulation of the reader's anxieties and sympathies." The sudden syntactic shifts, straight-faced interpolations of cliché, love of pyrotechnic display, and sheer inventiveness of the early novels are, by *The Lime Twig,* Guerard concludes, subordinated to story, theme, and vision.[49]

For James Green, Hawkes's nightmare landscapes are invested with an ironic reality that denies the innocence normally associated with dream. Focusing on the novella *Charivari,* Green identifies the recurrent images, actions, and mythic allusions as satiric devices that Hawkes employs to redeem the fairy tale from a childlike view of sexuality and to give form to his vision of the sterility of the modern age and the fundamental problems of human existence.[50] John Graham also resists the notion that Hawkes's novels are chaotic and points to the controls of observation and social structure that the author imposes in *The Cannibal* to compel the reader to resist all authority at all costs.[51] In a somewhat jargon-laden study that focuses on the reader's participation in Hawkes's rhetorical strategies, Thomas Armstrong leans heavily on an approach to the text he derives from the dialectic analysis of Paul De Man. Armstrong uses the example of *The Cannibal* to explore the discourse about language that "at once creates a world and continually reveals it as fictional." The reader is accordingly encouraged "to interiorize the rhythm of [a] passage even while rejecting its contents" and to acknowledge the shifting levels of the novel's narration.[52]

Among the techniques perhaps most frequently remarked upon in Hawkes's fiction is that of parody, whose ironic possibilities David Madden has identified in Hawkes's second novel, *The Beetle Leg,* where the author substitutes "repetition, suffocation, and finally paralysis" for the linear action of the traditional Western novel. Madden sees the prevailing image in the novel as a wasteland against which the dream of progress is converted into a nightmare of banality and exhaustion that is itself destroyed and that destroys its inhabitants.[53] Hawkes suggests the intent of the novel in the image of a character rescuing a dead human fetus from a flood. The act of examining the fetus before putting it back in the water Hawkes regards as "an analogue for what I think the artist ought to be able to do. We should feel a strong attachment to human life even in its most frightening forms."[54]

A static quality of narrative, a "defiantly remote" literary style, and a "refusal to create psychological complexity in his characters," are, for Lucy Frost, all characteristic of Hawkes's early novels. Nonetheless Frost finds dramatic vitality in the tension the novels generate between language and subject matter and in the comic spirit that informs them. Frost sees in *The Beetle Leg* the verbal equivalent of landscape painting, one which reveals an ironic vision of a disintegrating American culture patterned on the myths of Adam's fall and a new Eden, but which also enables Hawkes to fuse minimal movement with the timeless quality of the novel's striking images.[55] Alan Heineman, who also sees myth and symbolic dimensions as unifying elements in *The Beetle Leg,* finds implicit allusions to such classic American novels as *The Scarlet Letter, Huckleberry Finn, Moby Dick,* and *As I Lay Dying.* Within the family dynamic around which the novel centers, Heineman finds the dangers of repressed psychic lawlessness and a parodic treatment of such themes as fertility myths, the myth of the fall and redemption, Darwinian evolution, and the myth of the American West.[56]

Despite Hawkes's wish to dispense with plot, character, setting, and theme, Robert Scholes contends that, as his work has developed, Hawkes has "turned more and more to the unifying voice of a single narrator as a way of giving coherence to the events of his narrative." In moving from an emphasis on death and terror to a "lush eroticism," Hawkes immerses the reader in the abhorrent—projected in *The Owl* as a repressive fascism—only to expose and liberate the psychic realities "habitually concealed by habits of vision attuned only to the surface itself."[57]

For Leslie Fiedler, Hawkes's willingness to confront this dangerous psychic terrain instead of following the safe experimentalism for which modern fiction had settled, accounts in large measure for the neglect his work has continued to receive. In his somewhat contentious introduction to *The Lime Twig,* Fiedler describes Hawkes as a Gothic novelist whose achievement he attributes in part to the illusion of formlessness that Hawkes creates. Hawkes, Fiedler contends, employs a discontinuous style and indistinct contexts that nonetheless reveal that the final terror around which the novel is centered is that which emerges from the varieties of love.[58] Examining literary allusion in *The Lime Twig,* John Warner finds evidence of a mythic theme—the archetypal quest—internalized to reveal continuity with the early romantics. Warner draws on Harold Bloom's description of the two basic phases of this quest in which the double figure of the artist-hero initially adopts a Promethean involvement in and subsequently a relative disengagement from the world of the imagination.[59] Lawrence K. Boutrous sees the ambivalence in *The Lime Twig* more as a consequence of Hawkes's parodic treatment of the thriller and the detective story; Hawkes attempts to de-mythify the novel's subjects by scrambling character types and leaving all questions unanswered. Boutrous argues that Hawkes's fragmented, disjunctive narrative helps to destroy the unity of perception, extending the parodied genres by holding in suspension the elements of destruction and hope.[60]

Robert Edenbaum similarly sees *The Lime Twig* ending on a triumphant note. Edenbaum compares Hawkes to Nathanael West, in both of whom the reader finds a comic treatment of violence emerging from a fantastic landscape rooted in sexuality, a "horribly knowing innocence," and a "fondness for crossed expectations, so that, for example, the apparently deadly turns out to be harmless and the apparently harmless deadly." Unlike the horror in West's fiction, however, Hawkes's use of the "demolishing syntax of the devil" leaves intact human creativity as well as its destructiveness and this ultimately allows his characters' fantasies to turn into redemptive and so fulfilling action.[61]

Perhaps none of Hawkes's novels has provoked more critical disagreement than *Second Skin,* a reaction prompted, in part, by the author's insistence on the "truth of the fractured picture."[62] Focusing exclusively on *Second Skin,* John Graham assembled a useful selection of reviews, interviews, and essays, many of which were previously unpublished. Among the new essays are Lucy Frost's discussion of the techniques of juxtaposition and recurrence, William Robinson's examination of literary allusion as a structuring element of the novel, and Stephen Nichols's study of Skipper as an author dedicated to creation.[63] In addition to issues of unity and structure, much of the controversy surrounding the novel centers on the reliability of the narrator. Anthony Santore's view of Skipper as a menace who refuses to acknowledge his own impotence and possible homosexuality, and whose comic affirmation is based on self-deception, represents one extreme, closely followed by Thomas LeClair, who calls attention to Skipper's unreliability and hypocrisy and terms him a figure of "perverse, self-willed innocence."[64] In tracing the origins of the novel to Hawkes's story "The Nearest Cemetery," John Kuehl sees its dominant mood as one of "bitter-comic irony," whose most pervasive symbolism is associated with death.[65]

In adopting a contrasting view of Skipper, Ronald Wallace's emphasis on the comic aspect of the novel's distortion comes closer to the intention Hawkes has expressed. In addition to pointing to parallels with the mood of *The Tempest,* Wallace finds in Skipper a comic ambivalence whose innocence he places in the tradition of Dickens's Pip, Henry James's Maisie, or Joyce's Stephen Dedalus. Wallace argues that Skipper's humorous misinterpretations both heroically expose his humorous society and reflect the comic values of life, peace, integration, grace, and love.[66]

The attempt to discover unifying patterns in Hawkes's disjunctive form leads Norman Lavers to conclude that *Second Skin* deliberately exaggerates the archetypal formula that critics such as Leslie Fiedler or Richard Chase use to define the American novel, and that Hawkes does this to locate his work in the tradition of pastoral romance. Lavers finds that the principles of love and hate make up the structuring opposition of the novel, and he identifies in Skipper's triumph the passivity of a Christ figure.[67] Paul Witherington proposes parody as an alternative structuring principle of the novel. Suggesting that Skipper uses the secondary characters as a means of transference for his ambivalent sexual feelings, Witherington calls attention to the difference between Skipper's myopic celebration of his role as victim and the author's "witty and multilayered voice."[68] In another psychologically oriented study, Carey Wall concludes that in describing the psychological tensions that structure the novel, Hawkes destroys the easy distinctions between violence and love. Skipper's gradual understanding of the close relationship between those two forces, Wall concludes, forms the basis for the structure of the novel.[69] For Bruce Bassoff the unifying notion of *Second Skin* rests in the sacrificial act by which a godlike yet victimized and self-deceived Skipper transcends the violence of the novel and transforms it into good.[70]

That sacrificial figure, according to Patrick O'Donnell, becomes the artist who, like Prospero in *The Tempest,* magically transforms destructive or demonic objects through the exercise of imagination and the transformative power of language.[71] Donald Wineke also identifies Shakespearean parallels in *Second Skin,* whose double time-scheme supports a comic structure that Wineke finds at least as important as the novel's parodic elements.[72] For Mary Robertson, the comedy of *Second Skin* emerges in the play of language and the deliberate displacement of signs. Using terms drawn from Derrida, Robertson argues that Hawkes's style, at once intimate and distancing, employs discrepancies in syntax and voice, the ironic use of erasure, and the sense that any sign is a "supplement" to the idea it is intended to express and thus indicates a difference from it. Through these techniques, Robertson says, Hawkes preserves the contradictions of the text as possibilities and thus ensures its "undecidability."[73]

Although Hawkes has insisted on the comic impulse of *Second Skin,* commentators such as Richard Yarborough have looked to classical Greek tragedy to find the origin of the novel's violence and the narrator's attempt to redeem his history from an avenging fate, with Skipper substituting imagination for an understanding of his condition. Yarborough draws additional parallels in the novel between the immature narrator's use of language and John Berryman's *The Dream Songs,* in which the protagonist similarly manipulates memory into art in an attempt to deal with death. In his reply to Yarborough, Hawkes questions the view that Skipper mythologizes death. Describing

Skipper as an androgynous figure, and as such self-sufficient, Hawkes insists that despite all his weakness, Skipper is supposed to "embody the strength of knowing that there is nothing in the world except what he creates and the figures he discovers in his creation."[74] Hawkes replies as well to Ron Imhoff's examination of the unconventional structure of *Second Skin*. Where Imhoff maintains that Skipper attempts to establish himself as blameless, Hawkes indicates his intention to make Skipper a fully culpable narrator.[75]

Hawkes defends the detached approach that his novel seems to adopt toward emotional destructiveness, distinguishing destructiveness from indifference and linking *Second Skin* to his triad of novels—*The Blood Oranges, Death, Sleep, and the Traveler,* and *Travesty*—that focus on the situation of the artist, a theme that has informed his fiction since. "I think," Hawkes told Patrick O'Donnell, "many of the figures of my novels—Skipper and Sonny, Cyril and Hugh, Allert—are in some sense or other, benign or malignant versions of the artist."[76]

In four short plays Hawkes wrote between *Second Skin* and *The Blood Oranges,* Carol MacCurdy discovers evidence of just such a thematic interest. For MacCurdy these relatively minor works reveal an increased use of dramatic conflict not present in Hawkes's early fiction. In this dramatic form, Hawkes was able to work out his self-admitted preoccupation with innocence and its relationship to the imagination. Reversing the conventional notions of morality, the plays afford significant insights into a theme that evolves as central to his aesthetic.[77]

In the trilogy that followed the plays Enid Veron finds a comic design that she traces as a progression from the high comedy of *The Blood Oranges* to the low burlesque of *Death, Sleep, and the Traveler* and *Travesty*. The idyllic festival of *The Blood Oranges,* Veron argues, is transformed into farce in the subsequent two works, whose buffoonlike central figures argue for pornography and link sexuality with voyeurism and death. Ultimately, Veron concludes, king and scapegoat come together in a single figure that, through Hawkes's technique, compels us to laugh at our own ridiculousness.[78]

Paul Rosenzweig questions the role of aesthetics in the triad, where the central figures' attempts to impose order and so control experience result in a distortion of reality.[79] Dissolving the "traditional discrimination between man's unconscious fantasies and conscious acts," *The Blood Oranges, Death, Sleep, and the Traveler,* and *Travesty* mask the deviant and self-serving psychology of each narrator behind a facade of detached objectivity, only to reveal the narrator's fundamental impotence both in sexual life and in the face of death. In a companion essay that discusses *The Passion Artist* along with the trilogy, Rosenzweig notes the shift in Hawkes's work to more explicit sexuality, structural unity, traditional plot, and narrative self-consciousness, all of which reflect a stylized attempt at increasing narrative control. He argues that the third-person narration in *The Passion Artist* validates the central character's theories in a way that the first-person narrations of the triad do not. Rosenzweig finds that the novel exerts the very control over the material that the story repudiates, and concludes that Hawkes's increasing self-consciousness as an artist parallels the novels' increasing identification with the narrators and their visions, rather than indicates an awareness of the ironies implicit in the formal tensions of the novels.[80] John Guzlowski focuses on *Death, Sleep, and the Traveler* where, he maintains—as in the fiction of Thomas Pynchon, William Gaddis, and John Barth—Hawkes creates characters who reverse the traditional device of a sea voyage as a means of exploring the unconscious by masking their inner conflicts rather than confronting them.[81]

The attempt to control our psychic life without becoming lost in fantasy or divorced from experience is also the subject of an essay by Brenda Wineapple, who sees in Hawkes's novels a parallel with Hawthorne's cautionary tales of artistic isolation. Wineapple looks at *The Lime Twig,* in which the central figure attempts to create order through a sacrificial act rather than through the perspective of art, and at *Travesty,* which "exalts a 'pure' language." In Hawkes's fiction, Wineapple contends, the reader finds that language divorced from experience represents a confusion of art and life, and the pursuit of the abstract constitutes a travesty on both. "Too much control," Hawkes demonstrates "is as dangerous as too little." Wineapple concludes that Hawkes, like Hawthorne, links the actual and imaginary not by confusing art with experience but by opening a perspective through which each is able to draw upon and so enlarge the other.[83]

Two somewhat parallel approaches to *The Blood Oranges* appear in studies by Lois A. Cuddy and John V. Knapp. Cuddy places the novel in a pastoral tradition that holds in suspension the polarities of innocence, whose natural outcomes are sexual fidelity and marriage, and the possibility for erotic experience. Although Hawkes does not resolve these opposing ideas, Cuddy claims, they are ultimately collapsed into a concern with the darker aspects of experience and a "pastoral of the self."[83] Knapp regards *The Blood Oranges* not only as an expression of the lyric mode that looks to *Twelfth Night,* Milton's *Lycidas,* and Wallace Stevens, among other influences, but also as an intensely moral fiction in the manner of Plato's *Phaedrus.* Examining its patterns of imagery and the relations of the characters in several key scenes, Knapp concludes that Hawkes's intention was "to create a 'new' morality to supplant the outworn asexuality or a moribund Christianity," a morality in which sex and death are made to coexist.[84]

C. J. Allen deals with the difficulty of the moral stance of Hawkes's psychic journeys by displacing the destructive impulse in the trilogy with the imaginative act of the artist. The need for pattern and the narrator's attempt to objectify it, which begins with *The Blood Oranges,* is sublimated in a lack of conscious awareness in *Death, Sleep, and the Traveler,* whose narrator, Allert, does not understand or will not acknowledge his own motivation. A return to a highly conscious artistry is evidenced by the unnamed narrator of *Travesty,* who turns Cyril's tapestry of love into a "tableau of chaos" with his plans to crash his car and its passengers into a brick wall. The fascination with patterns, particularly as expressed in a sexual foursome, thus not only repeats the themes of the earlier novels but burlesques them as well.[85] *Travesty*'s claustrophobic violence is seen by Charles Baxter as an attack against the reader, who must learn the games invented by the author, particularly those involving "the imagination's moral powers." By deliberately withholding motivation, causality, and meaning, Baxter maintains, Hawkes imprisons the reader within a text that disregards the moral order of the outside world in order to elicit an innocent response rather than an agressive one of criticism or understanding.[86]

For William Van Wert, the exposure of unconscious needs and fears in the three novels reflects the movement from children's fears to adult fantasies. In another particularly suggestive reading, Charles Berryman finds in Hawkes's Gothic settings, poetic style, unity of effect, and unreliable narrators— especially as they appear in *Travesty*—close parallels to Edgar Allan Poe.[87] Hawkes's fiction increasingly reveals an affinity with Poe's ontological explorations of dream and death and their sexuality, as well as with Poe's treatment of the themes of fact and imagination, innocence and corruption, psychic division (doubling), and, perhaps above all, the conjunction of comedy and terror, which, as Poe claimed, went much deeper than Gothic conventions to reach the soul.

Seeing *Travesty* as an "inside narrative" whose events take place "within the teller's visionary imagination" is an idea developed by Donald Greiner, who contends that Papa, the narrator, is a composite of all of Hawkes's earlier storytellers. Greiner describes the narrative and the Papa's identification with the possibly imaginary characters within it as an expression of the desire for unity of erotic life and death. At the same time, Hawkes's control of the novel balances the chaos of the narrator's suicidal journey, pushing to its limits Hawkes's conviction that "imagined life is more sustaining than remembered life."[88]

In Hawkes's relation to the text and, in particular, to the innocence of narration, Heide Ziegler finds a form of fictional autobiography. Examining two of Hawkes's novels, *The Blood Oranges* and *Virginie: Her Two Lives,* Ziegler offers a poststructural reading that finds a development from an unselfconscious omniscience to an unreliable narrative posture. By *Virginie,* Ziegler contends, Hawkes explores the impossibility of storytelling to arrive at a postmodern form of the novel in which "character becomes the language of the text itself." Commenting on one another, Hawkes's novels increasingly abandon the posture of innocence, ultimately to reveal within the text the presence of an artistic consciousness.[89]

One of sixteen contributions to a 1983 special number of the *Review of Contemporary Fiction* devoted in part to Hawkes, Ziegler's essay confirms the continuing interest of European critics (several of whom also contributed essays to this volume), largely with a textual emphasis. Of particular note are the intricately argued essays of Marc Chénetier, Christine Laniel, and André LeVot, all three of which examine deconstructive acts of discourse in Hawkes's fiction. In Chénetier's dense study of the syntax and imagery of inscription in *Second Skin*, the circularity and doublings of the text ultimately yield the detachment of signs from objects and allow Skipper to neutralize desire. Writing of "the dead end of language" in *Travesty*, Laniel insists that while it exposes the self as "only the product of an ambiguous, treacherous, fraudulent flow of words," Hawkes's language achieves a metaphoric or poetic quality "creative only inasmuch as it is self-destructive." LeVot demonstrates the proliferation of signs without signification and the consequent dismantling of communication in *The Cannibal*, whose "choppy syntax without hierarchy or perspective" and dreamlike logic he regards as an example of the "post-apocalyptic imagination."[90]

A focus on the storytelling quality of Hawkes's fiction is also adopted by Patrick O'Donnell, who sees in *Adventures in the Alaskan Skin Trade* the author's regression to his textual past. O'Donnell identifies the theme of the novel as the paradoxical consequences of gender displacement on the search for identity. He maintains that Hawkes generates this paradox by multiple displacements through which he appears to "separate himself from the original, distinct authorial presence he has inscribed and signed in contemporary American letters, as well as to re-inscribe that presence, thus 'intertextualizing' it."[91]

Hawkes's technique is the subject of W. M. Frohock's study of violence in the early novels. Summarizing a number of the plots, Frohock points to Hawkes's strategy of supressing the information about motive or point of view on which the reader conventionally depends to understand events. Frohock locates this "technique of secretiveness" squarely in the experimental traditional of American writing and demonstrates Hawkes's use of rhetoric and syntax to expand the potentialities of the novel form itself.[92]

Marred by occasional though painful misreadings, Wayne Templeton's examination of Hawkes's novels through *The Passion Artist* emphasizes a synthesis of realism and fancy that informs the development of such themes as sexual sterility, victimization, and estrangement of modern society, and the connection between imagination (as it is expressed through art) and life. Although he acknowledges the sometimes convoluted style or strained narrative posture Hawkes adopts, Templeton admires the treatment of universal human relationships, the cinematic use of images, and the masterful if plotless interweaving of situations.[93]

The significance of Hawkes's fiction was signaled as early as 1963 by a special issue of *Critique* devoted equally to his work and that of John Barth, with which it has frequently been linked. Noting the dissimilarities in these two difficult writers, Alan Trachtenberg found they had both abandoned the traditional social novel in favor of more a more personal fable that in Hawkes's case takes the form of a haunting and dreamlike attempt to impose psychic order on a world marked by physical decay and spiritual decomposition.[94] (The issue of *Critique* also contained Albert J. Guerard's study of Hawkes's prose style, an analysis by Charles Matthews of Hawkes's fiction from *The Cannibal* to *The Lime Twig,* an essay on *The Cannibal* by D. P. Reutlinger, and a bibliography of Hawkes's works up to *The Lime Twig* by Jackson Bryer, containing an extensive listing of the reviews of Hawkes's first six novels.[95])

Parallels between Hawkes and Barth have also been drawn by Thomas LeClair, who focuses on *The Passion Artist* as part of a general assessment of Hawkes's work and career. Quoting Hawkes's stated goal of creating in the novel "a man who is more unsympathetic than any other character I've created and to make the reader share in artistic sympathy with him by the end of the novel," LeClair sees the central figure, Konrad Vost, as "the ultimate prisoner, like Hawkes's other characters captive of his childhood and repressions, his innocence and unconscious." LeClair concludes that the novel is about the liberation of women from the private obsessions that make up male sexual repression, and the imaginative transformations that allow Vost to transcend his victimization.[96]

In separate essays, Melvin Friedman compares Hawkes with two other writers he regards as central to American fiction since 1950, William Styron and Flannery O'Connor, neither of whom he judges as being as experimental as Hawkes. Friedman finds in Hawkes and O'Connor a common interest in the fiction of Nathanael West as well as in creating Gothic "landscapes of violence" and in "playing with such opposites as innocence and perversion, the sacred and the sexual." Although Friedman is reluctant to label either writer a *choisiste,* he notes that both share a "fascination with the surface of objects and acknowledge the importance of 'things.' Hawkes's baroque experiments with first-person narrative are contrasted with O'Connor's understated third-person narratives. In his feeling for the possibilities of language, however, Hawkes's debt is acknowledged to the French symbolists and to the fiction of Beckett and Joyce.[97] Friedman also finds a French connection in Hawkes and Styron. For Styron it rests in the French New Novelists Robbe-Grillet and Butor and in such existentialists as Camus; for Hawkes, in the symbolist poets and in the novelists Lautréamont and Céline. (In the latter's *Journey to the End of the Night,* Friedman finds a possible source for the title *Second Skin.*) Where Styron remains for Friedman a traditional storyteller, however, Hawkes "continues to grope for new forms and narrative possibilities."[98]

In an important survey of anti-realist writers, Albert J. Guerard links Hawkes with Jerzy Kosinski in showing how " 'psychology' functions in anti-realist rhetoric." Although Guerard contrasts Kosinski's overdetermined handling of sexual materials with Hawkes's condensations and displacements, he finds in both writers (though more noticeably in Hawkes), an "intense uncontrived correspondence between a deteriorated, literally menaced and menacing observed outer world and an inner world of childhood fears still wonderfully alive."[99]

In 1976 Hawkes shared another issue of *Critique*, this time with Vance Bourjaily. The issue contained the essay by John Knapp noted earlier, along with studies of *Death, Sleep, and the Traveler* by Donald Greiner and by Elisabeth Kraus, and a selected bibliography by Daniel Plung.[100] An important collection of essays and conversations, *A John Hawkes Symposium: Design and Debris* edited by Anthony C. Santore and Michael Pocalyko, constitutes the papers presented at an academic conference held at Muhlenberg College in Allentown, Pennsylvania, in April 1976. In addition to the essays by Veron and Graham already noted, this collection contains ten other pieces, several of which focus on narrative theory. James Frakes examines the anonymous narrative voices in Hawkes's first four novels and concludes that although there is no progression toward celebration or compassion, there is a recognition of the uniqueness of the individual. In a densely argued essay, Robert Steiner traces the archetypal figure of the storytelling traveler, whose use of the confessional mode in Hawkes's narrative results in decomposition and in a "literalness of contradiction" in which "the knowledge of loss is the essential element." Frederick Busch identifies the image of a sunken ship in a Hemingway short story as a powerful influence on Hawkes's imagination, ultimately emerging in *Death, Sleep, and the Traveler*, where it suggests the risk a writer undertakes in too-self-consciously allowing his life and early writing to surface in his work. The collection also contains an interview by Nancy Levine, one by the editors, a conversation between Hawkes and Albert J. Guerard,[101] and an examination of the opposition of Hawkes's aesthetic strategies of composition to his satiric intent by Marcus Klein that focuses on *Travesty*.

In an earlier study Klein, acknowledged the apocalyptic nature of Hawkes's vision but viewed his fiction predominantly in terms of comic satire that draws upon social and historical circumstances outside the invented landscapes.[102]

In his early full-length study, Frederick Busch focuses on the mythic elements and on the dominant imagery (largely animal) in Hawkes's novels through *The Blood Oranges*. The book includes one of the few discussions of *The Innocent Party*, Hawkes's collection of plays.[103] Another useful treatment of formal patterns and images is found in John Kuehl's *John Hawkes and the Craft of Conflict*, which demonstrates that a central conflict in Hawkes's fiction is the tension between Thanatos and Eros.[104] Finally, no survey of Hawkes scholarship would be complete without mention of Carol Hryciw-Wing's invaluable bibliography of primary and secondary sources through *Adventures in the Alaskan Skin Trade*, which contains useful annotations of each item and includes listings of reviews, interviews, and biographical material.[105]

Although Hawkes continues to receive some critical notice each year, the number of essays devoted to his work seems to have diminished from the high point during the 1970s. Hawkes's uncompromising explorations of the complex relation between aesthetics and ethics, and his insistence on the need for a sympathetic acknowledgment of what is most troubling and therefore most deeply concealed in human experience, have resulted in an artistic integrity critics frequently mistake for moral indifference. Hawkes does not unmistakably establish the laws by which the dislocation of his created landscapes may be understood, which is to say by which the characters within it operate. His world, like the psychic tensions it depicts, is subject to the innocence and the deceptions of the sexually charged imagination. Like John Updike or Philip Roth, two figures who surprisingly suggest parallels that invite further study, Hawkes explores the erotic as the source of a moral force. Deciding "the three most important subjects are consciousness, the imagination, and the nature of woman," Hawkes explains that he sees writing as "an act of eroticizing the landscape."[106] And though unlike more realistic writers Hawkes has concentrated on describing a psychic landscape, he is always aware of the importance of technique in structuring the imagination. "It isn't that I want any of Joyce's godlike omniscience," he told Patrick O'Donnell. "It's just that I want whatever one creates out of words to be so clearly something made, so clearly an artifice."[107] Perhaps because of the difficulties that artifice presents, recognition of his achievement to date continues to fall far short of what is demanded by his importance in American literary history and by the careful balance of poetic and novelistic methods that Hawkes brings to the development of innovative fiction.

Notes

1. "Books Briefly Noted," *New Yorker* 28 (28 January 1950): 85. Robert Gorham Davis, "Fiction Chronicle," *Partisan Review* 17 (May–June 1950): 522.
2. Janice Elliott, "Ice-cold," *New Statesman* (25 October 1968): 552.
3. Leslie A. Fiedler, introduction to John Hawkes, *The Lime Twig* (New York: New Directions, 1961), viii. For Hawkes's remarks see "'A Trap to Catch Little Birds With': An Interview with John Hawkes," in Anthony C. Santore and Michael Pocalyko, eds., *A John Hawkes Symposium: Design and Debris* (New York: New Directions, 1977), 171.
4. Roger Sauls, "I Am Pleased to Talk about Fiction," *New Lazarus Review*, Spring 1978, 6.
5. John Enck, "John Hawkes: An Interview," *Wisconsin Studies in Contemporary Literature* 6 (Summer 1965): 144–55. Hereinafter cited parenthetically in the text. Also appears in this volume.
6. Patrick O'Donnell, *John Hawkes* (Boston: Twayne, 1982), 2.
7. Sauls, "I Am Pleased to Talk about Fiction," 6.
8. Joseph Epstein, "Too Much Even of Kreplach," *Hudson Review* 33 (Spring 1980): 106.
9. Thomas LeClair, "The Novelists: John Hawkes," *New Republic* (10 November 1979), 27.
10. Donald Greiner, *Understanding John Hawkes* (Columbia: University of South Carolina Press, 1985), 8
11. John Hawkes, "Hawkes and Barth Talk about Fiction," *New York Times Book Review*, 1 April 1979, 31. (This exchange originally occurred at the University of Cincinnati on 2

November 1978 and is reprinted with some added material in *Anything Can Happen: Interviews with Contemporary American Novelists,* Tom LeClair and Larry McCaffery, eds., (Urbana: University of Illinois Press, 1981), 9–19.

12. Sauls, "I Am Pleased to Talk about Fiction," 10.

13. Adrianne Calfo and Richard Burgin, "A Conversation with John Hawkes," *New York Arts Journal,* November 1979, 8.

14. Andrew Fielding, "John Hawkes Is a Very Nice Guy, and a Novelist of Sex and Death," *Village Voice,* 24 May 1976, 47.

15. Robert Scholes, "A Conversation on *The Blood Oranges* between John Hawkes and Robert Scholes," *Novel* 5 (Spring 1972): 205.

16. George Meese, "Sensuous Rhetoric: John Hawkes's *Charivari.*" This essay was written expressly for this volume and is published here for the first time by permission of the author.

17. Bruce Bawer, "John Hawkes's Fan Club," *New Criterion* 3 (November 1984): 70–78. Reprinted in Bruce Bawer, *Diminishing Fictions: Essays on the Modern American Novel and Its Critics* (Saint Paul: Graywolf Press, 1989), 221–33.

18. Greiner, *Understanding John Hawkes,* 163. Patrick O'Donnell, *John Hawkes* (Boston: Twayne Publishers, 1982), 23.

19. Wallace Markfield, "Three First Novels," *Commentary,* April 1950, 392.

20. Vivian Mercier, "Moyenageux," *Commonweal,* 2 July 1954, 323. Also appears in this volume.

21. Joan Didion, "Notes from a Helpless Reader," *National Review,* 15 July 1961, 22. Also appears in this volume.

22. Claire Rosenfield, "John Hawkes: Nightmares of the Real," *Minnesota Review* 2 (Winter 1962): 249–54.

23. Stanley Edgar Hyman, "The Abomination of Desolation," *New Leader,* 30 March 1964, 24–25. Also appears in this volume.

24. Susan Sontag, "A New Life for an Old One," *New York Times Book Review,* 5 April 1964, 5.

25. John Graham, "John Hawkes on His Novels: An interview with John Graham," *Massachusetts Review* 7 (Summer 1966): 459.

26. Stanley Trachtenberg, "Counterhumor: Comedy in Contemporary American Fiction," *Georgia Review* 27 (Spring 1973): 40–42.

27. Roger Sale, "What Went Wrong?" *New York Review of Books* 21 October 1971, 3. Reprinted as "Hawkes, Malamud, Richler, Oates," in the author's *On Not Being Good Enough: Writings for a Working Critic* (New York: Oxford University Press, 1979), 30–32, 41. Also appears in this volume.

28. This exchange accompanied Sale's review, *New York Review of Books,* 21 October 1971, 36.

29. John Kuehl, "Interview," in his *John Hawkes and the Craft of Conflict* (New Brunswick, N.J.: Rutgers University Press, 1975), 169–72.

30. Paul Emmett and Richard Vine, "A Conversation with John Hawkes," *Chicago Review* 28 (Fall 1976): 168.

31. John Hawkes, "Notes on Writing a Novel," *Triquarterly* 30 (Spring 1974): 111.

32. Celia Betsky, "Author in Search of a Myth," *The Nation,* 18 May 1974, 630–31.

33. Greiner, *Understanding John Hawkes,* 121.

34. Emmett and Vine, "A Conversation with John Hawkes," 171.

35. Tony Tanner, review of *Travesty, New York Times Book Review,* 28 March 1976, 23–24.

36. Thomas LeClair, review of *Travesty, The New Republic,* 8 May 1976, 26–27.

37. Karen Osborne, review of *The Passion Artist, University of Denver Quarterly* 11 (Spring 1976): 137–38. Also appears in this volume.

38. Valerie Brooks, review of *The Passion Artist, Saturday Review*, 5 January 1980, 52.

39. Stanley Trachtenberg, "Perverse Charades," *Dallas Times Herald*, 27 June 1982, P4. Also appears in this volume.

40. Jack Beatty, "Uncle Jake and the Mosquito-Crazed Prospector," *New York Times Book Review*, 29 September 1985, 9.

41. Terrence Rafferty, "Postmodern Maladies," *Nation*, 16 November 1985, 496–98.

42. Bob Halliday, "Father and Daughter," *Washington Post Book World*, 29 September 1985, 5–6. Also appears in this volume.

43. William Veeder, "A Surprising Feminist View from Hawkes," *Chicago Tribune Book World*, 29 September 1985, 39.

44. Robert Taylor, "Tales of Alaskan Derring-Do and a Frozen-Out Family," *Boston Sunday Globe*, 13 October 1985, 91. Elliot Krieger, "Hawkes: Brown's Star Novelist," *Providence Sunday Journal*, 22 September 1985, Arts/Leisure section.

45. Rob Swigart, "A Great Bear of a Novel That Shakes You Up," *San Francisco Sunday Chronicle*, 22 September 1985, Review section.

46. Patrick McGrath, "Violent Horses and Violent Dreams," *New York Times Book Review*, 7 August 1988, 11.

47. Wendy Steiner, "Obscured Objects of Desire," *Times Literary Supplement*, 31 March 1989, 343.

48. Donald J. Greiner, "The Photographer's Sight and the Painter's Sign in *Whistlejacket*." This essay was written expressly for this volume and is published here for the first time by permission of the author.

49. Albert J. Guerard, "The Prose Style of John Hawkes," *Critique* 6 (Fall 1963): 19–29. Also appears in this volume.

50. James L. Green, "Nightmare and Fairy Tale in Hawkes' *Charivari*," *Critique* 13, no. 1 (1971): 83–95.

51. John Graham, "On *The Cannibal*," in Santore and Pocalyko, eds., *A John Hawkes Symposium*, 38–49.

52. Thomas Armstrong, "Reader, Critic, and the Form of John Hawkes's *The Cannibal*," *Boundary 2*, 5 (Spring 1979): 829–44.

53. David W. Madden, "The Unwinning of the West: John Hawkes's *The Beetle Leg*," *South Dakota Review* 19 (Autumn 1981): 78–91. Also appears in this volume.

54. Santore and Pocalyko, "'A Trap to Catch Little Birds With,'" 182.

55. Lucy Frost, "The Drowning of American Adam: Hawkes' *The Beetle Leg*, *Critique* 14 (1973): 63–74.

56. Alan Heineman, "'It Is a Lawless Country': Narrative, Formal, and Thematic Coherence in *The Beetle Leg*," *Review of Contemporary Fiction* 3 (Fall 1983): 136–48.

57. Robert Scholes, "John Hawkes as Novelist: The Example of *The Owl*," *Hollins Critic* 14 (June 1977): 1–10. Also appears in this volume.

58. Fiedler, introduction *The Lime Twig* vii–xiv. This essay, entitled "A Lonely American Eccentric: The Pleasures of John Hawkes," was originally published in *The New Leader*, 12 December 1960, 12–14.

59. John M. Warner, "The 'Internalized Quest Romance' in Hawkes's *The Lime Twig*," *Modern Fiction Studies* 19 (Spring 1973): 89–95.

60. Lawrence K. Boutrous, "Parody in Hawkes' *The Lime Twig*, *Critique* 15 (1973): 49–56.

61. Robert I. Edenbaum, "John Hawkes: *The Lime Twig* and Other Tenuous Horrors," *Massachusetts Review* 7 (Summer 1966): 462–75. Also appears in this volume.

62. Graham, "John Hawkes on His Novels," 449–61.

63. John Graham, ed., *The Merrill Studies in Second Skin* (Columbus, Ohio: Charles E. Merrill, 1971). Lucy Frost, "Awakening Paradise," 52–63; William R. Robinson, "John Hawkes' Artificial Inseminator," 63–69; Stephen G. Nichols, "Vision and Tradition in *Second Skin*," 69–82. The other essays in this collection are S. K. Oberbeck, "John Hawkes: The Smile

Slashed by a Razor," 45–52; Anthony C. Santore, "Narrative Unreliability and the Structure of *Second Skin,"* 83–93 (noted below); and Albert J. Guerard, *"Second Skin:* The Light and Dark Affirmation," 93–102.

64. Anthony C. Santore, "Narrative Unreliability, and the Structure of Second Skin," in Graham, *The Merrill Studies,* 83–93. Thomas LeClair, "The Unreliability of Innocence: John Hawkes' *Second Skin," Journal of Narrative Technique* 3 (January 1971): 32–39.

65. John Kuehl, "Story into Novel," in Graham, *The Merrill Studies,* 34–43.

66. Ronald Wallace, "The Rarer Action: John Hawkes's *Second Skin," Studies in the Novel* 9 (Summer 1977): 169–86.

67. Norman Lavers, "The Structure of *Second Skin, Novel* 5 (Spring 1972): 208–14.

68. Paul Witherington, "Character Spin-offs in John Hawkes's *Second Skin," Studies in American Fiction* 9 (Spring 1981): 83–91.

69. Carey Wall, "Solid Ground in John Hawkes's *Second Skin,"* in *Makers of the Twentieth-Century Novel,* Harry R. Garvin, ed. (Lewisburg, Pa.: Bucknell University Press, 1977), 309–19.

70. Bruce Bassoff, "Mythic Truth and Deception in *Second Skin," Etudes Anglaises* 30 (July–September 1977): 337–42.

71. O'Donnell, *John Hawkes,* 85–99.

72. Donald R. Wineke, "Comic Structure and the Double Time-Scheme of Hawkes's *Second Skin," Genre* 14 (Spring 1981): 117–32.

73. Mary F. Robertson, "The 'Crisis in Comedy' as a Problem of the Sign: The Example of Hawkes's *Second Skin," Texas Studies in Literature and Language* 26 (Winter 1984): 425–54.

74. Richard Yarborough, "Hawkes' *Second Skin," Mosaic* 8 (Fall 1974): 65–73. Hawkes's response appears in the same issue on pages 73–75. Both also appear in this volume.

75. Ron Imhoff, "On *Second Skin," Mosaic* 8 (Fall 1974): 51–63.

76. Quoted in Patrick O'Donnell, "Life and Art: An Interview with John Hawkes," *Review of Contemporary Fiction* 3 (Fall 1983): 115.

77. Carol MacCurdy, "John Hawkes's Plays: Innocence on a Limb." This essay was written specifically for this volume and is published here for the first time by permission of the author.

78. Enid Veron, "From Festival to Farce: Design and Meaning in John Hawkes's Comic Triad," in Santore and Pocalyko, eds., *A John Hawkes Symposium,* 64–76.

79. Paul Rosenzweig, "Aesthetics and the Psychology of Control in John Hawkes's Triad," *Novel* 15 (Winter 1982): 146–62.

80. Paul Rosenzweig, "John Hawkes's Novels of the Seventies: A Retrospective," *Arizona Quarterly* 38 (Spring 1982): 69–77.

81. John Guzlowski, "No More Sea Changes: Hawkes, Pynchon, Gaddis, and Barth," *Critique* 23 (Winter 81/82): 48–60.

82. Brenda Wineapple, "The Travesty of Literalism: Two Novels by John Hawkes," *Journal of Narrative Technique* 12 (Spring 1982): 130–38.

83. Lois A. Cuddy, "Functional Pastoralism in *The Blood Oranges," Studies in American Fiction* 3 (Spring 1975): 15–25.

84. John V. Knapp, "Hawkes' *The Blood Oranges:* A Sensual New Jerusalem," *Critique* 17 (1976): 5–25.

85. C. J. Allen, "Desire, Design, and Debris: the Submerged Narrative of John Hawkes' Recent Trilogy," *Modern Fiction Studies* 25 (Winter 1979): 579–92. Also appears in this volume.

86. Charles Baxter, "In the Suicide Seat: Reading John Hawkes's *Travesty," Georgia Review* 34 (Winter 1980): 871–85.

87. William Van Wert, "Narration in John Hawkes' Trilogy," *Literary Review* 24 (Fall 1980): 21–39. Charles Berryman, "Hawkes and Poe: *Travesty," Modern Fiction Studies* 29 (Winter 1983): 643–54.

88. Greiner, *Understanding John Hawkes,* 135.

89. Heide Ziegler, "Postmodernism as Autobiographical Commentary: *The Blood Oranges,* and *Virginie," Review of Contemporary Fiction* 3 (Fall 1983): 207–13. Also appears in this volume.

90. Marc Chénetier, "'The Pen and the Skin': Inscription and Cryptography in John Hawkes's *Second Skin,* 167–77; Christine Laniel, "The Rhetoric of Excess in John Hawkes's *Travesty,"* 177–85; André LeVot, "From Zero Degree of Language to the H-Hour of Fiction: Or, Sex, Text, and Dramaturgy in *The Cannibal,* 185–92. All three essays appear in *Review of Contemporary Fiction* 3 (Fall 1983).

91. Patrick O'Donnell, "Stories My Father Never Told Me: On Hawkes's *Adventures in the Alaskan Skin Trade."* This essay was written expressly for this volume and is published here for the first time by permission of the author.

92. W. M. Frohock, "John Hawkes's Vision of Violence," *Southwest Review* 50 (Winter 1965): 69–79.

93. Wayne Templeton, "Between Two Worlds: Experiencing the Novels of John Hawkes," *West Coast Review* 15 (Winter 1981): 3–22.

94. Alan Trachtenberg, "Barth and Hawkes: Two Fabulists," *Critique* 6 (Fall 1963): 4–18.

95. Albert J. Guerard, "The Prose Style of John Hawkes," 19–29; D. P. Reutlinger, *"The Cannibal:* 'The Reality of Victim,' " 30–37; Charles Matthews, "The Destructive Vision of John Hawkes," 38–52; Jackson Bryer, "Two Bibliographies," (which included John Barth) dealt with Hawkes' works on pages 89–94. All appear in *Critique* 6 (Fall 1963).

96. Thomas LeClair, "A Pair of Jacks," *Horizon* 22 (November 1979): 64–68, 70–71.

97. Melvin J. Friedman, "John Hawkes and Flannery O'Connor: The French Background," *Boston University Journal* 21 (Fall 1973): 34–44.

98. Melvin J. Friedman, "Dislocations of Setting and Word: Notes on American Fiction Since 1950," *Studies in American Fiction* 5 (Spring 1977): 79–98.

99. Albert J. Guerard, "Notes on the Rhetoric of Anti-Realist Fiction," *TriQuarterly* 30 (Spring 1974): 31–36.

100. Knapp, "Hawkes' *The Blood Oranges:* A Sensual New Jerusalem," 5–25; Donald J. Greiner, *"Death, Sleep & the Traveler:* Hawkes' Return to Terror," 26–38; Elisabeth Kraus, "Psychic Sores in Search of Compassion: Hawkes' *Death, Sleep & the Traveler,"* 39–52; Daniel Plung, "John Hawkes: A Selected Bibliography, 1943–1975," 53–63. All appear in *Critique* 17 (1976).

101. James Frakes, "The 'Undramatized Narrator' in John Hawkes: Who Says?" 27–37; Robert Steiner, "Form and the Bourgeois Traveler," 109–141; Frederick Busch, "Icebergs, Islands, Ships Beneath the Sea," 50–63; Nancy Levine, "An Interview with John Hawkes," 91–108; Anthony C. Santore and Michael Pocalyko, " 'A Trap to Catch Little Birds With' An Interview with John Hawkes," 165–184; Marcus Klein, "The Satyr at the Head of the Mob," 154–164. All appear in Santore and Pocalyko, eds., *A John Hawkes Symposium.*

102. Marcus Klein, "Hawkes in Love," *Caliban* 12 (1975): 65–79.

103. Frederick Busch, *Hawkes: A Guide to His Fictions* (Syracuse, N.Y.: Syracuse University Press, 1973).

104. John Kuehl, *John Hawkes and the Craft of Conflict* (New Brunswick, N.J.: Rutgers University Press, 1975).

105. Carol A. Hryciw-Wing, *John Hawkes: A Research Guide* (New York & London: Garland, 1986).

106. In an interview with Thomas LeClair, "The Novelists: John Hawkes," *The New Republic* 181 (10 November 1979): 26–29.

107. O'Donnell, *John Hawkes,* 3.

REVIEWS

◆

Three First Novels
[Review of *The Cannibal*]

WALLACE MARKFIELD

Here are three first novels by young writers; the youngest, as the book-jacket proudly states, is twenty-three. These are not the customary immature products to be jabbed with rusty critical knives. They show strict control, with none of those qualities of youthful ebullience and sentimentality which so often pervade the work of first novelists. Yet the admirable restraint, the scrupulous attention to craftsmanship in Frederick Buechner and Paul Bowles seem only to disguise a basic lack of creative energy, especially when juxtaposed against an imagination as rich and overpowering as that of John Hawkes. Both their novels have the same basic theme—the anguish of the modern intellectual, who, unable to communicate his need for love, is condemned to isolation in a world which he can only analyze and endure. But the tragic significance of this theme is never captured, for the human beings who move through these novels are merely the shadowy backdrop against which the real hero, entitled perhaps "The Modern Dilemma," is illuminated. . . .

The Cannibal is a far more experimental venture than *A Long Day's Dying.* On the most simple reading, it is the story of one day in the history of a small German town, told with utter disregard for orthodox chronology and sequence. The year is 1945, and the life of the town is as diseased and sluggish as its choked sewers. ("The undertaker had no more fluid for his corpses; the town nurse grew old and fat on no food at all.") It is policed by one American soldier on a motorcycle, who represents the authority of the Occupation. When the day ends, he has been ambushed and assassinated.

Tormented by memories, the characters are passive, somnambulistic victims of history. Their world is distorted and hallucinatory, haunted by grotesque specters from the past; even as one of them strangles a chicken, the face of the old Kaiser is dimly seen pressed against a window; another runs wildly down a street in pursuit of an open carriage, shedding his identity with each step and emerging finally as Princip, the young assassin of Sarajevo. Vague childhood fears become a terrorizing reality as decayed bodies assume obscene

Reprinted with permission by Wallace Markfield and *Commentary* from *Commentary*, April 1950, 391–92; all rights reserved. Additional novels treated in the review are *A Long Day's Dying* by Frederick Buechner and *The Sheltering Sky* by Paul Bowles.

gestures that mock the living, as ghosts clamber out of the turrets of rusted, overturned tanks.

Hawkes does not focus the novel upon a single character. He attempts rather to portray the obsessions of many different minds submerged in a nightmare. The seeming ludicrousness of many of his images serves only to heighten our sense of horror as we perceive their full import—the dead monkey rising from the heap of bodies, tail coiled about his neck, screaming "Dark is life, dark, dark is death," children sliding down staircases on their stumps— these symbols serve to concentrate our vision upon a scene of desolation as terrifying as anything in modern literature. We cross the border of fantasy into another universe: the tiny village becomes not a microscopic representation of Occupied Germany and the rest of the world; instead, it is these larger entities that assume the dimensions of Spitzen-on-the-Dien.

Hawkes gives the impression of a talent rich, diffuse—and virtually uncontrollable. His preoccupation with filth and decay is extreme. ("All during the day the villagers had been burning out the pits of excrement, burning the fresh trenches of latrines where wads of wet newspaper were scattered . . . where pools of water became foul with waste that was as ugly as the aged squatter.") The macabre aspect of his humor is sometimes over- worked, and the cocoons undulating in the mouths of corpses give one the feeling of a malevolent child displaying a boxful of worms. Nevertheless, Hawkes is a cold and brilliant writer, with a superb eye for visual and olfactory detail. He has succeeded in carrying off the prize which has up to now eluded the grasping fingers of the Kafka cult: namely, the achievement of truth through distortion.

Improvised Alibis
[Review of *The Innocent Party,*
The Beetle Leg, and *The Lime Twig*]

JOHN HOLLANDER

John Hawkes's reputation in the United States is rather high at present. He emerged with *The Lime Twig* and *Second Skin* from underground, where for many years he had been considered a unique flank of the avant-garde. His novels seem self-born, his protagonists ambiguously picaresque, even for post-war American fiction, and, above all, his style darkly idiosyncratic. It was inevitable that the Ford Foundation's drama fellowship programme, designed to entice real Writers (rather than merely Playwrights) into the enfeebled American theatre, should have turned to him. His sojourn in 1964–65 with the San Francisco Actor's Workshop resulted in four short plays, published as *The Innocent Party* with a fatuous introduction by Herbert Blau, one of the theatre's former directors. The best of them is "The Undertakers," which offered Mr Hawkes a chance to rework in uncharacteristic ways material that had already been imaginatively given—for example, the suicide of the father of Skipper, the protagonist of *Second Skin.* It revolves, like all these plays, about an elaborated single confrontation, with both of the characters playing meta-roles in the course of the scene. In this case, the 40-year-old son, remembering and purging the event, plays himself as a boy of 12, for whom his widowed father, in a ludicrous and grisly scene of bargaining, gets into drag as the boy's mother.

"The Innocent Party" is the longest, most ambitious and least successful of these plays. It has, like all of them, a young innocent; in addition, we have a brace of parents, a dike-type aunt, and an aggressive Symbol in the "dried-out swimming pool partially filled with debris" which, at a final moment of knowledge and freedom, fills up with water. The actual nastiness of the situation is one which a writer like Paul Bowles could have handled beautifully in a few pages. But the effects of the dialogue here are neither brilliant nor lingering enough to sustain several episodes and the passage of time.

In one way, these plays are almost counterpoint exercises in what to do with a pair of characters, one conventionally stronger than the other. The language is almost transparent: a reasonable approximation to some kind of

Reprinted with permission from *Listener* (London) 18 July 1968, 85–86.

American speech-style is established for each character immediately, and the surface of that style, even in occasional set-pieces, is never violated as the dialectic of the situation progresses. But this stylistic clarity is unusual for Mr Hawkes, whose style-from-a-despair is often oppressive.

The Beetle Leg, an early novel, was first published 17 years ago, while its author was learning to write. It is characteristic of his work in its ritualised situations and hovering figures (a man buried alive in a western dam, a brother guarding the burial place for years, their folk-doctor father returning to his sons). It anticipates as well his almost puritanical refusal to psychologise or admit the fictional reality of motives; this is not balanced, however, as in the *nouveau roman,* by a care for objects in space, and interiors and landscapes are imprecise. Also, it is lamentably written. Literally impenetrable syntax ("they broke the law all right, directly they couldn't quiet down and talk when I was near enough to see"), factitious vernacular speech, overt referential solecism ("septic pencil" for "styptic" where the malapropism is only Mr Hawkes's)—all of these, multiplied excessively, annoy without revealing.

There are some good paragraphs, but they emerge from the welter of the rest trailing clouds of *Cold Comfort Farm* asterisks. It is almost as if, groping for the right sort of tone for his peculiar paranarratives, he were deliberately affronting articulation in order to exorcise all mere gesture. Since then, he has learned to manage both an accordion-pleat kind of narrative chronology and an almost rhetorically neutral density of prose. In *Second Skin,* even his naval solecisms work to reinforce the notion that fiction is really like a hysterical, lying, improvised alibi, a notion so powerfully illuminating in his imaginative world. There is a touch of the Statue of Liberty's "flaming sword" of Kafka's *Amerika* about much of his local colour. But in *The Beetle Leg* (its title, incidentally, defines the quantum of motion per annum as a huge dam creeps downstream) the reader's hard going goes unrewarded.

The Lime Twig, which has been reissued in England after six years, represents a tremendous advance, stylistically and imaginatively, over the earlier books. Leslie Fiedler, in an introduction to this new edition, is reminded of *"Brighton Rock* rewritten by Djuna Barnes," and I suppose that this does say something about the book's texture: a racetrack-gang, shoot-em-up-bang plot and one of Mr Hawkes's disturbingly discontinuous surfaces of experience are yoked by violence together, this second-order violence being of language rather than of action. Eschewing the exploration of motives with his accustomed, almost puritanic zeal, Mr Hawkes sets this particular nightmare in a contemporary England which he makes up out of better whole cloth, or with more sharply honed shears, than he used for his previous American fictional worlds. There are fewer solecisms, more telling and economical use of details, a more clearly sexualised set of relations between his dreaming innocents and the thugs who do violence to them, and the old American gothic prop of that very violence itself (the best sustained scene in the book may be that of the subsequently fatal beating of a young woman). In any event, the violence and the anti-suspense plot are purgative enough to clear the air, sharpen the prose, and focus the sighting (I do not say "vision" advisedly) inside this novel's narrow, stuffed room.

"Moyenageux"
[Review of *The Goose on the Grave*]

VIVIAN MERCIER

"Fifteen-love, and the game's tennis," a friend of mine used to say. It always struck me as a very profound remark. In literature, as in sport, one should always know not merely what the score is but what game is being played. Dante put the same idea into rather different words in *Il Convivio* when discussing the four different ways of understanding a book—the Literal, the Allegorical, the Moral and the Mystical: "But in demonstrating these, the Literal must always go first, as that in whose sense the others are included, and without which it would be impossible and irrational to understand the others. Especially is it impossible in the Allegorical, because in each thing which has a within and a without, it is impossible to come to the within if you do not first come to the without."

"The Owl," the first of the two novels under review, left me so unsatisfied at the Literal level that I posponed any inquiry into the Allegorical one until I had gone off and read Mr. Hawkes' two previous books, *The Cannibal* (1949) and *The Beetle Leg* (1951), to see if the praise of them quoted on the new volume's wrapper had any justification. Well, it has.

The Cannibal is a busy little book about an imaginary German town in 1945 and 1914. A strange mingling of realism and surrealism, it herds a bunch of comic-strip Germans through some sharply visualized, though unreal, horrors. Nowadays, everything that makes no sense realistically is reputed to be symbolic, so that comparisons to Kafka were tossed around freely by Albert J. Guerard in his introduction to the book. The difference between Mr. Hawkes and Kafka is fairly easily defined: Kafka takes basically simple imagined situations and gives them multiple and complex symbolic meanings; Mr. Hawkes' situations are complex, but his meanings—those that reach this reader, anyway—are fundamentally sophomoric; furthermore, Kafka is much more understandable and believable at the Literal level.

The Beetle Leg, a comic-strip Western, represents a great improvement on *The Cannibal.* As in many of Faulkner's books, the reader feels that he, an outsider, has been allowed to sit in on one of those interminable conversations

Reprinted from *Commonweal,* 2 July 1954, 323. Copyright Commonweal Foundation. The book *The Goose on the Grave* contains two short novels.

that apparently flow on year after year in hotel lobbies, saloons and courthouses all over the South and West. None of the speakers ever feels the need to stop and explain anything, for the facts and the persons involved have been familiar to them all their lives. If the Easterner keeps his mouth shut, he may eventually get the hang of about half of what is going on.

The Beetle Leg, which I hope to re-read soon, has some of Al Capp's grotesque, wry humor, but in "The Owl" we are plunged into the humorless cliché-world spawned by the anonymous illustrators of horror comic books. The narrator and central figure is an executioner—tall and thin, inevitably—who domineers over a vertical, elaborate, impossibly medieval Italian hill town. Wedded to his gallows, he carries out an execution and fails to take a wife. The French have a contemptuous word, *moyenageux,* which perfectly describes the story's phony medievalism. After reading Mr. Hawkes' other books, I still remain indifferent to the Allegorical significance of "The Owl," if it has any.

"The Goose on the Grave," the slightly longer of the two stories, eludes me even at the Literal level; this is infuriating to one who considers himself a practiced and sensitive reader, so perhaps it is impossible for me to be fair. Here, at any rate, are a number of moderately vivid scenes of a war-time Italy, mostly viewed through the eyes of a motherless boy, Adeppi; certain characters appear, disappear, reappear, but their motivation has to be supplied by the reader as they fight, sing, pray and die. Mr. Hawkes seems to be deliberately covering up all the clues to motive that other novelists would sprinkle around.

Three things *The Beetle Leg* has which these new stories have not. First, it unfolds in a vernacular that, like Faulkner's, may *somewhere* have been spoken *by* somebody *to* somebody; "The Owl," which has a straightforward enough story line, is undone by rhetoric; the novel form, after all, has been colloquial, not rhetorical, since its seventeenth and eighteenth century beginnings. Second, *The Beetle Leg* contains within its covers all we need to know about its people, though mingled with much that is irrelevant, and scattered in a disorder which we, as readers, have to set in order; "The Goose on the Grave," however, leaves me with the feeling that the author is holding out on me somewhere, as Stendhal failed to inform his readers that the hero of his *Armance* was impotent. Third, there is something in *The Beetle Leg* worth knowing, for the dead man buried under the dam, both as an individual human being and as a symbol, offers an unknown territory that we are happy to explore. I suggest Mr. Hawkes back-track to where he was when he wrote *The Beetle Leg* and start afresh.

Notes from a Helpless Reader
[Review of *The Lime Twig*]

JOAN DIDION

If I skim over John Hawkes' *The Lime Twig,* it is in despair at my inability to convey its imaginative brilliance, its appreciation of the possibilities that lurk somewhere outside Eliot House. If you have ever read *Brighton Rock* while in a peyote trance, you may have some notion—I don't know—of what *The Lime Twig* is like. It is peopled by characters who come to live out their own nightmares: Hencher, the inveterate lodger, the man who lives vicariously, finally kicked to death by the horse he had arranged to steal; Cowles, his throat cut in the oppressive white anonymity of a steam bath; Michael Banks, throwing himself on the track before a field of horses; Margaret Banks, dreamily beaten almost to death ("she realized . . . it was something they couldn't even show in films") and finally freed from her ropes by a man in a steel vest, whose next step is to slash her wrists. (" 'You cut me.' He said only: 'I meant to cut you, Miss . . .' ") And Larry, the killer in the steel vest, the love-death made manifest, the nightmare lover, his women begging to see the bullet proof vest: "Larry turned slowly around so they could see, and there was the gun's blue butt, the dazzling links of steel. . . . 'For twenty years,' shouted Dora again through smoke opaque as ice, 'for twenty years I've admired that! Does anybody blame me?' "

As in a dream, gratuitous horror mounts upon gratuitous horror; every scene unfolds like those nightmares in which, as one tries to cope with the rattlesnakes underfoot, a faceless body hurtles down an air shaft somewhere in the distance. But the power of *The Lime Twig* is that the action takes place exactly on the *brink* of nightmare: it is not quite hallucination, and therefore nothing from which you can wake up; it is every waking wish carried to its logical extreme, and what Dora and Larry and Hencher and Michael and Margaret are screaming is simply *mon semblable, mon frère.* In brief, *The Lime Twig* made me more than happy, for the first time in some time, to set aside the *Hollywood Reporter.*

Reprinted with permission from *National Review,* 15 July, 1961, 22. © National Review, Inc., 150 East 35th Street, New York, NY 10016.

The Abomination of Desolation
[Review of *Second Skin*]

STANLEY EDGAR HYMAN

John Hawkes is a remarkable phenomenon in our letters. He has written, and New Directions has published, six short novels in five volumes since 1949. These do not make the slightest concession to any reader—their vision of life is shattering and their forms are shattered—as a result of which Hawkes is almost unread. I do not enjoy Hawkes' novels or think that they succeed; more accurately, they succeed all too well in Hawkes' aims, which I think to be mistaken. Nevertheless, his unique role and utter integrity demand serious consideration.

Hawkes' first novel, *The Cannibal* (1949), is perhaps the most depressing and compelling of them all. It tells of Germany in 1945, with a long flashback to 1914. The book is one vast surrealist image of what the Bible calls "the abomination of desolation": Germany is seen as a gutted ruin full of well-poisoners and madmen. When a dance is held in a deserted asylum, the dancers assemble dutifully: "some with bones broken off-center, some with armpits ringed as black as soot."

In what plot the novel has, the narrator, a German nationalist and anti-Semite named Zizendorf, assassinates the sole Allied overseer of the region, an American Jew named Leevey. After this triumph, Zizendorf is full of grandiose schemes for national liberation, and he prints up illegible manifestoes, but the only practical result is that by the book's end the patients have started to file back into the asylum.

The Beetle Leg (1951) has been described by Hawkes as "a panoramic and humorous vilification of the American West." Its title (Hawkes is a wonderful titlist) represents the infinitesimal. The novel's story, if it has a story, tells of the effects that the landslide death of a dam-worker named Mulge Lamson has on various people. *The Beetle Leg* seems to me the most Faulknerian of Hawkes' novels, in the bad sense of the word: syntax tormented, diction strained, participles dangling. It may in fact be a deliberate parody of Faulkner.

The novel includes all the properties of Westerns, from a senile sheriff to a

Reprinted with permission from *New Leader*, 30 March 1964, 24–25. © The American Labor Conference on International Affairs, Inc.

licentious Indian girl, as well as one brilliant invention: a group of young nocturnal motorcyclists called the Red Devils. The Red Devils sometimes seem human and sometimes seem artificial creatures made of rubber and leather; they are given to crashing through plate glass windows and making sudden invasions of the town's main street; in the last scene three of the characters hunt them down with shotguns. There are very funny things in the book—surely the Old West will never be the same after we have seen a cowboy stride up to a bullet-scarred bar and bark: "Bowl of chowder and shot of muscatel"—but I think that the ultimate effect of *The Beetle Leg* is less humorous than macabre.

Hawkes' third book, *The Goose on the Grave* (1954), contains two short novels, *The Owl* and *The Goose on the Grave*. *The Owl* is about a city-state, apparently based on San Marino, which is ruled by a hangman, the narrator, who has a great owl and simultaneously *is* a great owl. The action consists of an escape by a prisoner about to be hanged, his recapture, and his hanging. I suspect that Hawkes is trying his hand at the Gospel story: the owl-hangman can be seen as God the Father; the prisoner is an innocent man who when captured bore a note reading, in part: "No outmoded punishment should be practiced upon me in the name of the Spirit"; there is a "judgment supper" at which the council of 12 and the hangman dine ceremonially on 13 little fish; after the torture and hanging the owl retreats into a tree, and the book ends with the announcement that a new "covenant" has been made.

The emphasis throughout is on life-denying ceremonial: on the walls are "proclamations hundreds of years old, still readable, still clear and binding"; the council members wear ruffs and have antique gavels of rolled calfskin; there is a ritual combat between a man and a dog that is like an evil dance; the hanging is the occasion for a civic feast. If *The Beetle Leg* is Hawkes' most Faulknerian novel, *The Owl* is his most Kafkaesque: a dark fable of pointless sacrifice and divine indifference.

The Goose on the Grave is set in Fascist Italy. The title comes from the folk belief (which I may have invented) that gooseflesh is a sign that a goose has walked across one's grave. This novel is full of a covert homosexuality that never quite becomes overt. Jacopo and Edouard, the two men who cultivate the boy Adeppi, have an ambiguous past with each other; a man named Nino seems at one point to be confessing to a priest something about himself and Adeppi; and the same priest later imprisons Adeppi naked in his cell.

The framework of the book has a beautiful anticlerical simplicity: in the first pages three priests carry off Adeppi's mother; in the last pages they burn her. A flashback reveals that as novices two of the priests once stripped an old woman and sewed her into a hair shirt of raw ratskins; she is perhaps the old mother in the novel, who wears a hair shirt so old and worn now that "little punishment remained in it." What these two novels bound together have in common is a vision of authority as Rack, Noose, and Stake.

The Lime Twig (1961) deals with racetrack crime in England. The title refers to bird-catching, but "lime" in the book has additional meanings as, for the protagonist, the bitter taste of gastric juices in the mouth, while for his antagonist it symbolizes a tropical paradise. The plot involves a couple named Michael and Margaret Banks, whose conventional London middle-class life is transformed when William Hencher, their boarder, persuades Michael to join him in stealing an aged racehorse. As a consequence of this act, Hencher is kicked to death by the horse, and a racetrack gang wrecks the Banks' flat, kills or nearly kills Margaret, and drives Michael (after granting him a fantastic night of sexual athleticism with the gang's girls) to a spectacular suicide under the horse's hoofs during the big race.

Hawkes' new novel, *Second Skin* (New Directions, 210 pp., $4.00), is the first of his books to have a happy ending, and the title is fittingly regenerative. In it a soft fat grandfather called "Skipper" gradually loses all his kin: his father blows out his brains in the bathroom, while the boy plays Brahms on the cello to dissuade him; his mother dies incommunicado; his alcoholic wife kills herself in a cheap motel; his homosexual son-in-law is savagely murdered by some soldiers he has picked up; his beloved daughter Cassandra jumps off a lighthouse because she is pregnant by a repulsive Maine fisherman.

Skipper's reaction to these willed deaths is to affirm life. After Cassandra's death, he flees from the freezing Maine island to a paradisal tropical island, taking along his Negro friend Sonny. There Skipper and Sonny make their living by the artificial insemination of cows (ah, life!), a trade practiced in the course of long drowsy mixed picnics, as it might be in the works of Gauguin. Skipper (or Sonny) has a child by Catalina Kate, a young Negro girl not addicted to wearing clothes, and this child and a number of bleating calves are the evidences that Skipper has conquered the family death drive. (If this sounds silly in synopsis, it is because it is silly in the novel; when Kate announces her pregnancy by bringing Skipper and Sonny a pound of good old American hot dogs, we are back home in Capoteland.)

Skipper has always been the victim of the world's cruelty. When he captained the U.S.S. *Starfish* during the war, a mutineer put him over a barrel and raped him; Cassandra sadistically had Skipper's chest tattooed with the name of her unfortunate husband. Now on the tropical island the memory of the rape has diminished as Skipper's naval uniform is reduced to a frayed cap with cockroaches in the sweatband; his misery about Cassandra has faded as the tattoo has faded on his tanned chest. Skipper's second skin is more invulnerable, since it is all scar tissue.

Hawkes' books are nightmares, grotesque metaphors for our bad times and the timeless human condition, but along with the power they have the shapelessness of nightmare. Leslie Fiedler, whose skill in formulating an issue is matched only by his consistency in choosing the wrong side once the issue has been formulated, writes approvingly in his introduction to *The Lime Twig:* "The order which retrospectively we *impose* on our awareness of events . . . Hawkes decomposes." So he does, but this ordering, form, is the necessary ordering of art. Hawkes' books are shredded fables, jumbles of apocalyptic visions. They would be true novels only if he went through a third stage, *re*composing.

Nevertheless, some of the individual scenes are remarkable. My favorites include: the mayor in *The Cannibal* betraying Pastor Miller to his death because he is terrified of the red eyes and sharp claws of the American eagle on the colonel's uniform; the attack on the car by the enraged rattlesnake in *The Beetle Leg; The Goose on the Grave*'s self-destructive insects called "two-heads"; the three naked soldiers lining up to kiss Cassandra in *Second Skin*. Sometimes Hawkes' supernatural portents chill the blood. A dead monkey suddenly screams "Dark is life, dark is death," or two harpies flap by in the Italian air, wings and beaks quivering. At the end of *The Lime Twig* there is a dreadful suggestion that Margaret is not really dead, but, drained of blood, has become a living zombie.

Hawkes' new book shows cheerfulness breaking through, but not form. The chronological order of its story seems to have been disarranged at random, as by a shuffle of pages. John Hawkes seems to me to have most impressive talents, hobbled by the mistaken theory that Yvor Winters calls "the fallacy of imitative form" (you must disintegrate your poem to convey disintegration). I wish that Hawkes' integrity were in a better cause, and perhaps it will be yet.

What Went Wrong?
[Review of *The Blood Oranges*]

ROGER SALE
WITH RESPONSE BY GILBERT SORRENTINO
AND REPLY BY ROGER SALE

John Hawkes's *The Blood Oranges* fails because it is the work of a contemptible imagination. Hawkes has always seemed to me more an unadmitted voyeur of horror than its calm delineator, but in this new novel the pretense that what is being described is horrifying is dropped, and we have only the nightmare vision of a narrator unable to see how awful he is. He is a "sex-singer," a middle-aged expert in love who is frequently delighted to tell us in what good shape he is, how he looks in his trunks, how skilled he is in bed. He and his wife want and capture other people, in this case another couple, and they insist the world should learn to have its sex with the same impersonal, erotic ennui that is their staple emotion. Their insistence that they are flexible and free is belied by the rigid emptiness of their daily round: sit on the beach, climb a hill to see a peasant or a goat, screw expertly.

There is cruelty here that, because unadmitted, is not even palliated by the relish of sadism. The two men see a peasant girl in a barn and the narrator says: "Perfect, let's hunt her down." They do, and force her to strip so they can take pictures of her, and the other man is delighted by things like the hairs on her chin because he is making a collection of photographs of peasants: "That's perfect. Now let's just shove her over against the beam." Great fun.

And when the friend decides later on that he doesn't much like the idea of the two couples making a sexual foursome, we get lectured: "Need I insist that the only enemy of the mature marriage is monogamy? That anything less than sexual multiplicity (body upon body, voice on voice) is naïve?" When the other man wants to keep his wife to himself, when the other woman collapses after the death of her husband and the departure of her children, they are to shape up, and to *this* standard: "It is simply not in my character, my receptive spirit, to suffer sexual possessiveness, the shock of aesthetic greed, the bile that greases most matrimonial bonds, the rage and fear that shrivels your ordinary man at

Reprinted with permission from *New York Review of Books*, 21 October 1971, 3. © 1971 NYREV, Inc. Gilbert Sorrentino's response and Roger Sale's reply were published in the *New York Review of Books* 1 December 1971, 36.

the first hint of the obvious multiplicity of love." This deeply *un*receptive narcissism has so little aesthetic greed, furthermore, or even mere desire to write well, that we find, on almost every page, something like "The sun was setting, sinking to its predestined death," or "And already the seeds of dawn were planted in the night's thigh."

Hawkes has many admirers, which means some will note that I have completely missed the fact that it is all a put-on; some others will suspect I am guilty of all those sins that Hawkes's narrator so cleverly exposes in your ordinary man. So be. But when horror becomes a pastime it should announce itself or at least know itself; when reticence and shyness become the great human vices, then their opposites should be clearly and ably defended; when the man who does not want his wife sleeping around makes her wear a rusty and viciously designed chastity belt, then narrator and author should not imagine it is chastity's fault; when life is insistently joyless it should not be called good, or even particularly tolerable; when people stop mattering to a novelist, the writing will suffer and the writer should stop.

GILBERT SORRENTINO RESPONDS

Must we, at this late date in the history of the novel, be subjected to the kind of silly frothings at the mouth found in Roger Sale's assault on *The Blood Oranges* [*NYR*, October 21]? "We have only the nightmare vision of a narrator unable to see how awful he is," says Mr. Sale. But the narrator, through the elaborate meanderings of his tale, through his self-justifications, through his insistence on the glory of his adulterous life, *is* showing us "how awful" he is, through (one is almost ashamed to point this out) the artifice that is Mr. Hawkes' novel. How is it possible that a reviewer cannot know that a first-person narrator is also an invention of the author, as much as setting or conversation is? One suspects, with a sinking feeling, that Mr. Sale is representative of hiddeen thousands, that he somehow thinks that fiction is "real," or worse, that it should be.

Mr. Sale goes on to say that many of Mr. Hawkes' admirers "will note that I have completely missed the fact that it is all a put-on." *The Blood Orange* is, of course, not a put-on, but a wholly realized tale of meanness and tragedy, related by a narrator who is revealed (not to Mr. Sale, I assure you) to be as mean and tragic as the tale itself. "When horror becomes a pastime," Mr. Sale notes, "it should announce itself or at least know itself." The "announcing" and the "knowing" are both accomplished—by the novel that Hawkes has given us.

Yet further, Mr. Sale speaks of the "narrator and author" as if they are one. One is amused at what Mr. Sale might have to say of the inseparability of John Dowell and Ford Madox Ford, or, for that matter, of Nick Carraway and Scott Fitzgerald. Mr. Sale's cheaply trite attack on Hawkes' masterpiece is a disgrace to a profession that, one thought, has already sufficiently disgraced itself.

Roger Sale replies

It had to happen. The least I can assure Mr. Sorrentino is that his anger and contempt are not surprising. A few years ago, when I complained that Mary McCarthy's *The Group* was a tedious book. I was told by a number of her admirers that of course the narrator is tedious, that is the *point*, etc. I remember someone coming, or so he thought, to the rescue of Ian Fleming after Fleming had been attacked as a vulgar, showy, sadistic writer, and the terms of the rescue were the same: of course James Bond is vulgar, showy, sadistic, that is the *point*, etc. If you can't call it a parody, call it a careful study of the vices in question.

It is clear that Mr. Sorrentino and I have read the same novel; I would know much less easily how to reply if he had questioned my moral sensibilities rather than my critical capacities. If he is happy imagining that John Hawkes is cunningly, knowingly, carefully standing aloof from his narrator, fine. I can't really see what difference it makes. A novelist thus aloof is the same thing as no novelist at all. Certain Bay Area people like to think of the San Francisco *Chronicle* as a secret underground newspaper, and presumably they are delighted to read it that way. I find it dull and depressing either way, just as I did *The Blood Oranges*; imagining it to be all intentional helps not at all, because that intent, if there, changes nothing on the page, informs and shapes nothing.

What is happening in *The Good Soldier* or *The Great Gatsby,* or *All the King's Men* or *The Turn of the Screw* is different because in each case the authorial pressure on the narrator is there, demonstrable, not the least hypothetical. I perhaps give myself away, though, by adding that I find none of these books as good as many people do precisely because so much investment is being made in the narrator as a character and the narrators are not very interesting. There are, of course, great first person narrators—Ishmael, Huck, Nelly Dean, Pip—but I suspect that after Flaubert, James, and others made the world self-conscious about all such matters the self-consciousness itself began to become the interest, and relatively minor matters like authorial distance and narrative stance began to seem of prime importance. Ralph Ellison in *Invisible Man* practically destroyed a great novel—in the eyes of many he did do so—by all his fussing about just these matters.

But all this is almost irrelevant to *The Blood Oranges* where, on both Mr. Sorrentino's account and mine, we have a boring, hateful narrator. To imagine John Hawkes standing either squarely behind him or at a great and cunning distance from him changes nothing; in either case the man doing the manipulating is dabbling in the boring and hateful, understanding what he is doing only in ways that seem to me, to repeat, contemptible. Much more interesting books along the line of the book Mr. Sorrentino says Hawkes is writing have been written by Charlotte Armstrong and Margaret Millar.

Author in Search of a Myth

CELIA BETSKY

Life is full of questions. People wonder about the future, scrutinize their present. Most agonizing are questions about the past. Allert Vanderveenan, the Dutch anti-hero of John Hawkes's new novel, is especially dominated by his past, both real and imagined. He—and only he—seems to understand his enigmatic present, but it is his past that plagues him, and memory is the struggle to which he is forced to submit. Why, he wants to know, did his wife desert him? And "why did she wait this long to tell me that I am incapable of emotional response and that she cannot bear my nationality?" More important, "why did she refuse to join me on the white ship and so abandon me to death, sleep and the anguish of lonely travel," for as his marriage is disintegrating his wife Ursula sends him off on a cruise to parts unknown and unspecified.

Allert may not want to accept the lot to which his wife has abandoned him, but in the work of John Hawkes this lot is familiar territory, mapped out here in the title itself. Death, sleep and travel underlie most of Hawkes's stories in one guise or another and play central roles in this novel. Allert is haunted by the undignified death of his friend Peter, a psychiatrist with whom Allert shares his wife, and by the death of a young girl with whom Allert had a shipboard affair and whom he is accused and then acquitted of having murdered. Images of death pervade his frequent dreams, for in true Hawkes fashion sleep and dreams figure as tangibly in Allert's life as the world of waking. Like many an earlier Hawkes character, Allert too is a traveler. He has embarked on an unpleasurable pleasure cruise against his will, a Flying Dutchman drifting from dream to dream, from nightmare to reality, from question to question as Skipper explored the world's loneliest beaches in *Second Skin*, as the American Leevey criss-crossed the ruins of postwar Germany on his motorcycle in *The Cannibal*, as cowboys roamed the badlands in *The Beetle Leg*, and the hangman scoured Italy for victims and love in *The Owl*.

Allert's voyage becomes a trip through disillusion and disgust; as he describes the geography and situation of each island the ship visits, it becomes clear that these ports are symbols for aspects of his own life. Islands and a ship compose the topography of his travels; isolation forms the framework of his life.

Review of *Death, Sleep, and the Traveler* reprinted with permission from *Nation*, 18 May 1974, 630–31. © 1974 *The Nation* magazine/The Nation Company, Inc.

Allert's closest companion on the cruise is a promiscuous young woman, Ariane. This modern Ariadne is no heroine of tragedy. The thread she gives Allert is a trail of quick moments of sex with him and with others. They leave the ship only a few times. At the beginning of his journey, Allert examines an island which is his first sight of solid ground. But the place is arid and rocky, inhabited only by mangy goats hunting for grass and the memory of Ariane's mysterious smile when she tells Allert that the island is hers. Next they visit a nudist colony, the dreary embodiment of Allert's sexual fantasies and his hobby, a pornography collection. Then they go to a zoo where they gawk at a cage full of bats performing auto-fellatio. Horrified, Allert sees himself in the bats, finds the zoo "the true world of the aimless traveler" such as himself and Ariane. The bats' blind self-gratification is a good symbol of the kind of sex that Allert, his wife, his friend and the two couples in Hawkes's previous novel, *The Blood Oranges,* enjoy—or at least engage in.

Two major elements from Hawkes's earlier work are missing from this novel and the last: violence and the memory of World War II. The psychic and physical wounds of war and a brutal violence lent a kind of horrible truth to Hawkes's original surrealistic material. The horror gone, much of what seemed significant truth is gone, too—the truth about human nature reflected in a world created by a writer fascinated by the grim heritage of global holocausts.

The war being fought in Hawkes's last two novels is a sexual one. It is an ugly war, but strangely empty and mechanical; Allert's pornography collection is boring, even to him. Hawkes writes not about love but about sex. People who don't experience love have little understanding of human beings; Allert realizes about his wife that he had "known her in every way and yet not at all." He regrets the failure of his marriage, but no one else can. It wasn't a marriage. Allert cares more about Peter's feelings for his wife and his ideas about Peter than he does about Ursula.

Allert and Hawkes have an even more intense relationship with another area of human experience—the landscape of dreams and nightmares that seems more real than the vague home Allert inhabits during his marriage, or the floating opera in which he acts on board the ship. Hawkes likes to explore the strange land between waking and sleeping, and this habit gives a surrealistic twist to even so prosaic a story as *Death, Sleep & the Traveler.* To Allert, the world is a "stage," and he "dreams rather than lives" his life. In dreams as in life he is an incurable *voyeur* and, according to Ursula, he is afraid of life itself.

Through Allert's dreaming mind, Hawkes takes us where we've been with him before: funeral processions and coffins, death and decay, a violent struggle to re-enter the womb, memories of a childhood confused by a conflict of sexual identity. Allert escapes into dreams and Hawkes runs right along with him, a copy of Freud clutched under his arm. Allert spends as much time dreaming his fantastic dreams as he does leading his pointless life. Hawkes spends as much time describing these dreams as he does fleshing out his sketchy characters. Dreams explain and come out of daily life; Hawkes becomes so involved in thinking up dreams for his hero that he forgets to give anyone the life that inspires them.

Is Allert mad? The world of Hawkes's fiction certainly does not preclude this possibility. "I am," "I did," "the reason was," Allert seems to say often enough, but his matter-of-fact descriptions are never quite believable. In a discussion he has with Peter the themes of death, sleep and travel merge into an analysis of madness that does not lie far from Allert's later predicament. The two men are talking about a form of therapy so dangerous that it was eventually discontinued at Peter's clinic. He explains:

> . . . by subjecting the patient to deeper and deeper states of coma we brought him increasingly close to death's door . . . the patient was traveling inside himself and in a kind of sexual agony was sinking into the depths of psychic darkness, drowning in the sea of the self, submerging into the long slow chaos of the dreamer on the edge of extinction. . . . The greater the agony with which he approached oblivion, then the greater and more profound and more joyous his recovery. . . . The only trouble was the possibility of the patient's death. On the other hand, coma and myth are inseparable. True myth can only be experienced in the coma. Perhaps such an experience is worth the necessary risk of death.

Hawkes sending Allert on his voyage is an author in search of a myth. Although he does not succeed in finding a resonant myth, his excursion into questions of insanity raises welcome echoes of the surrealism that characterized his earlier work.

More than twenty years ago Albert J. Guerard praised the surrealistic qualities in Hawkes's writing, but predicted that Hawkes would change from a surrealistic to a realistic writer. Sadly, Guerard was right. Despite details and careful descriptions, Hawkes's new realism is not real. In his earlier work people were grotesque types who lived in an anti-realistic world, but they were interesting and unique. Now Hawkes writes about such things as human emotions and psychological motivations, yet his people remain flat, his style heartless. Cyril in *The Blood Oranges* and Allert in the current novel are large, very fat men, as though Hawkes had to compensate with physical size for what these men lack in substance.

Hawkes does not have the support of a literary tradition, or, one suspects, a personal heritage colorful or varied enough to strengthen the kind of ordinary material with which he deals in *Death, Sleep & the Traveler*. He makes Allert a Dutchman, because without that foreignness he might be too dull a figure—but he cares so little about the authenticity of Allert's Dutchness that he gives him a last name that could never exist in Holland. John Hawkes has proved himself capable before of creating his own literary tradition, a surrealistic style that made his earlier books very special works of American art. It was a pity to see him forsake that talent in *The Blood Oranges* and now in this latest novel. It is disappointing to watch Dali turn into Daphne du Maurier, to watch a good writer handle his material in a new way that makes us wish for the old.

Review of *Travesty*

THOMAS LECLAIR

Travesty is an interesting minor work of a major novelist, an ironic palinode to Hawkes' recent fiction. It completes the trilogy of "sexual extension" begun in *The Blood Oranges* and continued through *Death, Sleep, and the Traveler* by reducing the dense materials of those two novels into a parodic fable of failed eroticism. Like Barth's recycling *Chimera*, *Travesty* has its own tale in its mouth, is a self-reflecting, self-consuming, choking-joking little thing. It will amuse Hawkes' faithful readers, but others may miss the humor of a novel that is more figure than carpet.

While Barthelme and Barth are our best known parodists, Hawkes has long enjoyed the "guilty pleasures" of twisting literary forms. *The Beetle Leg* reruns the American Western, *The Lime Twig* subverts the detective story, *Second Skin* mocks the classic American Adam tale, and *The Blood Oranges* reworks the romantic pastoral. Hawkes' purpose has been to expose and employ the dark sides of these forms. In *Travesty*, a 128-page suicide note, Hawkes begins with negation and forces it to a foolishness that the reader can never quite trust. Parodying what Anthony Alvarez has called the "art of suicide," Hawkes also examines some of his own basic impulses as a writer.

The novel is the uninterrupted monologue of an unnamed speaker who is driving his car very fast toward a "private apocalypse," a smash-up that will kill him and his passengers—his 24-year-old daughter Chantal and his poet friend Henri. He has in mind "an 'accident' so perfectly contrived that it will be unique, spectacular, instantaneous, a physical counterpart to that vision in which it was in fact conceived. A clear 'accident,' so to speak, in which invention quite defies interpretation." Camus spoke of logical suicide. This is suicide as high art, the crafted event without a message, deceptive disruption, Dada of the flesh.

Having estheticized death, this "privileged man" finds common human claims trivial. He comforts his traumatized daughter, whimpering in the back seat, that this "is a warm and comfortable way to go." Henri, lover of both Chantal and the narrator's wife Honorine, is assured that no banal motivations —jealousy, revenge, torture, despair—are in effect. The narrator heads off all questions, objections and possible interpretations of his act. He is not a

Reprinted by permission from *New Republic*, 8 May 1976, 26–27. © 1976 The New Republic, Inc.

murderer, not even a suicide: he maintains he is just a lucid man who has arranged this "form of ecstasy, this utter harmony between design and debris." The serenity of his speech, the clarity of his perceptions, and the clever sophistry of his arguments give the narrator a remarkable seductiveness: ah yes, the *frisson* of suicide. Of course he's a madman. And all suicide notes are travesties. But Hawkes makes his voice hypnotic while it is absurd.

The model is Camus' *The Fall,* which supplies an epigraph, but the materials of *Travesty* are Hawkesian distillates. He has always created a context of absence by subtracting causality, ordinary people, workaday actions, identifiable settings, social niceties and a popular culture from his fictions. The result is an extraordinary focusing of attention, a distorted clarity: "the greater the silence, the louder the tick." In *Travesty,* constriction is extreme: we have only glimpses of a dark external world, normalcy is compulsion, the past a fiction. A single voice yarns away. He is the familiar Hawkesian explainer, an "innocent" victim like Cyril of *The Blood Oranges,* a bemused failure like Allert in *Death, Sleep, and the Traveler.* But now he is a killer, the Hawkesian coward evolved to his logical extreme, a travesty of those earlier narrators who tried to eroticize the landscape or dreamt the worst of dreams.

The "privileged man" says he would rather see "two shadows flickering inside the head than all your flaming sunrises set end to end." The head is Hawkes', its metaphor the car. One shadow is the poet Henri, from whom the narrator has learned his "cruel detachment." The irony is that Hawkes' own imagination, which he insists be poetic and detached, has created the other shadow, the speaker, who has pressed an esthetic to murder, who threatens to destroy shadows and head. The book is Beckett's *Endgame* with Clov at the wheel, a parodic psychodrama, a metafiction with no survivors.

Always concerned with the physics of fantasy, Hawkes in *Travesty* exaggerates the elements of his fiction some readers have found repugnant and thus demonstrates his awareness of the dangers and limits of his ruthlessness. His holding up the mirror to the mirror is not so much self-indulgent as generously, albeit ironically and bleakly, self-revelatory. While the novel lacks some of the pleasures of Hawkes' best work—resonating verbal texture, chambered structure, largeness of mind—it does have the gouging insistence of its simplicities and a witty contempt for itself. Its narrator seeks only silence. Hawkes, even in this brief sport, still seeks to articulate the dream that will liberate us from our nightmares and our daily banalities. Though disfigured by exaggeration and often private, *Travesty* does this and, perhaps more importantly, provides a remarkable and welcome coda to Hawkes' major novels.

Review of *The Passion Artist*

KAREN OSBORNE

John Hawkes has repeatedly explored the workings of myth within the human imagination, but in his most recent novel, *The Passion Artist,* he confronts Eros anew and produces a work more profoundly disturbing than any he has yet written. A word of caution seems only fair: reading this novel, despite the joys of its style, is not a pleasant experience. Brilliantly conceived and beautifully written (Hawkes has been for some time one of the best prose stylists ever to use the English language), this novel unleashes an energy neither pleasant nor contained. Its energy captures the reader as would a demon lover, alternately frightening and seductive. This is the energy of nightmare, a surrealistic voyage something like Djuna Barnes's *Nightwood,* lyrical and unnervingly provocative. It both horrifies and condemns; like *Nightwood, The Passion Artist* leaves the reader with a burden no more welcome than the tale of the Ancient Mariner, and the effect is a sense of devastation. Nonetheless, the burden of awareness Hawkes offers is something one feels compelled to accept. He startles the reader into unforgettable reactions of horror, disgust, and sympathy. He reinvents Eros in a bold series of dramatic revelations and speaks directly to the danger which lies at the heart of love.

Hawkes's career has been haunted by this theme, and *The Passion Artist* is an exciting culmination. His most recent novels—the trilogy which includes *The Blood Oranges; Death, Sleep, and the Traveler;* and *Travesty*—employ first person narrators. Although the narrators are different in each book, by the time the reader reaches *Travesty* this device begins to wear thin. In *The Passion Artist* Hawkes wisely chooses the third person. The main character, Konrad Vost, is not allowed to speak directly to the reader. A nameless narrator unfolds the horrifying comedy and pathos with effective dispassion.

Konrad Vost is a man who loves women. He is an Eros figure, half man, half symbol. Virtue becomes disgrace, and the androgynous Vost is imprisoned in his love for women, in his own myth. Like Kafka's hunger artist, he is captive to his art, and ultimately it destroys him. He lives in a town near the prison where his mother has been incarcerated for the murder of his father. The women in the prison eventually revolt. But even before they do, Konrad's ordered world, dominated by his obsession with his mother, his dead wife, and

Reprinted with permission from *Denver Quarterly* 14 (Winter 1980): 146–47.

his daughter, is shattered when he discovers the daughter is a prostitute. "Surrounded by the music of such names, it was inevitable that Konrad Vost should himself become one of the children menaced by the nightingales."

Throughout his life Vost is victimized by women, yet still he persists in clinging to a sinister innocence. As in an earlier Hawkes work, the play *The Innocent Party,* such innocence is willed. Vost had inherited an "instinct for innocence," and cultivated "the purest habits and coldest turn of mind," and yet he has repeated encounters with cruel, vicious women: "dung and snow," the reader is told, "were the essential ingredients in the crucible of his innocent and detested childhood." The series of incidents from Vost's childhood is distributed among elements of the present narrative action, which describes his painful journey to liberation. During this journey the novel moves back and forth from realism to surrealism, exploring the relationship between art and life. Vost's "inner landscape" becomes "externalized." His hand turns into silver and then changes back again: the illusions of art are stripped away when a woman removes his glove.

Hawkes writes with the evenhanded condemnation of an old satyr figure. He goes beyond D. H. Lawrence and uses mythic materials with a powerful, organic irony that spares absolutely no one. The pain inflicted by the satyr has its purpose. Konrad Vost's story is a series of painful humiliations, but gradually he learns to see, rather than to impose his interior idols on what he sees. "Passionate sensation depends on sight," he is told by the large woman who instructs him at last. "In no other way . . . can a woman so reveal her eroticism as by an act of the will . . . As for you, the force of amorous passion is respect. You are now aware of your own respect and mine." Vost learns to accept himself and then can love, or so it is implied.

Throughout the book Hawkes describes sexual encounters in blunt, graphic terms. He renders the human anatomy ludicrous, grotesque. Suggestions of incest abound. If the child mythologizes, the adult must strip away illusion and reinvent myth based on honest recognition, willed perception. Finally, Vost is brought to an ironic "liberation": "Thus in a city without a name, without flowers, without birds, without angels, and in a prison room containing only an iron bedstead and a broken toilet, and with a woman who had never trussed herself in black satin, here . . . Konrad Vost knew at last the transports of that singular experience which makes every man an artist: the experience, that is, of the willed erotic union. He too was able to lie flat on his bed of stars. He too was able to lie magically on his bed of hot coals."

Hawkes undercuts the significance of the action in the very language which describes it and in the ending of the book which follows. Although the ending is logical and inevitable, and although the reader has been well prepared, it still comes as a surprise. The reader's reaction after the final page is turned provides a measure of Hawkes's genius: the reader, too, has been caught up in the confrontation with Eros, investing something personal in this novel which shows that nothing can be trusted, that art will always appropriate life,

life art, and that neither is necessarily fair. When Konrad is freed by the women and leaves the prison, we learn to beware not only the nightingales but also their keepers.

Hawkes is at his best in *The Passion Artist*. It is a work full of bitter irony and comic, often brutal revelation. Read it, and you will be both humbled and touched; afterwards you may be haunted by the vision of an Eros reborn out of the chaos and destruction men and women have wreaked upon each other. The book is unforgettable, and deserves its rightful place along with *Nightwood* and the best novels of D. H. Lawrence. It is an erotic education, and should become a classic.

Perverse Charades
[Review of *Virginie: Her Two Lives*]

STANLEY TRACHTENBERG

In "Virginie," John Hawkes continues to explore the frightening terrain of the mind and its elusive fictions of horror, erotic fantasies, nightmare visions, death.

To bring together these fragmented images, Hawkes uses a precocious 11-year-old who keeps two journals. One chronicles her adventures as the companion of an 18th-century French nobleman known only as Seigneur. The other takes place just after World War II, when Virginie reappears as the sister of a Bocage, an earthy Paris taxi driver. Each household has assembled a group of women and their partners who act out perverse charades of love.

For Seigneur, whose story is told in 1740, the year of DeSade's birth, love and lust are interchangeable. He devises a series of cruel dramas in order to train women through sexual humiliation into figures of obedience he terms Noblesse. Seemingly, these games are designed to release the anarchy of buried sexual longings. Their real purpose, however, is to impose a stylized working out of Seigneur's passion for symmetry and order through what he terms a Tapestry of Love.

The depravity of Seigneur's ménage is parodied in coarse mirror images by Bocage and his friends, who invest them with the carnival atmosphere of a sex arcade where Seigneur deals with Oedipal fears and allegorical warnings. Bocage celebrates the lusty variety of sex in Rabelesian catalogues. Both make use of a literary tradition that includes the French troubadors and the Fabliau, in which a mixed company entertains itself with bawdy tales, and extends to the novels of Charlotte Brontë.

In both households there is a forbidding maternal presence who attempts to suppress incestuous longings. In one case, her disapproval is mute, in the other it issues in angry whispers which we are for the most part unable to catch but which finally are responsible for ending the revels and rescuing Virginie while at the same time denying the fulfillment she desires.

Virginie remains an ambiguous symbol of willing decadence and unaffected innocence. There is even a suggestion that both charades are merely

Reprinted with permission from *Dallas Times Herald*, 27 June 1982, 4.

constructs of her own imagination, exaggerated in much the way a child might see things. We are not in her mind but in her story. Through its unreliability, Hawkes draws attention to the distortions not only of her mind but of the literary attempts to shape its vision.

Little remains of the ordinary world or of the reassuringly familiar landmarks on which we depend to get along in it—landmarks of place, of speech, of modes of behavior; above all, perhaps, of some reliable perspective to put them all into recognizable relation. Hawkes' pictorial style allows the conflicts to emerge in surprising juxtapositions which resemble the composition of a multi-paneled painting. The scenes are spread out, linked by repetition rather than progression, and by related imagery, recurring circumstances, symmetrical patterns of events.

Objects appear in the vivid yet indistinct manner in which they occur in dreams, framed in common Freudian images such as going up in flames, beheading a long-necked bird, or extracting a tooth. We are carried across a hallucinatory landscape of magical castles, strange cloisters, nightmare cities, deserted except for dark buildings which conceal ghostly amusement parks or houses in which innocence is surrendered to couples who vanish the next day, vanish without a trace.

Seemingly innocent details are magnified, brought close so that they are made to appear threatening, while the human world behind them shrinks into the distance. The attempt to depict these perverse demons brings the novel to the exploitation of pornography. We do not participate; we witness what even the characters regard as performance. The natural impulse struggles with artificial control, with civilized arrangement. Artifice and awareness are made to substitute for innocence and nature: yet Hawkes never allows us to become too confident about which pair is the more destructive—and the more necessary.

In this obscure but compelling fiction, Hawkes dramatizes the conflict between the two. He creates a tension whose source we can never fully know, but which reaches the deepest fears we have about ourselves. And he projects his discoveries in the often terrible, often comic disguises that make them bearable.

Father and Daughter
[Review of *Adventures in the Alaskan Skin Trade*]

BOB HALLIDAY

Longtime admirers of John Hawkes' fiction who have had trouble with his past two novels can relax: his new book, *Adventures in the Alaskan Skin Trade,* is one of his very best. Hawkes' name is a magic word for anyone who cultivated a taste for new fiction during the 1950s and 1960s. The landscape he discovered in early novels like *The Cannibal* and *The Lime Twig* was exciting in a way modern American imaginative prose had never been before: shadowy and out of focus, but very precise in its ability to evoke equivocal emotions for which no names exist.

As his style matured, each new work appeared to become more realistic, progressing from the dreamlike blur of *The Cannibal* to the solid but refracted reality of *Second Skin.* In this last-named novel and the next few to follow it, Hawkes described a world that resembled that of more conventional novelists, but which could suddenly split apart to reveal terrifying, irrational emotions seething beneath the surface. Something seemed to go wrong, however, when *The Passion Artist* appeared in 1979. Sexual ideas which had been intriguing in Hawkes' earlier work moved to center stage, and the novel came across as curiously obsessive and shrill. *Virginie, Her Two Lives* (1982) struck at least this reader as even less satisfactory: an elegantly written but thin erotic caricature. *Adventures in the Alaskan Skin Trade* marks a return to the great days.

Readers who pick up the novel will get yanked in so quickly that they may forget who it is they're dealing with: a writer whose true subject is the irrational reality that lies under the surface of things. In this case, the surface is the adventure-packed memoir of an Alaskan whorehouse madam with the unlikely name of Sunny Deauville. Underneath, it is a psychological study of a disturbed father-daughter relationship, so powerful and acute that it bears comparison with Christina Stead's great *The Man Who Loved Children.*

Like Sam Pollit, the demonic father in Stead's novel, John Burne Deauville, Sunny's father, is an irresistibly magnetic figure. After bringing his wife and daughter to Juneau in 1930, he chases around after adventure, casting

Reprinted with permission from *Washington Post Book World,* 29 September 1985. ©. The Washington Post.

his family in whatever roles he finds necessary to fulfill his fantasies, and disappears without a trace in 1940. Sunny narrates all of this from the standpoint of 1965, when she is 40 years old and desperately trying to leave Alaska, the land of her father's disappearance, and travel to France, where he was born.

A large portion of the novel is made up of Sunny's retellings of her father's accounts of his adventures, spun out to family and friends each time he returns home. The tales themselves are whoppers: killing giant bears, pulling teeth for suffering Indian chiefs, rescuing prospectors driven mad by mosquitos, but it quickly becomes clear that Sunny's feelings will not permit her to recount his narratives accurately. She is possessed by her memories of her father, wounded by his unexplained disappearance and abandonment of her to a degree she can't begin to express directly, and her portrait of him is grotesque with the distortions wrought by 25 years of tortured and unresolved speculation about him. He emerges as a kind of spring-wound incarnation of the Boy Scout Oath, a monster of manly virtue and relentless self-conscious moral purity, who speaks a laundered macho idiom straight out of boys' adventure fiction as he unconsciously destroys those who are closest to him.

From the outset, John Deauville sets up impassable barriers between his family and himself. He is especially creative in using nicknames to undermine natural relationships: his daughter becomes Sunny; his wife, Cecily turns into Sissy, and he himself

"a few months prior to going to Alaska . . . renicknamed himself Uncle Jake. . . . My father, then, was Uncle Jake. I was not allowed to call him Father. I was never allowed to call him Dad. Especially was I never allowed to call him Dad. But if my father was to be blamed for humorously renaming the unoffending population of his little world, and most of all denying to his daughter what was rightfully hers—the name appropriate to that man who was her sole spell-caster—how much more was I to be blamed, since I too called my mother Sissy."

He is also ambivalent in his perception of pain in those who love him. He never becomes aware of Sissy's crushing unhappiness in Alaska, and even though he suffers mightily as she is being treated for a toothache, he fails to observe the symptoms of the heart disease which will kill his wife after five years in the inhospitable territory.

Although Uncle Jake is a handsome and dashing man, he is so oblivious to sexual identity that he spends years in the vicinity of a Juneau hotel swarming with prostitutes without ever realizing that they are anything other than friendly women who know how to give a warm greeting if you meet them in the corridor. He knows how to mix a wicked punch, but will never touch anything stronger than ginger ale, and emphatically forbids family and friends from sipping even a beer. He never questions the presumed natural inferiority of American Indians, one of several firmly held prejudices that Sunny records without comment.

Her judgment on all of this is her chosen style of living, which is in effect a gigantic reaction against Uncle Jake. In response to his puritanism she constructs the Alaska-Yukon Gamelands, a kind of theme park brothel which caters to the supermales which populate Sunny's Alaska. After her father's disappearance she wastes little time in sacrificing her virginity to an Indian named Sitka Charley, and she has no aversion at all to alcohol.

But this rejection takes a toll. Fight it as she may, Sunny is still Daddy's girl. The first word of her memoir is "Dad," despite the injunction, and throughout her account she unwittingly romanticizes her father extravagantly. Her account of his courtship of Sissy, for example, is an elaborate paraphrase of the Cinderella story, complete with malicious sisters and fateful footwear. More poignantly, he haunts her dreams. Even those who know the surrealist methods of Hawkes' first novels will be amazed at the power of the nightmares he creates for Sunny: tight formulations of failure and guilt which embrace the reader with the suffocating pressure of real dreams. In each of them she rather impassively watches Uncle Jake die a gruesome death as he requests her help with equal impassiveness.

All refer to his request that "when I go—when it's my turn to go—you're the only person I want at my funeral. Not even [my partner] Fran, Sunny, just you." Sunny can never really move on until she participates in some form of funeral for him, even if it is just an understanding of his disappearance. Such a revelation does occur, and it forms the crux of the novel, heralding Sunny's liberation from her guilt and acceptance of herself.

Sunny is a fascinating character, and she keeps the book constantly and vigorously alive. Some of her reminiscences jolt with their perverse originality, such as her account of how the most virile of her lovers was stolen by the astounding Martha Washington, an amazon aviatrix and adventuress whose penny-dreadful life succeeds in all the areas where Uncle Jake's fails. But Hawkes' greatest success in *Adventures* is the depth with which he permits the reader to understand Uncle Jake despite the narrator's various blindnesses. He passes the fact of Uncle Jake's vast vulnerability right over Sunny's head to the reader, showing the deep scars left by the neglect, the suicide of loved ones and other forms of emotional abandonment which had been part of his upbringing. ("Innocence in Extremis," a long story by Hawkes recounts an incident from Uncle Jake's childhood that makes a passing but important appearance in the novel.) Uncle Jake's compulsive bravado and unintentional cruelty come to seem inevitable and pathetic. One episode dealing with his fear of heights is particularly wrenching, as is a hint midway through the book that he already foresees his end.

But Hawkes captures his Alaskans alive; he never makes the book hold still for a session of character analysis. It zips along like the page-turner it is, and it is only in retrospect that one really appreciates its profundities. *Adventures in the Alaskan Skin Trade* is the most moving and accessible novel yet from one of the most distinguished of American writers. It should be with us for a long time.

INTERVIEW

♦

John Hawkes: An Interview, 20 March 1964

JOHN ENCK

For many critics, your books show, if not the direct influence of, then affinities with, European works—perhaps more so than do most American novels. This connection may be a tie to a kind of internationalism noticed in the 'twenties, 'thirties, and 'forties, but less common now. Do you think American writers can learn anything from European writers, or is that period over?

Your word "affinities" seems to me more to the point than "influences." Certainly it's true that in many ways my own fiction appears to be more European than American. But the fact is that I've never been influenced by European writing. The similarities between my work and European work— those qualities I may have in common with, say, Kafka and Robbe-Grillet and Günter Grass—come about purely because of some kind of imaginative underworld that must be shared by Americans and Europeans alike. I don't think writers actually learn from each other. But obviously we tend to appreciate in European writers what we sometimes fail to recognize in our own writers—that absolute need to create from the imagination a totally new and necessary fictional landscape or visionary world.

You mentioned Céline earlier this morning.

Yes, Céline is an extraordinary writer, and his *Journey to the End of the Night* is a great novel. His comic appetite for invented calamities suggests the same truth we find in the comic brutalities of the early Spanish picaresque writers, which is where I locate the beginnings of the kind of fiction that interests me most.

Let's turn to the older writers in the United States. For example, James, Hemingway, Fitzgerald, or Faulkner. Do any of these writers seem particularly significant to you at the present time—do they seem more or less significant than they did in the past?

As a writer I'm concerned with innovation in the novel, and obviously I'm committed to nightmare, violence, meaningful distortion, to the whole panorama of dislocation and desolation in human experience. But as a man—as reader and teacher—I think of myself as conventional. I remember that after

Reprinted with permission from *Wisconsin Studies in Contemporary Literature* 6 (Summer 1965): 141–55. © The University of Wisconsin Press. For a note on how this interview was conducted, see *Wisconsin Studies in Contemporary Literature*, Winter–Spring 1965, 1–2.

Faulkner's death, which followed so closely on the death of Hemingway, there was a kind of journalistic polling of critics and reviewers in an effort to assess our position and re-assess our writers in terms of influence and reputation. I think that at the time there was a general inclination to unseat the accepted great contemporary writers in America, to relegate Faulkner, Hemingway, and Fitzgerald to history, and instead to acclaim, say, Norman Mailer and James Baldwin. And we've also seen at least one recent effort to debunk the achievement and pertinency of Henry James. I myself deplore these efforts and judgments. James gave us all the beauties, delicacies, psychic complications of a kind of bestial sensibility; Fitzgerald's handling of dream and nightmare seems to me full of rare light and novelistic skill; Faulkner produced a kind of soaring arc of language and always gave us the enormous pleasure of confronting the impossible at the very moment it was turning into the probable. I think of all these achievements as the constants of great fictional ability. I think these writers will always survive shifts in literary taste and changing conditions in the country, and will always in a sense remain unequaled. Incidentally, after my reading last night a man asked me if there was anything of Faulkner or Faulkner's influence in my work. He was thinking of the passage from *Second Skin,* and I answered that I didn't see much Faulkner in that book. But as a matter of fact, while I was reading from *The Lime Twig* last night, I became quite conscious again of echoes of a Faulknerian use of inner consciousness and expanded prose rhythms. The echoes are undeniable, I think—Faulkner is still the American writer I most admire—though at this point I ought to insist again that in general my work is my own, and that my language, attitudes and conceptions are unique.

Such a view, then, would link you to the experimental writers of the avant-garde. As you know, the "avant-garde" was a rather popular concept about twenty years ago, but seems to be less so now. Do you have any views on the writer as experimenter?

Of course I think of myself as an experimental writer. But it's unfortunate that the term "experimental" has been used so often by reviewers as a pejorative label intended to dismiss as eccentric or private or excessively difficult the work in question. My own fiction is not merely eccentric or private and is not nearly so difficult as it's been made out to be. I should think that every writer, no matter what kind of fiction writer he may be or may aspire to be, writes in order to create the future. Every fiction of any value has about it something new. At any rate, the function of the true innovator or specifically experimental writer is to keep prose alive and constantly to test in the sharpest way possible the range of our human sympathies and constantly to destroy mere surface morality. What else were we trying to get at?

The concept of the avant-garde.

America has never had what we think of as the avant-garde. Gertrude Stein, Djuna Barnes, whose novel *Nightwood* I admire enormously, Henry Miller—no doubt these are experimental writers. But I don't think we've ever had in this country anything like the literary community of the French Surrealists or the present day French anti-novelists. And I'm not sure such a community would be desirable. On the other hand, in the past few years we've probably heard more than ever before about an existing avant-garde in America—we've witnessed the initial community of Beat writers, we're witnessing now what we might call the secondary community of Beat writers, recently many of us have defended *The Tropic of Cancer*. But I confess I find no danger, no true sense of threat, no possibility of sharp artistic upheaval in this essentially topical and jargonistic rebellion. Henry Miller's view of experience is better than most, Edward Dahlberg is a remarkably gifted writer who has still not received full recognition, I for one appreciate Norman Mailer's pugilistic stance. But none of this has much to do with the novel, and so far Beat activity in general seems to me to have resulted in sentimentality or dead language. My own concept of "avant-garde" has to do with something constant which we find running through prose fiction from Quevedo, the Spanish picaresque writer, and Thomas Nashe at the beginnings of the English novel, down through Lautréamont, Céline, Nathanael West, Flannery O'Connor, James Purdy, Joseph Heller, myself. This constant is a quality of coldness, detachment, ruthless determination to face up to the enormities of ugliness and potential failure within ourselves and in the world around us, and to bring to this exposure a savage or saving comic spirit and the saving beauties of language. The need is to maintain the truth of the fractured picture; to expose, ridicule, attack, but always to create and to throw into new light our potential for violence and absurdity as well as for graceful action. I don't like soft, loose prose or fiction which tries to cope too directly with life itself or is based indulgently on personal experience. On the other hand, we ought to respect resistance to commonplace authority wherever we find it, and this attitude at least is evident in the Beat world. But I suppose I regret so much attention being spent on the essentially flatulent products of a popular cult. A writer who truly and greatly sustains us is Nabokov.

I think many Beat writers have a kind of popularity. Whom do you think of as your audience, and what sort are you looking for?

The question of audience makes me uncomfortable. I write out of isolation, and struggle only with the problems of the work itself. I've never been able to look for an audience. And yet after a number of years spent in relative obscurity, I'm pleased that my books are gaining readers. I think that works of the imagination are particularly important now to younger readers, and I think it's clear that my fiction is being studied in colleges and universities. Apparently it's being read even by New York high school students. But at any rate I care about reaching all readers who are interested in the necessity and limitless possibilities of prose fiction, and I think there must be a good many of them. I'm trying to write about large issues of human torments and aspirations, and I'm convinced that considerable numbers of people in this country must have imaginative needs quite similar to mine.

One kind of reader is the critic. At its best, do you find any particular kind of criticism helpful—criticism appearing in larger circulation magazines or in smaller magazines? Does criticism mean anything at all to you as a writer?

I think the critic's function is mainly in terms of the reader. The critic makes the work more accessible, meaningful, and hence essential to the reader. I happen not to share the contempt for literary or academic criticism which appears to be current now. The critical efforts of the magazine *Critique,* for instance, which devoted one of its special issues to John Barth's novels and mine, are enormously helpful and gratifying. Generally I think I've benefited from criticism, though over the years what I've gained specifically from the critical judgment of a friend like Albert Guerard is almost too great to mention. I won't pretend not to be affected by newspaper reviews—in this area I'm easily outraged and just as easily pleased—but despite some of the silences and some of the more imperceptive or hostile responses, I have the impression that reviewers and readers alike in America are becoming increasingly receptive to original work. Certainly I've fared far better in America than in England where in one of the few sympathetic notices of my work to appear in that country I was described as a "deadly hawk moth."

What do you think of the Sunday New York Times *book review section?*

The problem is so old I'm tempted to call it one of our dead horses. But I don't read the *New York Times* book review section (or any other book review section for that matter), and I could be very wrong. I think the scene is changing momentarily—perhaps the *New York Times* book section will become serious one of these days and give the lie to us all. It would be a welcome irony. It may sound paradoxical, but if they ever gave my own work the attention it deserves I'd be deeply moved.

An aspect of your work that I have always appreciated, which I think many other critics have not, is the comic element. You have referred several times to comic writing—would you like to say something more about what you regard as the importance of comedy in your work?

I'm grateful to you for viewing my fiction as comic. Men like Guerard have written about the wit and black humor in my novels, but I think you're right that reviewers in general have concentrated on the grotesque and nightmarish qualities of my work, have made me out to be a somber writer dealing only with pain, perversion, and despair. Comedy puts all this into a very different perspective, I think. Of course I don't mean to apologize for the disturbing nature of my fiction by calling it comic, and certainly don't mean to minimize the terror with which this writing confronts the reader—my aim has always been the opposite, never to let the reader (or myself) off the hook, so to speak, never to let him think that the picture is any less black than it is or that there is any easy way out of the nightmare of human existence. But though I'd be the first to admit to sadistic impulses in the creative process, I must say that my writing is not mere indulgence in violence or derangement, is hardly intended simply to shock. As I say, comedy, which is often closely related to poetic uses of language, is what makes the difference for me. I think that the comic method functions in several ways: on the one hand it serves to create sympathy, compassion, and on the other it's a means for judging human failings as severely as possible; it's a way of exposing evil (one of the pure words I mean to preserve) and of persuading the reader that even he may not be exempt from evil; and of course comic distortion tells us that anything is possible and hence expands the limits of our imaginations. Comic vision always suggests futurity, I think, always suggests a certain hope in the limitless energies of life itself. In *Second Skin* I tried consciously to write a novel that couldn't be mistaken for anything but a comic novel. I wanted to expose clearly what I thought was central to my fictional efforts but had been generally overlooked in *The Cannibal, The Lime Twig, The Beetle Leg.* Obviously Faulkner was one of the greatest of all comic writers—Nabokov is a living example of comic genius.

Do you have any comments on Flannery O'Connor as a comic writer?

For pure, devastating, comic brilliance and originality she stands quite alone in America—except perhaps for Nathanael West. Both of these writers maintain incredible distance in their work, both explode the reality around us into meaningful new patterns, both treat disability and inadequacy and hypocrisy with brutal humor, both of them deal fiercely with paradox and use deceptively simple language in such a way as to achieve fantastic verbal surprise and remarkable poetic expression. No doubt Flannery O'Connor is a more ruthless writer than West. But in an essay of mine called "Flannery O'Connor's Devil," which appeared in *The Sewanee Review,* I tried to suggest some of these similarities and also mentioned that I first read West and Flannery O'Connor at the same time and from that moment on felt a sustaining involvement with both of them. About six years ago I visited Flannery O'Connor in Milledgeville, Georgia, and have been writing to her since then. She's an extraordinary woman with what I like to think of as a demonic sensibility. I've been trying to persuade Flannery O'Connor that as a writer she's on the devil's side. Her answer is that my idea of the devil corresponds to her idea of God. I must admit that I resist this equation. Certainly in her two great short stories, "A Good Man Is Hard to Find," and "The Life You Save May Be Your Own," as well as in her brilliant first novel, *Wise Blood,* it's the unwavering accuracy and diabolism of her satiric impulse that impresses me most. At any rate, her imaginative authority, her absolute originality of voice and language, her unflinching, unsparing treatment of the reader as well as her materials—all of this suggests the importance of her fictional gifts. I do think that Nathanael West is the only other American writer whose fictional spirit is comparable to hers.

To continue perhaps with your opinions on contemporary American authors, would you comment on Carson McCullers? What do you think is her place in the literature of our time?

I admire her compassion and the fine warm mordant tones and slow cadences of her writing. It seems to me that Carson McCullers deals more directly and consistently with the materials of childhood fantasy than perhaps any other American writer, which might help to account for her power. It's as if she's telling stories about legendary children to other children who have already died. But the differences between Carson McCullers' humor and Flannery O'Connor's black wit, which is like a steel trap snapping shut on the reader's mind, make me aware again of the loss involved in grouping writers together under such terms as "Gothic." I'm sure we could go on at length about Saul Bellow and Bernard Malamud, but obviously these are two of our most important comic novelists. I think that *Henderson the Rain King,* which seems to have flowered enormously and wonderfully out of his perfect short novel *Seize the Day,* is Bellow's finest work. Malamud is one of the purest creators I know of.

There are some personal questions here about how you write and you may answer them or not as you like. The first is, do you outline your novels before you start writing?

I've never outlined a novel before starting to write it—at the outset I've never been aware of the story I was trying to handle except in the most general terms. The beginnings of my novels have always been mere flickerings in the imagination, though in each case the flickerings have been generated, clearly enough, by a kind of emotional ferment that had been in process for some time. I began *The Cannibal* after reading a brief notice in *Time* magazine about an actual cannibal discovered in Bremen, Germany (where I had been, coinciden- tally, during the war); I started *The Lime Twig* when I read a newspaper account of legalized gambling in England. My other novels were begun similarly with mere germs of ideas, and not with substantial narrative materials or even with particular characters. In each case what appealed to me was a landscape or world, and in each case I began with something immediately and intensely visual—a room, a few figures, an object, something prompted by the initial idea and then literally seen, like the visual images that come to us just before sleep. However, here I ought to stress that my fiction has nothing to do with automatic writing. Despite these vague originations and the dream-like quality of some of these envisioned worlds, my own writing process involves a constant effort to shape and control my materials as well as an effort to liberate fictional energy. *The Beetle Leg* and *The Lime Twig,* for instance, underwent extensive revision. I spent four years revising *The Lime Twig* which, as you know, is a short book. And I must say that once a first draft is finished I certainly do resort to outlines, sometimes to elaborate charts and diagrams. I suppose this writing method involves considerable wasted motion. But since I'm compelled to work with poetic impulses there seems to be no alternative.

Would you say something about your working conditions?

Like most people, I've written under a variety of conditions. I wrote my first novel in a writing class when I returned to college after the war; I wrote a short novel in the cab of a pick-up truck in Montana; I've written at night after work and in the early mornings before going to work; the first draft of *The Lime Twig* was written during my first academic summer after I began teaching; *Second Skin* was written last year on a kind of paradise island in the West Indies. In his book *Enemies of Promise,* Cyril Connolly said that one of the greatest obstacles to the young writer was the "perambulator in the hall." But I was married at a fairly early age and have always felt that the conditions of ordinary life, no matter how difficult they might prove to be, were the most desirable conditions for writing. My prose might be radical, but my habits are quite ordinary. On the other hand, I admit that I did have mixed feelings when a Guggenheim fellowship and several grants allowed me to take a year off from teaching at Brown—it was difficult to face the prospect of a year of ideal writing conditions without a certain amount of anxiety, especially since I had always resisted the notion of making special allowances for writers. However, I confess that now after those arcadian months in the West Indies—I worked on *Second Skin* every morning and spent the afternoon in the water washing away the filth of creative effort—I feel very differently about complete freedom and ideal writing conditions. *Second Skin* couldn't have taken the form it did without the time and locale made possible by the grants. I'm reminded that a few years ago Irving Howe gave a lecture at Brown in which he said that if Raskolnikov tried to commit his murder today he'd receive a special delivery letter announcing that he'd been awarded a Guggenheim fellowship. It's an amusing and accurate comment on our own special artistic state of affairs and the risks existing today for the subsidized artist and subsidized culture. Subsidy seems absurdly contrary to the integrity of the writer's necessary anti-social stance. But personally I think foundation gifts are worth the risks involved. My own grants were unexpected boons which I look back on with nothing but considerable gratitude. I think that writers—and especially younger writers—should receive as much help and encouragement as possible.

To a certain extent you anticipated a few moments ago my next question, but I'll ask it, anyhow. To what degree are you worried about structure in your novels? Do you generally think of your novels in terms of a formal structure of the narrator, or do you discover structure as you write?

My novels are not highly plotted, but certainly they're elaborately structured. I began to write fiction on the assumption that the true enemies of the novel were plot, character, setting, and theme, and having once abandoned these familiar ways of thinking about fiction, totality of vision or structure was really all that remained. And structure—verbal and psychological coherence—is still my largest concern as a writer. Related or corresponding event, recurring image and recurring action, these constitute the essential substance or meaningful density of my writing. However, as I suggested before, this kind of structure can't be planned in advance but can only be discovered in the writing process itself. The success of the effort depends on the degree and quality of consciousness that can be brought to bear on fully liberated materials of the unconscious. I'm trying to hold in balance poetic and novelistic methods in order to make the novel a more valid and pleasurable experience. Of course it's obvious that from *The Cannibal* to *Second Skin* I've moved from nearly pure vision to a kind of work that appears to resemble much more closely the conventional novel. In a sense there was no other direction to take, but in part this shift came about, I think, from an increasing need to parody the conventional novel. As far as the first-person narrator goes, I've worked my way slowly toward that method by a series of semi-conscious impulses and sheer accidents. *The Cannibal* was written in the third person, but in revision I found myself (perversely or not) wishing to project myself into the fiction and to become identified with its most criminal and, in a conventional sense, least sympathetic spokesman, the neo-Nazi leader of the hallucinated uprising. I simply went through the manuscript and changed the pronouns from third to first person, so that the neo-Nazi Zizendorf became the teller of those absurd and violent events. The result was interesting, I think, not because *The Cannibal* became a genuine example of first-person fiction, but because its "narrator" naturally possessed an unusual omniscience, while the authorial consciousness was given specific definition, definition in terms of humor and "black" intelligence. When I finished *The Beetle Leg* (a third-person novel), I added a prologue spoken in the first person by a rather foolish and sadistic sheriff, and this was my first effort to render an actual human voice. Similarly, Hencher's first-person prologue in *The Lime Twig* (also a third-person novel) was an afterthought, but his was a fully created voice that dramatized a character conceived in a certain depth. This prologue led me directly to *Second Skin* which, as you know, is narrated throughout in the first person by Skipper who, as I say, had his basis in Hencher.

On the matter of structure would you comment on the relationship of Sidney Slyter to the main action of The Lime Twig?

As soon as he read the manuscript of *The Lime Twig,* James Laughlin, the publisher of New Directions (who, by the way, has been a sustaining friend since I began to write), suggested that this novel might be more accessible if it had some kind of gloss or reader's guide. I believe that he even suggested the idea of a newspaper sportswriter as an appropriate kind of "chorus" to comment on the action of the novel. I don't know how I arrived at the sportswriter's name (I may have been trying to echo comically the common

English term "blighter"), but at any rate that's how Sidney Slyter came into being, with his snake-like character embodied in the ugly sibilance of his name which was also related, of course, to Sybilline, the dark temptress in the novel. To me it's interesting that Sidney Slyter's column was in effect another afterthought, since actually his sleazy character and cheap column afforded me perhaps the best opportunity for dramatizing the evil inherent in the world of *The Lime Twig*. Slyter's curiosity, his callow optimism, his lower middle class English ego, his tasteless rhetoric, his vaguely obscene excitement in the presence of violence—all this makes him one of the most degrading and perversely appealing figures in the novel. I would say that in reporting the criminal actions of the novel, Slyter carries degradation to its final end. I've been told that he's an authentic type, which pleases me since I've never known such a man and have only a passing interest in horse racing sheets. Perhaps Sidney Slyter is some indication of why *The Lime Twig* was overlooked or ridiculed in England.

What is the relationship between William Hencher and Michael Banks? Is Hencher some sort of prologue for Michael Banks? One of the most shocking parts of the book is to find Hencher killed so early.

I thought his death was amusing. But given my need to parody the novel form, in this case to parody the soporific plot of the thriller, Hencher's death seems to me an appropriate violation of fictional expectation or fictional "rules." However, *The Lime Twig* begins and ends with Hencher; his early violent death is analogous, I think, to all that follows; and to me he reappears as Cowles (the murdered fat man) and as the constable. I meant the pseudo-mystery of his death to pervade the novel. On the thriller level, Hencher is literally a member of Larry's underworld gang, is an instrument of Michael's fatality. Like Michael Banks, Hencher—because of his need for love—is killed by the race horse; if we understand Michael's own story then we understand Hencher's death. But of course you're right that Hencher's introduction serves as a prologue to all the episodes of the novel in which Michael's fantasies become real. Michael and Margaret Banks were conceived as representing England's anonymous post-war youth (the borrowing of the hero's name from the Mary Poppins series has obvious significance), while I saw post-war England itself as the spiritless, degraded landscape of the modern world, in this case dominated by the destructive fatality of the gambling syndicate. But it seemed to me that the drab reality of contemporary England was a direct product of the war, and that Michael and Margaret were in a sense the innocent spawn of the war. However, since Michael and Margaret were mere children during the war, incapable even of recalling the bombing of London, the problem became one of dramatizing the past, of relating wartime England to post-war England, of providing a kind of historical consciousness for characters who had none of their own. Hencher served this function. He became the carrier of Michael and Margaret's past as well as of their future; I thought of him as the seedbed of their pathetic lives. To me Hencher is a thoroughly sympathetic character, though some readers would probably consider him (wrongly, I think) to be merely crippled, perverse, distasteful. My own feeling is that Hencher's innocence, like Michael and Margaret's, can only suffer destruction by ruthless victimizers in a time of impoverishment. But paradoxically, in *The Lime Twig* as in my other novels, even the victimizers have "their dreams of shocking purity," to quote Albert Guerard.

Does teaching creative writing at Brown influence your own work in any way? Have you noticed any changes?

I think not. It may be that teaching has made clearer to me the possibilities for disrupting conventional forms of fiction, and no doubt I've benefited considerably from the imaginative exchange that occurs between teacher and student. There's a reassuring immediacy in students' needs and abilities. But it seems to me that the pleasures of teaching have to do with other people's writing and discoveries, rather than with your own. As you know, writing students are infinitely capable; the very variety of their work demands an appreciation from the teacher which forces him away from his own personal bias, and this, I think, is one of the most important aspects of academic life for the writer. There's a special value in a student's own work, and in his resistance as well as his enthusiastic response to the teacher.

This anticipates, then, the next question, which is whether as a teacher you discern any trends among students as writers or whether you find all kinds and don't see any general patterns among them.

I've always tried not to generalize about students. Ten years ago the most exciting students were as unpredictable as they seem to me today. The trends and patterns that do appear to be developing among student writers strike me as superficial. As far as the undergraduate sexual revolution is concerned, I don't find it evident in student writing. That is, I've known unusually gifted and mature younger writers throughout my years of teaching.

Are there any younger writers whom you think undervalued?

It seems to me that Grace Paley has not received the recognition she deserves. Three very different but promising first novels, *This Passing Night* by Clive Miller, *Seven Days of Mourning* by L. S. Simckes, and *Run River* by Joan Didion should have received more appreciation, I feel. On the other hand, William Melvin Kelley, who began to write in a class of mine at Harvard, wrote a first novel, *A Different Drummer*, which received an award from the National Institute of Arts and Letters—obviously a hopeful indication that early encouragement is perhaps more prevalent now than it used to be. And Susan Sontag's first novel, *The Benefactor*, has received appropriate attention, though I must say I disagree with those reviews that described the prose in this book as an easy imitation of French style. Susan Sontag's writing is often pure, controlled, disturbing in the best sense, and highly pleasurable. Her novel assumes a genuinely significant attitude toward sexual experience, her use of a first-person male narrator reveals an extraordinary kind of imaginative knowledge.

We are back almost to where we came in with internationalism and French influence.

I would still say that internationalism rather than influence is the point. Malamud and Nabokov are international writers, but their work really doesn't raise the question of influence. I think that a younger writer like Susan Sontag is promising precisely because of those moments in her novel where she's turning philosophical abstraction into concretely rendered life and is overcoming mere influence through her own imaginative pressures.

Would you want to say a few words about what you think is the ideal relationship between the writer and the university where he teaches?

It pleases me that Flannery O'Connor wrote her first novel in the writing program at Iowa and that so many writers, including for instance Malamud, Nabokov, and Susan Sontag, either are or have been teachers. I suppose the university world is a good one for the writer because it provides him with a literal experience in which he's both involved and detached in terms of life materials and intellectual and artistic effort. I think the writer, like other faculty members, should teach with commitment and offer what he can to the life around him; I think the university should encourage the writer's work with time off. There's no question any more about the place of the writer or artist within the university; the only question concerns the extent to which the university is equipped to foster artistic activity. Personally—and despite what I said earlier—I wouldn't give up teaching entirely even if I could.

I don't know quite how to phrase this, but it seems that in your work one of the things that is unique, in comparison with other modern writers, is the setting of your novels in an alien situation, one which you personally have never experienced as far as the actual milieu is concerned. You have never been in England, for instance, and the setting of The Beetle Leg *and the others is far from literal. Is there any particular reason for this? Do you feel you are getting at important matters more effectively than you would have out of your own, more immediate world?*

I take literally rather than figuratively the cliché about breaking new ground. Or I take literally the idea that the imagination should always uncover new worlds for us—hence my "mythic" England, Germany, Italy, American west, tropical island, and so on. I want to write about worlds that are fresh to me. But in his preface to *The Secret Agent,* Conrad speaks of the sights and sounds of London crowding in on him and inhibiting his imagination. And this danger of familiarity is something I've tried almost unthinkingly to avoid. As I've said, my writing depends on absolute detachment, and the unfamiliar or invented landscape helps me to achieve and maintain this detachment. Such a landscape provides an initial and helpful challenge. I don't want to write autobiographical fiction, though I admire Agee's *A Death in the Family* or the ways in which Conrad or Ford Maddox Ford transform elements of personal experience and elements of subjective life into fiction. I want to try to create a world, not represent it. And of course I believe that the creation ought to be more significant than the representation.

We can have a last question. In The Lime Twig *you killed off Michael Banks and Margaret, the gang survive, at the end the detectives do not accomplish much. Despite what you've said about comedy, this novel doesn't appear to be very hopeful. Would you care to comment on this problem?*

For me the blackest fictions liberate the truest novelistic sympathy. When Michael is killed the whole world collapses with him, and comically—that is, the race track is littered with the bodies of the fallen jockeys and horses. And at the moment of Margaret's death, Larry, the head of the gang, is speaking comically about his hopes of journeying to a new world full of lime trees. (It's a journey which he won't be able to take of course, since his gigantic plan has failed.) But at any rate Michael has destroyed the "golden bowl" of earthly pleasure and destructive dream and has atoned for his betrayal of Margaret. This ending along with the novel's general pairing off of sensual and destructive experiences to me suggests a kind of hope. The fictional rhythm itself is in a way hopeful. But I admit I'm reluctant to argue too strongly for the necessity of hope.

What about the detectives? Are they anything more than comic?

The detectives represent law and order, or the baffled and banal mind at large. Specifically, and along with Sidney Slyter, they may be seen as images of the absurd and lonely author himself. Even the author is not exempt from judgment in my fiction. But at least the detectives, in trying to learn what the reader has presumably learned already (and it's clear, I think, that these obtuse men from Scotland Yard will never solve the "crime"), are attempting to complete the cycle of mysterious experience. At least they, like ourselves, will go on hunting for clues.

ESSAYS

♦

Notes on Writing a Novel

JOHN HAWKES

A scholarly, gifted, deeply good-natured friend once remarked that "Notes on Writing a Novel" is a deplorably condescending title. And I think he's right.

At that moment, as one more brief illumination gave way to typical frustration, I thought of a metaphor with which I'd ended a talk on fiction ten years ago at Boston College, when I said that "for me, the writer of fiction should always serve as his own angleworm, and the sharper the barb with which he fishes himself out of the darkness, the better."

But when I proposed "The Writer as Angleworm" as an alternative, my friend pointed out that preciousness is worse than condescension.

"Notes on Writing a Novel" is condescending because of its deceptive simplicity. In fact it represents everything that I deplore in any discussion of fiction, since it suggests that the writing of fiction is really a very off-hand matter; that we all do it, all the time, between various chores; but worst of all, that the writing of fiction is an orderly process. The implication is that if you learn the tools of the trade you'll be able to build the house, which may be true enough for certain carpenters but not, it seems to me, for writers and artists. That is, the learning of the craft does not necessarily result in authentic art or writing. (Here I ought to say that if a student used that homely "house-building" metaphor, I'd be outraged, and rightly so. But we are all our own worst betrayers.)

The other idea—of the writer serving as his own angleworm and fishing himself out of the darkness—raises the problem of the relationship between the writer and his fiction, and implies that fiction is simply about the writer or that the fiction writer can only write what he "knows," which is another popular misconception about the dazzling and painful process of writing. On the one hand there's the thoughtless notion that the finished novel is simply a book at best produced by some long-forgotten machine instead of by a living or once living person. And on the other hand there's the equally misleading notion that the ultimate key to the novel lies in the life of the writer, which is untrue.

Reprinted with permission from *Triquarterly* 30 (Spring 1974): 109–26. © John Hawkes. This piece appeared, in somewhat different form, in *Brown Alumni Monthly*.

At any rate it's the "dazzling and painful process" that I'm trying in one way or another to expose.

My novel *Second Skin* was written in eight swift magnificent months in 1962–63, when my wife and children and I were living in the natural lushness and clarity of an island in the Caribbean. But this novel actually had its genesis in the distant past of my childhood, was related to other fiction I'd written by that time, appeared to depend on a few strange moments when literal event and imagined event coincided, and underwent a fairly extensive metamorphosis several years before we lived on our splendid island. So for me *Second Skin* lends itself in special ways to the discussion of the fiction process.

There are other more specific reasons why I like talking about *Second Skin* and why I've tried (unsuccessfully) more than once before to reconstruct its beginnings, and why I'll no doubt continue in the future to try (unsuccessfully) to convey how this novel was written. *Second Skin* was the first novel I knew I wanted to write entirely in the first person; it was a novel I finally managed to write with genuine ease and considerable pleasure; it was the first novel in which I was explicitly attempting to write comic fiction. (I might add that I'm no longer interested in writing comic novels, that I'm wary now of the "safety" inherent in the comic form, that from now on I want to come still closer to terror, which I think I'm doing in the short novel I'm trying to write at the moment.) Furthermore, *Second Skin* does, as I say, have some of its sources in actuality. But whereas much of my earlier fiction was concerned with what Albert J. Guerard has called "landscapes of sexless apathy" (and it was in Albert Guerard's class at Harvard that I wrote my first two short novels), *Second Skin* reveals for the first time in my work a kind of sexual affirmation, since it's told by a 59-year-old ex-Navy lieutenant, junior-grade, who is an artificial inseminator of cows on a tropical island, and since the novel ends with the birth of a black child—all of which I still find pleasurable, despite my longings for pure terror.

In brief, *Second Skin* is about the futile efforts of its narrator, who is known variously as Skipper or Papa Cue Ball, to prevent the suicide of his only daughter, Cassandra. Skipper tells his "naked history," as he calls it, while living in idyllic timelessness on a floating tropical island with his Second World War mess boy, Sonny. As he waits for the birth of Catalina Kate's child, who may have been fathered both by Sonny and by Skipper, and as he lyrically impregnates great Brahmin cows or swims in the clear limpid midnight sea, Skipper recalls how he attempted but failed to save the life of Cassandra who, on a small cold island off the New England coast, finally jumped to her death from an abandoned lighthouse. The juxtaposition of the two islands, the juxtaposition of Cassandra's death and the eventual birth of Catalina Kate's black child—these are the essential opposites of *Second Skin*.

As I say, this novel is certainly not autobiographical. I myself have only seen the unhappily banal process of artificial insemination. And the true sources of fiction—interesting fiction—no doubt lie buried in some inaccessible depth of the psyche. And yet the two islands in *Second Skin* share obvious similarities with two quite real islands, while many images and the deepest thematic preoccupations of this novel do have their shadowy counterparts in memory.

Here, then, is something of the personal chronology that lies behind *Second Skin*. When I was a thin, horseback-riding, asthmatic child of about eight years old, we were living in a small old-fashioned Connecticut village on the edge of Long Island Sound. And one of my earliest and strongest recollections is of a girl, a first cousin, who now for me is only myth but whom I loved as a child.

When I was about 17, I happened by accident to enter a room in which a relative of mine was threatening to commit suicide. Or perhaps this moment was merely a dream.

When I was 22, Sophie and I were married at the end of one summer that was all the more beautiful because we lived it in the brilliant barrenness of Montana. It was there in Montana, while waiting with fierce eagerness and fierce anxiety for the moment of marriage, that I first turned to fiction and wrote about half of my first short novel, *Charivari*, a highly surrealistic vision of a middle-aged couple, Henry and Emily Van, who are embarking on marriage with all the fear and innocence of youth. Emily's father is a general, Henry's a parson. The projections and transformations are obvious, though I was fairly unaware of them at the time.

When I was 24 and finishing my first novel, *The Cannibal*, in Albert Guerard's course, and also finishing my last two years at Harvard (I was always a poor student and had lost several semesters thanks to the war), Sophie and I became friends with a younger student, an enormous life-filled humorous artistic person whom we loved until his death, and still do.

When I was about 30, I began to teach at Harvard, where Sophie and I became friends with Edwin Honig—who helped to allay those earliest terrors of teaching, who gave us his poetry, who talked even then of an island off the New England coast where he had spent one perfect isolated year writing poetry.

The next year Edwin Honig came to Brown. The year after, I too came to Brown. The following spring Sophie and I read a poem of Edwin Honig's called "Island Storm." And that was the summer we managed to spend on the island of Edwin's poem, where we ate blueberry pancakes while watching smaller off-shore islands emerge out of the dawn, and where I began to try to write a novel which—abortive, unfinished—became the written genesis of *Second Skin*.

Two years later, in the spring, our life-filled friend from Harvard committed suicide. That fall Sophie and our by now four young children and I went to our coral-ringed island in the Caribbean. There at last I had *Second Skin* firmly in mind and wrote it.

From this brief personal chronology, I would infer so far that if we're lucky our friends are poets, while events of the imagination precede and sometimes even outdo the events of life itself. I say this because my life owes much to poets and because in the case of the New England island, at least, I experienced some version of it as a child, imagined a truer version of it as a young man writing *Charivari,* glimpsed in the real island the one I had already written about, found this island most real in Edwin Honig's poem, then tried to create it one last time from the vantage point of its opposite—which was a serene and spice-scented island in the tropics.

By now it's obvious that I'm obsessed among other things with the sea and with islands, and whereas Donne says that "no man is an island," I myself believe that we're all islands—inaccessible, drifting apart, thirsting to be explored, magical.

I remember very little of my marvelous mythical cousin. She was tall, she was beautiful, she was energetic, no doubt she was to me another version of my own mother. But in light of the imagination, at least, and incestuous implications aside, surely she must have been my first love.

I can't remember anything about my cousin and me—the slender invisible girl and the skinny child—except that we walked. Again and again I see the two of us walking, merely walking, and always down the same empty lane in the twilight toward the water and, most important, into a great abandoned half-built house on the very edge of that gray darkening ocean. I remember longing in some vague way for the love of my cousin. Now it seems to me that she must have spent all of her adolescence taking me on exactly the same thrilling but also dreadful walk at the end of each of the days of my childhood. And what kind of lovely and lonely adolescent girl would want to spend her afternoons taking her little cousin into the empty rooms of a monstrous castle-like hull of a house that was built so close to the sea and so imperfectly, so incompletely, that the ocean would suddenly roar up inside the unfinished room where we stood holding hands, great waves smashing onto the black rocks actually visible below us at the edge of the unfinished floor, and then receding and leaving spumes of foam lying around our wet shoes? The wind and the sea used to roar through that hopeless house, and I would be terrified and more in love with my cousin than ever.

I don't know what kind of person she was. She was probably only an ordinary young girl helping her aunt by occasionally taking her aunt's little boy on a walk. But that same girl led me happily into the terrors of a microcosmic New England, into the world of dead houses with beams like great bones, and toward the ocean that lies vast and ominous at the end of a country road. She embodied what I've feared and yearned for ever since, and the abandoned house she used to take me to is clearly the source of three related visions or images that have obsessed me as long as I can recall: the abandoned lighthouse, the abandoned ocean liner leaning on its side in low tide far from shore, and the New England fishing village on an island.

The island fishing village is something I've long pursued, then, in the imagination, in fiction, and finally in actuality. And in various forms it appears in *Charivari*, "The Nearest Cemetery" (the fragment preliminary to *Second Skin* and written on the island where Edwin Honig lived), and lastly in *Second Skin*. The abandoned lighthouse is central to Cassandra's death in *Second Skin*. But my vision of the ocean liner hasn't appeared as such in my fiction, and still remains what it's always been: a personal waking dream in which I stand alone at the edge of a straight empty shore at low tide and gaze with both fear and longing at an enormous black derelict or damaged ocean liner that looms in awful silence in knee-deep water about a mile from shore. A few lifeboats hang halfway down the side of the ship from their davits; on the ship there is no movement, only the black immensity and the smokeless funnels and the occasional small flash of some piece of metal on the deck or in the rigging. And then I am compelled to walk slowly but deliberately into the muddy shallow water and toward the ship.

In this waking dream I know that I am going to have to walk the entire distance from shore to the listing ship. I know that I am going to climb somehow to the tilted deck of the abandoned ship. I know that I must discover its vast world, must pry open some metal door rusted half ajar and enter the ship until I discover what it contains—either its treasure, if childhood hopes prevail, or its emptiness, its floating corpses.

The vision, no matter how personal, is one of potential and desolation. It suggests the undiminishing power of childhood experience, it defines what I'm most interested in writing about, it becomes suddenly literal in *Second Skin* when Skipper happens to see a long dark ship drifting by on the horizon and finds himself filled with both joy and dread.

Charivari, from which we get our word "shivaree" (the comic and vulgar rites for harassing newlyweds), is about marriage. In this youthful short novel (which is to say that it's whimsical, surrealistic, clumsy, indulgent, often poetic in quite the wrong way), Henry and Emily Van are, as I've said, a strange and lonely pair of middle-aged people newly married. At the hands of each other, and especially at the hands of their aged parents, they undergo a kind of double suffering—of the indignities of middle-age and of the vulnerabilities of youth. Whether *Charivari* was at the time an accurate self-portrait thinly veiled in wild distortion and surging prose (since at the time of our marriage I thought of myself as dourly old), or whether it was instead a kind of terrifying glimpse into the future (some of my friends still consider me deplorably adolescent), nonetheless even *Charivari* evokes its share of universal burdens of desire and anxiety framed in the rituals and conditions of married life.

One of Henry Van's worst fears is the possible loss of Emily, and one section of *Charivari* is devoted to the moment when Henry's fears come true and Emily disappears. In a violent storm and in a small archaic fishing village,

Henry does catch a sudden dream-like glimpse of the missing Emily, only to lose her.

The wind shot down the main street, oscillating, shimmering from side to side, pulling with its giant tail armfuls of driving rain from the doldrums; it broke off in tangents to be drawn into a chimney flue, to swirl madly, trapped in a dead end, or to fly swiftly and vertically up the crevice between two houses, to be spent in the still aimless air high above. The main blow beat its way down the narrow street, tearing leaves from trees and rattling windows, smashed between two warehouses and jumped out to sea, tearing frantically at the waves. The rain was almost impenetrable; it beat like nail heads on the rotting wood, and covered cobblestones with a running slime.

Henry lost his nerve. Pummeled he stood heaving to and fro, floundering, flapping wildly, in the middle of the street before her house. His hands shifted and beat the air, thrusting outward to clutch at lost supports, to maintain a precarious balance; he hung by the good graces of the wind. He laughed and felt himself shoving off at last, but he simply couldn't go to the house.

The door opened and she came out and walked easily into the storm. For a moment she was but thirty feet from him. Miraculously the black hat stayed in place. He could almost see the features of the face, oh, Emily, yes, yes, the howling wind, the shadowed mouth open to gasp for air behind that wind, the eyes covered by a constant veil, the hair beating upon the open throat. Fish were being hammered against the logs, clouds collided with mountains of water, the fishing nets tore loose, and wandering, flying, flung themselves on teakwood ribs, sky, and rocks.

For one brief moment his hope and desire came together, to walk up to her, hold her, speak to her, hold the blowing hair. The taste of salt was on his lips. Then he turned and was carried off down the street. Once he turned back and saw that she was following.

This was his gigantic hold, the town of water. He noticed each blurred metallic color or lack of color, each gray and black, each wet shadow, salt and iron of the sea and blood. Drawn to her, he fled from her, happier in each dolphin-winged spasm, careening along with pillaging, battling black birds. To catch fish. To catch grain. To shed the strengthening water. He bent his body and ran disjointedly for cover. The inn door. Pieces of driftwood were pounding on the shore; a deep loud voice from the doldrums. Sailors from Madagascar, ships from the Caribbean, the Puritan, iron hulks from Liverpool, plunging their crimson sails and tarred lines through the surf, they hovered in the harbor. No sun, no moon, only hurling starfish and fine foam, water hauling in the wizened lives.

Leather rots; rubber comes alive; the beach erodes; the fungus grows; the sound of the wailing bell. And always that barely remembered woman behind him, the faint flush of youth and scrubbed cheeks.

Despite the many embarrassing moments in this passage, this is at least the first moment when my imaginary island fishing village became fictional. The passage embarrasses me for its awful adverbs, for its colloquialisms

("Henry lost his nerve," which is a shocking lapse from the rhetoric of "running slime"), for the extremely youthful lapse into Henry's interior consciousness ("oh, Emily, yes, yes"), for its sentence fragments, for its lapses into iambic pentameter. All of these are distracting indulgences, the extremes of inexperience. They're all to be avoided.

And yet Henry's "town of water" is precisely my own seaside Connecticut village and that empty half-built house echoing with the sound of waves at the water's edge—though while writing *Charivari* I'm sure I never gave a thought to my childhood. Then too, this passage reveals the beginnings of my own fictional insistencies (the wind and rain become animated and start to take over the passage, the writer dwells lovingly on images and details of decay and corruption) and reveals too the beginnings of my own writing voice (heard, I think, in such phrasing as "beat like nail heads on the rotting wood"). But the association of the "barely remembered woman," who is idealized for her "faint flush of youth," with a vast violent world of death, sexlessness, and misogyny, is in fact the thematic center of all that I've written. And what I realized some time ago was that the language of this passage had served as an unconscious source for much of the language in *Second Skin*.

A few moments after catching his glimpse of Emily in the storm, Henry watches while a group of hip-booted old men haul up Emily's drowned body in a basket stretcher from the low tide at the end of a rotting pier. And yet by the end of *Charivari* this death is revealed to have been merely hallucinatory, and Emily lives. Emily Van is the only pseudo-victim in my fiction. All the other victims stay maimed or dead, as the case may be.

In the spring of 1960 Edwin Honig gave Sophie and me a copy of his then newly published book of poems, *The Gazabos*. And it was at that moment, when I first read aloud to Sophie Edwin's poem "Island Storm," that the island (or lost New England world) of my own preoccupations leapt out from the page—as real, as tangible, as powerful as it has ever been, before or since.

My reading of "Island Storm" was and still is personal, selfish, since while being aware of the poem as a gift of art, I was most elated at the sudden shocking appearance of a specific imagined world which I took as real, as suddenly created by another writer out of the rain and sea, and as mine.

When I read this poem I felt that I too was a version of its narrator, and that I too was surviving the battering rain, the darkening storm in a place I recognized and wanted to be in—despite its cataclysmic chaos, its unavoidable terror. And even then I thought that the poem had already made inevitable our actual journey to the "cold, Atlantic island," as Skipper calls it in *Second Skin*.

Here, then, is "Island Storm":

All morning in the woods I heard the bushes choke
  Among dead boughs that creaked and groaned,
And no other murmur than the flurry of live prey
  Grappling in the wind's slow teeth.
A starling toppled near the river-run, black
  As stone. A garter snake shivered
Up a root and instantly turned brown. It began
  On such a day prophets used
To rave about—"Stiff-necked mankind, remember
  Sodom and God's frown!" Through miles
Of tensing acreage only two eyes peeped when it
  Came down. The road became a falls
Where hubbubs fell to foam across a glazed surrendering
  Of channelled stone. In the hollow beat
Of some annihilating warmth, tumorous old stumps
  Were ground to muck. "Will it be day
Again?" I heard the brittle window ask the lightning
  Flash, and tremble three full hours
As it spoke. Often, while the sea coughed distantly,
  Infamous last words of misanthropes
Ransacked my brain for counter-prayers. Below the eaves,
  Crackling like a greasy frying
Pan, only a floral lampshade quavered hope.

When at last the silence trickled in, I found
  The fungi like great plastered wounds,
The stupefying sweetness everywhere. And when
  The weather turned gigantically
And padded off, I found the world it left nearby:
  On the bloated attic floor
Two drowned mice; through the skylight, one fir
  Permanently bowed; above the flooded
Garden, the first fierce dart of an exploratory crow.*

This, it seems to me, is a dark and unmistakably New England world, ringing with loneliness and all the destructive frightening cadences of the old puritanical voice, which is "saved" or finally destroyed by the poet's own voice. I like the moments of awesome sound in this poem, I think its beauty depends magnificently on the way the world of nature is first mythologized, or personified, and then "collapsed" to a few palpable details of concrete reality. But I myself quicken most of all to the "tumorous old stumps" and to the fungi "like great plastered wounds," since these images make me think of *Charivari* ("Leather rots; rubber comes alive; the beach erodes; the fungus grows; the sound of the wailing bell"), and since this special sympathy for decay, deterioration, destruction (and for the maimed, the victimized) is one of the essential qualities of the imagination, evident as it is in "The Ancient Mariner," say, or in the mammoth, bruised and battered and aged tortoises of Melville's *Encantadas*.

And then, and only a few weeks later, we went to the Atlantic island. On a cold, bright, early summer morning we sailed with our then three young children on an old white fishing boat converted to carry passengers and, on its spongy, wooden deck, a single car, until we had crossed the 11 necessary miles of brilliant sea, with the boat smelling of dead fish and engine fumes, and our little five-year-old girl seasick down below in her mother's arms in the dark and foul-smelling cabin, until we sailed down the length of the island and rounded a promontory and for the first time saw my imaginary fishing village clustered around its shimmering boat-filled harbor (as I had known it would be), and then docked and carried ashore our little girl who was already a victim—poor thing—of the island I myself was so terribly drawn to.

This was what the imagination had suddenly and at last produced: the sun, the black shining sea, the cluster of bleached houses, the bright boats, an enormous abandoned white house on another promontory, and overhead the marvelous white scavenging gulls. And only a few miles from the village we saw for ourselves the row of "permanently bowed" fir trees from "Island Storm."

So for that summer we lived on the island, eating our blueberry pancakes on a veranda overlooking the sea and a few smaller islands, sleeping in bedclothes that smelled of mothballs in a small clapboard house with wrinkled linoleum on the kitchen floor and a playable, wooden pump-organ in one of the small rooms. The privy was like an upended coffin, there were stunted apple trees on the slope between the porch and the sea, we lived in the rhythms of bright sun and heavy fog. We walked, we explored the island, the children painted designs on rocks and pieces of driftwood, and up under the eaves of one of the narrow bedrooms (that smelled of camphor and dead insects) I wrote about 50 pages of the fragment called "The Nearest Cemetery" that immediately preceded *Second Skin*.

The landscape, charged as it was with personal meaning, the landscape at once familiar and unfamiliar, the constant dream-like appearance of symbols in nature (the gigantic rocks like human skulls, the foreboding trees), and that strange psychological pull exerted by the unexpected confluence of sloping farmland and open sea—in the context of all this I was, for the first time, prompted to try to write fiction out of the very world I was living in. I was so moved by the vivid mythical atmosphere of the island that I thought I could overcome the dangers inherent in immediacy. And perhaps in *Second Skin* I did finally overcome the risks of immediacy.

An anecdote, a real woman, and a few rumors cohered to give rise to the story of "The Nearest Cemetery." We hadn't been on the island a week when I heard an anecdote about a local barber who had been accused of molesting a child and who managed to jump overboard and drown himself when he was being taken from the island back to the mainland for arraignment and trial.

And then there was a woman, the wife of a summering New Yorker who lived somewhere up the island road from us, who daily passed our cottage wearing a pale blue kerchief and waving and calling out in a lovely voice to the children. The rumors (and I disagree with Mary McCarthy's notion that fiction is a form of gossip, yet sometimes can't help valuing the malice and humor of good gossip), the rumors were that this marvelous woman in the blue kerchief was in fact known throughout the island. She was known, according to the rumors, in culverts, in fields, in dank places among the trees, in abandoned farm houses filled with rotting mattresses and broken whiskey bottles. She was everywhere, we heard, this defenseless and unhappy and smiling woman, and I thought of her as everywhere and pure. I called her the Princess. I used to sit in the privy and think of the Princess or hear her voice, as she called out to our children from the country road, and imagine her blue kerchief which she always wore when the wind was blowing and when it was calm. The fiction that came to mind was about a woman called the Princess who had many lovers and was murdered by the local barber. "The Nearest Cemetery" begins with a kind of stage setting and Faulknerian cast of characters:

SCENE OF NARRATION:	a small state penitentiary in New England.
CHARACTERS:	
THE PRINCESS:	summer visitor to Bloody Clam Shell Island; unhappy wife of a New York meatpacker; woman of beauty; victim of the local barber.
MILDRED:	the barber's wife.
CAPTAIN RED:	lobsterman in his fiftieth year; first lover of the Princess.
BLUD:	lighthouse keeper; Mildred's brother; second lover of the Princess.
JOMO:	off-island gas station attendant and vicious smalltown sport; third lover of the Princess.
THE BARBER:	narrator; fourth and final lover of the Princess. He loved her from afar and killed her.

My notion was that three ordinary men—Captain Red, Blud, Jomo— had all committed various crimes for the sake of the Princess, with whom they had all experienced extravagant and not entirely loveless sexuality, and so at the time of the barber's narration were to be imprisoned; and also that the barber, whose love for the Princess was purely imaginary, had finally murdered the Princess in order to preserve his ideal love. At the time of his narration, then, the barber was to be imprisoned with the other three, was to spend his days cutting their hair and waiting for the inevitable moment when he, the barber, was to be revengefully murdered by the other three. In my mind, at least, the barber had buried the dismembered remains of the Princess in the town dump, and was a doomed romantic worthy somehow of compassion.

Here's an example of the barber's interior voice, of the barber talking to himself at night in his prison cell, obsessed with the dead Princess and with his own wife (Mildred, the New England Puritan) and aware of his own approaching murder by the men who actually did have some kind of crude capacity to love.

So the mind lies between the echoing coffins of the ears—a barber's ears—and you try to calm it in the midst of all that roar and whisper while a shadow falls through the bars and sweeps your chest. But then I raise my hands; I hold one ear; I hold both of them; I press with my palms. Because then it is not Mildred's voice I hear—not the voice, though I hear it often enough—but rather Mildred playing steadily on the church organ, Mildred pumping her feet, Mildred pushing the keys and Mildred making the reeds and seagulls shriek. And in each of Mildred's chords is the heavy harmony of the Lord and bass voice of Mildred's other brother who died from drink. And I cannot bear to listen. The barber cannot bear to listen to Mildred pumping and marching with the Lord at the town's church organ. The Lord and Mildred deafen me. They make me think of lying dead and naked beside the body of the shipwrecked woman on Crooked Finger Rock at the height of the gale.

Short as the watch that ends the night is what I hear, and *Time like an ever-rolling stream, Bears all its sons away* is what I hear, the phrases filling the mind with their monotony and fear, and *They fly, forgotten, as a dream Dies at the opening of day*—all of it this booming, this beating of hymn on slick shingles and empty beach, and the Lord and Mildred are bearing me away to the Rock. Singing. Bearing off the naked barber to the heart of the hymn that is the gate, carrying me away at the center, easily, while the plankton spurts aloft into the dark of the storm, and I fly, fly, while Vinny cranks his truck in the wind and Mildred sings with the lost brother.

The barber. But even the barber has his tongue and toes and fingers, his hidden hair. The barber too has his lungs of twisted and dampened paper, his ears in which the islands float, his eyes that gleam, his sensitivity to skin, his touch. And sometimes I think I am all water. Hair and water. What the crack leaps upon, leaping to deform the image further, is nothing and my shop is on Bloody Clam Shell Island—closed, safely boarded up—while I am here.

No doubt this is the rhetoric of tormented sexlessness and a punitive religious preoccupation with death. These are the guilt-ridden lofty cadences of someone beguiled by but also hating New England puritanism. I like this deadly situation and hymn-book prose (deriving as it does from *Charivari* and, more important, serving as the immediate source of the language in *Second Skin*). But the fact of the matter is that the very intensity or inflation of this interior monologue was the reason "The Nearest Cemetery" failed.

By the summer's end I gave up on the barber, partly because I couldn't sustain his relentless interior monologue, partly because I had already heard another anecdote, this time of a man who with remarkable tenderness and selflessness was devoting his life to a futile attempt to save his daughter from the oblivion of emotional illness. And suddenly I was much more interested in the selfless father (who couldn't be entirely blameless for the emotional state of his daughter) and in the deteriorating girl who was to become the object of her father's steadfast care and unwitting love.

For the next two years I thought about this story of an older man's unsuccessful efforts to preserve his daughter's sanity on a New England island.

And then in the spring of 1962 I came down with pneumonia (when Providence was a place of iron and ice and fever and dead morality rattling in the bitter wind). And in that same terrible and often delirious season we heard by telephone that our humorous, artistic, life-filled friend from Harvard had committed suicide. Weeks later I knew that I wanted to write a novel about an older man attempting to preserve his daughter not from insanity but from suicide, that the real center of the novel had to be sexuality and suicide, that the novel would be comic, and that I wanted to write it not in infectious Providence but on a tropical island, where we would all flourish in the sun and I, incidentally, would gain new detachment from the Atlantic island.

Thanks to a Guggenheim Fellowship and, once again, Edwin Honig, who gave us a ten-year-old guide book called *Paradise Isles of the World,* we did indeed flee Providence for the West Indies—where all of our children became violently sick when we drove from the airport over the mountains and through the rain-forests to our crescent of perfect beach, and where we did flourish (on the beach, in the clear sea, surrounded by tropical wildflowers and humming-birds and the underwater coral beds of the earth's navel), and where I spent my timeless mornings sitting on a veranda in the trade winds (wearing gangster-style dark glasses and holding a clipboard against the wind) and writing *Second Skin.* Surely *Paradise Isles of the World* is final proof of the poet's invulnerability and unerring vision, since the island we found was in every way as lyrical as the one we read about, which means that Edwin's own poetic vision somehow "corrected" a guide book ten years out of date.

In those eight months of warmth and clarity I felt suspended, free, detached, confident (as if life itself had become a fiction or the purest kind of ritual), and it gave me a secret, even crafty pleasure to invoke the cold dark Atlantic island while sitting amidst the light and spices of a tropical world, or to fictionalize Skipper's tropical landscape while having freshly in mind some recently written scene of New England coldness and brutality. Skipper was now a heavy benevolent middle-aged disreputable Prospero creating both his present and past life on a wandering tropical island (since my fictive plan was once again invaded by actuality—Brahmin cows, towering sugar cane, sea fans waving in the depths of the clear water, candles burning at night in a sunken cemetery—so that now I had to write about the southern idyllic island as well as about the northern one); and the Princess became Skipper's daughter Cassandra; the barber's wife Mildred became the heavy-set seductive landlady who fails to win Skipper and so plots to involve Cassandra with Captain Red and Jomo, knowing that these sexual liaisons will lead inevitably to Cassandra's suicide; while Captain Red remained the same, as did Jomo—except that I had the pleasure of deciding that Jomo would be one-handed, so that the steel hook that served as his missing hand would also exemplify the ruthlessness of his sexual greed. On the tropical island I believed more strongly than ever that the Atlantic island was filled with men like Jomo and Captain Red. They carried knives, they had long black sideburns, they lolled on the wharves and back roads leading to abandoned trysting places, their skin was made of fishscales—and they were poor, violent, isolated, admirable. In the sun of the tropical island the dangerous death-ridden landscape of the Atlantic island loomed with a beauty quite the equivalent of the Caribbean island paradise.

I'd like to leave you with a final vision of the abandoned lighthouse which in its desolation organizes the fears and longings of childhood, but also remains standing everywhere in New England—in the form of old houses, fallen tombstones, half-sunken boats, and most of all in the endless long-empty factories still somehow suggesting the piety and callousness and expended energy that no longer exist.

In this passage Skipper is climbing up the inside of the abandoned lighthouse in his futile effort to prevent the last sexual encounter between Jomo and Cassandra. But Jomo and Cassandra have already made love at the top of the empty lighthouse. Jomo has already fled the scene. Cassandra has already leapt naked from the top of the lighthouse to her death on the rocks below—a fact which Skipper knows but can't admit.

The iron gut of the tower remained intact, and I crawled to the top and crawled back down again without mishap, without a fall. But the damage was done. I knew it was done before I reached the top, and I began to hurry and began to whisper: "Cassandra? He's gone now, Cassandra, it's all right now . . . you'll see. . . ." I heard nothing but the echoing black sky and tiny skin-crawling sounds above me and the small splash, the eternal picking fingers of wave on rock below. "Cassandra?" I whispered, and tried to pull myself up the last few shaky steps, tried to fight down dizziness, tried to see, "you're not crying, are you, Cassandra? Please don't. . . ."

But the damage was done and I was only an old bird in an empty nest. I rolled up onto the iron floor in the smashed head of the lighthouse and crawled into the lee of the low wall and pulled myself into a half-sitting position and waited for the moment when Dog's Head light must tremble and topple forward into the black scum of the rising tide far below.

"Gone, Cassandra? Gone so soon?" I whispered. "Gone with Gertrude, Cassandra? Gone to Papa? But you shouldn't have, Cassandra. You should have thought of me. . . ."

The neat pile of clothing was fluttering a little in the moonlight and it was damp to the touch. . . .

I clutched a couple of the thin rusted stanchions and in the gray moonlight started out to sea. The shoals were miles long and black and sharp, long serrated tentacles that began at the base of the promontory and radiated out to sea, mile after square mile of intricate useless channels and breaking waves and sharp-backed lacerating shoals and spiny reefs. Mile after square mile of ocean cemetery that wasn't even true to its dead but kept flushing itself out on the flood tide. No wonder the poor devils wanted a lighthouse here. No wonder.*

I hope very much that all this says something—and something affirmative—about the writer, the angleworm, the barb, and the darkness. I hope too that we can all keep finding our islands.

Note

*Reprinted by permission.

The Prose Style of John Hawkes

ALBERT J. GUERARD

The critic's natural impulse, faced with such a macabre and inventive writer, is to confine himself to the enormities of conception and incident. This is a fictional world in which violence, anxiety and regression are everyday norms, and our deepest fears and most antisocial impulses are dramatized fairly openly. Oral fantasies and castration fears, inversion, murder and mutilation, dread of impotence and dread of sex—these appear either manifestly or beneath thin disguises. The compulsive, somnambulistic, often well-meaning personages are intimately allied to us. This is our underground life—more truly conveyed, I think, than in the usual psychological novel or in the dry interior notations of the French anti-novel. Moreover, these absurd victims form "societies" in each book, and ironically reflect or discredit our actual public world. I think this side of Hawkes may have been overstressed by critics anxious to find links with real reality. But *The Cannibal* does indeed convey one Germany as few realistic novels have, and *The Lime Twig*'s sordid, damp England is as authentic as Graham Greene's.

All this is worthwhile. But it is well to attend also to the language that informs and at last redeems the enormities: one of the most personal of contemporary prose styles. The style naturally underwent some changes between *The Cannibal* of 1949 and *The Lime Twig* of 1961, as Hawkes became more conscious of his art and vision. The movement has been from murky, groping, brilliant, eccentric expression to deliberate rhetorical manipulation of the reader's anxieties and sympathies. Hawkes, a most gifted critic and teacher, could hardly fail to examine his own procedures. In the change there has been some loss of obsessive visionary power, but there has also been much gain.

In the present essay I shall note a few aspects of this development, and a few continuing characteristics. A fuller analysis would turn to other things: to the recurrences of imagery, for instance; to syntax, to the positioning and post-positioning of adjectives; and to the effects of abrupt or modulative transitions. And to much more.

Reprinted from *Critique: Studies in Contemporary Fiction* 6 (Fall 1963): 19–29, with permission of the Helen Dwight Reid Educational Foundation. Published by Heldref Publications, 4000 Albemarle St., N.W., Washington, DC 20016. Copyright © 1963.

The Relative Abandonment of "Literary" Display

Some of the prose of *The Cannibal* is involuntarily crabbed and awkward; much of it, attending only to its subject, is marvelously evocative. But there is also (as in many young writers of great talent) a love of verbal adventure and display. Our early view of Stella Snow is prettified, feminine, self-conscious and epigrammatic in the manner of Djuna Barnes, or in the manner of Faulkner's *Soldier's Pay:* "She craved candies imported from France and Holland, heard lovers sing in raucous voices, and punting, seemed the image of the passing swan. She had a mouth that inverts envied, and when the first thuds of cannonade rocked the country, the mouth closed and she began to read. She loomed like a waxed noncommital saint when her mother fell before her in the street from marketing, a piece of metal jutting from the bosom, while the airplane crashed."(12)* Some ten thousand words later the effects still remain slightly literary. But the authorial voice now attends more to Stella than to its own riches. A great deal more is compressed into relatively few lines. For Stella is indeed the Teutonic earth-mother possessed of historical prescience, as she waits the caress of Ernst's clawed left hand. The roasted apples, so far as I know, are left unexplained. But the irony of "token pellet" and the dehumanization of the mother (her reduction to a stain dry and black as onyx) are highly characteristic:

> The orchestra filled out the room behind her, roasted apples fell from the bosom of an oracle, burnt and golden, and gradually the three men drew closer, warm with all the taste of a chivalric age. She covered the glass before her with the golden hair and saw for a moment in its swirling depths, the naked cowardice of the fencer, the future fluttering wings of the solitary British plane leaving its token pellet in the market place, her mother's body rolling around it like a stone stained forever, the stain becoming dry and black as onyx.(65)

The impulses to verbal play and gnomic utterance are, fortunately, not wholly abandoned. But—for better or worse—language is largely subjected to story, theme and vision in *The Lime Twig*. In *The Beetle Leg* of 1951 there still remained a good deal of amusing pyrotechnic display. An expository paragraph on Lou Camper resembles closely in its methods Lawrence Durrell's epigrammatic early evocation of Scobie as an old salt. Each of Hawkes' sentences has its several surprises: its twists and turns of syntax, its ridiculously unexpected words, its clichéd and inappropriate gnomic saws—and the *few* broken fingers, the prowess struck off *like a head of hair.* The whole ends with a confident and epigrammatic summation:

> He had an old man's kidney. He had an old man's tumorous girth and thickly dying wind, a hardening on the surface of his armpits. Chest and shoulders were solidified against youth, bulged in what he assumed to be the paunch of middle

age; he was strapping, suffered a neuralgia in winter, a painful unlimbering in the spring. A few fingers were broken, snubbed, since an old man labors from stone to knife to saw to possible tractor accident and back to the single burning of a match flame short in argument. He could laugh, sparsely, at the exploits of men over fifty who enacted, he believed, all they claimed; his own prowess, he told them, had been struck off, like a head of hair, by maturity. And he was, except for a few patches that had to be shaved monthly by a barber, bald; lost by pernicious exposure to the sun, kept from water and finally pulled out one night in a troubled sleep by bloody, rasping fingertips. He mimicked, with unclean, pyretic dignity, the limp folds under the chin, the cockles in the cheeks, the gasp of wisdom and inflammation, the rock-like, seasoned cough of the prime, half invalided buck.(55)

This is a highly controlled set-piece, "written" rather than "spoken," bemused by its own absurd inventiveness. There are also occasional instances in the first two novels of the sentence or the paragraph being wholly carried away—the conception visibly growing as the author writes. Such at least is the effect of the apocalyptic dogs chasing a train in *The Cannibal,* who before the end of the paragraph have leaped on board, become paying passengers, and leaped back into the night and the pack. I find the same effect in a paragraph on shower stalls in *The Beetle Leg.* The passage begins quietly enough: "The stalls were made of planking from the scaffolds." But six sentences later—"the river was filled with the lattice of new lumber, white sawdust fell on the muddy current and the prairie ranchers, riding out of the dunes and through the tents on the bluff to watch, saw wood come into the sand country and not only cut, but cut to special sizes." The creative necessity (so evident in Faulkner) is to magnify and vivify everything, to leave no part of one's fictional world neutral and inert.

This freedom from inhibition—or, this compulsive and exuberant inventiveness—diminishes slightly as we move from *The Cannibal* to *The Lime Twig.* There is substituted for it a more controlled and more sinister accent.

THE APPEALS OF IRONY AND CONTROL

At his best John Hawkes is a master of rich syntax and of the punctuated pause. There is ironic and nervous pleasure in a carefully-paced, orderly, understated recitation of horror. In the Winter 1962 issue of *The Minnesota Review* Claire Rosenfield called attention to the macabre humor of Hattie Lampson's burial near her son, who had died in the Great Slide while building an irrigation dam, and who was accidentally incarcerated in it. The pauses are very effective; and, as Dr. Rosenfield remarks, the humor "makes obscene those vague abstractions we are taught to revere—in this instance, human dignity, religious burial, motherhood": "Face down, eyes in the dirt, she peered through the sandy side toward her son below, where he too lay, more awkward than she, feet up and head in the center of the earth." This is from *The Beetle Leg*. But Hawkes had shown a similar control of syntax and pause in an even more grotesque sentence of *The Cannibal*. There is fine black humor as well as terror in the movement from the detached, traditionally moralizing "without thoughts of trade" to the visualized face knocked backwards, and thence to the grossly anomalous "angry, disturbed." The next sentences bring other fictional pleasures of the Hawksian kind: "There the Merchant, without thoughts of trade, dressed only in grey, still fat, had died on his first day at the front and was wedged, standing upright, between two beams, his face knocked backwards, angry, disturbed. In his open mouth there rested a large cocoon, protruding and white, which moved sometimes as if it were alive. The trousers, dropped about his ankles, were filled with rust and tufts of hair."(115)

The strategies of such irony—of this formal pace and dry measuring of horror, of a calm that itself becomes a component of terror—may be extended to a whole scene; or even, as in *The Lime Twig*, to virtually a whole novel. The passages quoted so far have been relatively open and direct, reasonably innocuous. But in more ambitious scenes powerful displacements occur; the material becomes generally menacing and specifically sexual, with both castration and sexual inversion at stake. In *The Goose on the Grave* (1954) the novices in a monastery are irritated by an old woman demanding religious instruction, and at last they fashion for her a hair shirt made of uncured rat skins with the fur turned in toward the body. They strip her to the waist and sew it over her body. In the telling the episode is made extraordinarily sadistic. The narrator tells us the old woman was not pierced as the pelts were sewn over her, with the first pelts "covering the dugs." But the tone of the passage, as conveyed by language and pauses, suggests that she was.

It is interesting to follow the highly controlled treatment of sexually charged writing from *The Cannibal* through *The Lime Twig*. The most audacious displacement occurs in a crucial scene of *The Cannibal*. The Duke (who is the cannibal of the title) has throughout the novel, and wandering through this ruined town, been in homosexual pursuit of a boy. But the boy, caught at last, has turned into a fox, and the Duke methodically hacks the body to pieces. The passage of about 800 words, from which I extract a few parts, almost reads like a parody of Hawksian horror. The Duke's inhumanity is magnified by his occasional moments of human irritation: his sword cane is "impractical" for dissecting purposes; it had been "another mistake" to leave his glasses at home; he is angry because he lacks practical knowledge of anatomy, and should have "studied the thing out beforehand"; he regrets having brought no "phial for the blood, some sort of thermos or wine bottle perhaps." The ironic chilled measuring prose depends for its effects on great formality of syntax (the parallel clauses, the use of the conditional at a crucial moment, the carefully punctuated pauses). It depends too on a large incidence of abstract words, words relevant to high intellectual discourse, and, of course, on the incessant tendency to classify and order. The passage (excessive as it doubtless is) yet serves as a remarkable evocation of the stolid methodical Teutonic mind, a mind scholarly even in its atrocities:

. . . He should have had a rubber apron like a photographer or chemist, he should have had short sharp blades instead of the impractical old sword cane. The whole business bothered him, now after three or four hours of running about the town in the darkness. For the Duke was an orderly man, not given to passion and since there was a 'von' in his name, he expected things to go by plan. But the odds of nature were against him, he began to dislike the slippery carcass. It took all his ingenuity to find, in the mess, the ears to take as a trophy, to decide which were the parts with dietician's names and which to throw away. At one moment, concentrating his energies, he thought he was at the top of it, then found he was at the bottom, thought he had the heart in his hand, and the thing burst, evaporating from his fingers. . . .
It lost all semblance to meat or fowl, the paw seemed like the foot, the glove the same as the shoe, hock and wrist alike, bone or jelly, muscle or fat, cartilage or tongue, what could he do? He threw them all together, discarding what he thought to be bad, but never sure, angry with his lack of knowledge. . . .
The task was interminable and not for a layman, and the English, he realized, never bothered to cut their foxes up. They at least didn't know as much as he. He sliced, for the last time, at a slender stripped tendon. It gave and slapped back, like elastic, against his hand. It would be pleasant, he thought, to pack these tidbits, be done with them, on ice. Someday, he told himself, he'd have to go through a manual and see exactly how the thing should have been done. The Duke put the blade back in its sheath and making a cane, he hooked the handle over his arm. The organs and mutilated pieces gathered up in the small black fox's jacket, he tied the ends together, used his cane as a staff, and trudged up the hill, his long Hapsburg legs working with excitement. (180–82)

There are ritual, methodical, formal scenes of dancing in each of Hawkes' novels. One of the most interesting, from *The Owl* (1954), resists any easy symbolic interpretation, though the overall burden seems homosexual and the immediate drama one of bondage, sexual or not. Pucento and a dog, last of a breed trained to ritual dancing, execute a fandango and a gavotte. (The concern with cruelty to animals is another strain running through the five novels.) The voice here is obviously a subtler and more personalized one than the voice that described the dissection of the fox. And the overall act of displacement is more oblique. Again it is necessary to select from and break in on carefully modulated prose:

"To the hind legs!" Pucento shouted and proceeded slowly toward the center of the green. His walk was stiff, slow, itself determined by the beauty of the aged provincial combat between man and dog, the mastery of training over the temptation and distraction that plagued the low species. . . .
The dog was muzzled. To the tip of the muzzle into a ring fastened at the end

of the snout was hooked the leash which Pucento and the animal kept taut between them, a thin rein of brilliant red. . . .

On their leaning instruments the musicians played the seldom heard "March of the White Dog." This whole breed had once been deprived and whipped, tied ascetically by the lay brothers on the slopes. The bitches were destroyed. And the rest, heavy of organ and never altered with the knife, day after day were beaten during the brothers' prayers, commanded to be pure unmercifully. The dogs tasted of blood given in mean measure but were not permitted the lather, the howl, the reckless male-letting of their species. Beaten across the quarters, they were taught by the monks the blind, perfectly executed gavotte.

The sole remaining dog moved and balanced as the first packs, flawless, the long wail of refusal still in his throat and still denied him by the muzzle. The dog followed Pucento on the end of the tight rein, a heavy animal, the white coat become tarnished and cream with age. . . . The joints were round, distended, polished to silver, thick though the legs were slim, worn and delicate with the hours of balancing. (62–64)

The dance ends with a peculiar effect of stasis, of frieze, vaguely obscene; or, in Hawkes' own word, "unnatural":

The dog shuddered and swung backward in brutal symmetry, lifted, stood on two legs, then leapt, once, thrice, and each time a single leg only touched the earth, quivering, burdened, unnatural. On the one leg, the dog propelled itself upward again without falling, and the bones pressed through the fat. Even Antonina's mother did not regret the sight.

The dog stopped. As bidden, its front paws came to rest lightly upon Pucento's back on each side of the neck. Thus they remained rigidly, heads damp, white, lifted into the sun, while the musicians dragged their viols onto the field and the girls raised and silently shook their clutches of rose campions. (64–65)

Hawkes' general strategy (to convey inward conflict through hallucinatory atmosphere and nightmare plot, as well as through physical process) is at work in each of the novels. The emphasis is on processes that would in themselves disturb most readers—the extraction of rattlesnake poison, for instance, or an injection. But this primary overt innocent fear is related to fears living deep in the psyche. There is often a strange counterpoise of minutely described horror and saving humor. If we compare passages from *The Beetle Leg* and *The Lime Twig*, both humor and horror seem intensified in the later book.

In the first passage, the movement is from exact physiological notation, to a psychological commentary in more elevated language, to an absurd analogy. Much of the effect of Hawkes' ironies depends upon such shifts. These sentences follow upon a detailed account of preparing the boy's leg for puncture, and upon comments on the prevalence of rattlers in the region:

The blade turned blue. Luke once more picked up the leg and sank the point quickly in and out until two crosses had been cut and, the knife still hanging from his fingers, Camper holding the child's shoulders, he relaxed his face and posture and sucked the wounds, his eyes growing heavy in the headlights, staring, as if the venom had a hard and needy taste to a man who, in all his youth on the infested range, had never himself been bitten. He took it as one of his four drays copped the bar of salt, hung it over, and kept it from the rest. (27–28)

In *The Lime Twig* we are told of the many times Larry has had to give Sparrow injections. But they operate, thanks to the prose, as murderous or castrating, or at the very least sadistic, injections. "He had tended to Sparrow in alleys, bathhouses with crabs and starfish dead on the floors, in doorways, in the Majesty, and the back of horsedrawn wagons on stormy nights. He had jabbed Sparrow in the depths of a barroom and upright in the booth of a phone. . . ." The reader is spared no detail of the injection, but the ironies of the fifth and sixth sentences—the tattoo, the long shadow and the comment on shoulders that would please a master tailor—gradually disengage us from an obsessively close watching:

"This ought to do it," he said, and leaned forward, pinched as much of the flesh on Sparrow's arm as he could into a chilly blister. Then he punctured it, slid the needle beneath Sparrow's skin, gently pushed down the plunger. For a moment he could see the fluid lying like a pea just under the skin, then suddenly it dropped into a duct or into the mouth of a vein and was gone. He withdrew the needle and there was a tiny heart of blood on the tip of it. He watched, and in the middle of the tattoo—a headstone with "Flander's Field" in scroll beneath it—his pinch marks and the nick of the needle were still visible. He was casting a long shadow across Sparrow's torso, and the substance of his own head, the lines of his shoulders—constructed to catch a man's love for master tailoring—these lay lightly on the man in his agony. (87–88)

VOICE

Every good writer has his particular voice, which will be heard at least faintly in everything he writes. In Hawkes as in many modern writers there is interplay—alternation, conflict, or rich ironic juxtaposition—between the elevated prose of an "implied author" and the more relaxed colloquialism of a personalized narrator. The narrator of *The Cannibal* is also the political leader of a resurrected Germany (resurrected into madness) but is really satisfactory in neither role. He was an authorial afterthought, and seldom controls the quality of the diction or rhythms. But the naive sheriff who begins the narration of *The Beetle Leg* sets a tone—laconic, absurdly moralistic, naive—that will prepare the reader for the richer prose of the later chapters. The narrators of *The Owl* and

The Goose on the Grave speak "in character" rather more than is usual in Hawkes, and speak less ironically. But even such realism does not preclude the use of the author's own colder and richer verbal inventions, when these seem desirable.

The narrative situation in *The Lime Twig* is very interesting, and involves more careful modulations of tone than in any of the earlier books. The long first chapter, narrated by Michael Hencher in a highly individual, wholly credible voice, is Hawkes' longest flight of sustained realism—realism in spite of the psychological regressions expressed symbolically, and in spite of such improbabilities as the airplane slowly descending in a back yard. It is standard first-person introspective narration of the most expert kind; and some of the qualities of this voice carry over, after Hencher's death, into the implied author's main narrative. Meanwhile each chapter is prefaced by a gloss: nominally a column by the racing writer Sidney Slyter. His voice too is absolutely authentic—though it is also a mysterious voice (and consciousness) oddly blending racing journalese, an infectious note of curiosity, authorial irony, and an occult foreknowledge of events.

The temptation to quote from *The Lime Twig,* as indeed from any of the novels, is unsubduable. A final passage will have to do, and one which contains a sudden pleasing shift in voice, in tone and rhythm—a shift occurring with the recollection of Cowles' college days. Speaking voice and organizing imagination and terrifyingly precise notation work together. The variations in sentence length and structure, and in levels of diction, accompany a movement from exact rendering of present scene to almost poetic recollection of another murder. At this point in the novel Banks is about to discover, in a crowded steam-filled Turkish bath, the body of the slain Cowles:

And he himself was creeping off again, feeling his foot drag through a limpid pool, feeling the sediment on his skin. His hair was paste smeared across his scalp. He felt how naked he was, how helpless.

Then, still on all fours, he came to the corner. Under the wooden shelving, lying half-turned against a stretch of soapstone, bent nearly double at the angle of meeting walls, crowded into this position on the floor of the Baths was Cowles' body with the throat cut. Banks crept up to him and stared and the trainer was a heap of glistening fat and on one puffy shoulder was a little black mole, growing still, Banks realized, though the man was dead. And though this Cowles—he had had his own kill once, kept dirty rooms in a tower in the college's oldest quad, had done for the proctor with a fire iron and then, at 4 A.M., still wearing the gown darned like worn-out socks, had stolen the shallow punt half-filled with the river's waters and, crouched heavily in the stern with the black skirts collected in his lap, had poled off under the weeping willow trees and away, lonely, at rest, listening to the fiends sighing in nearby ponds and marshes— though this Cowles now lay dead himself his blood still ran, hot and swift and black. His throat was womanly white and fiercely slit and the blood poured out. It was coming down over the collar bone, and above the wound the face was drained and slick with its covering of steam. One hand clutched the belly as if they had attacked him there and not in the neck at all.

Just as Banks caught the lime rising at the odor of Cowles' blood he felt flesh striking against his flesh, felt a little rush of air, and Jimmy Needles lunged at him in passing and fled, hunting for the door. Before he himself could move he heard a sound from the wood above Cowles' corpse, glanced up, and peered for several moments into the congealed blue-tinted face of the constable: an old man's naked face reflecting cow and countryside, pint-froth and thatch in all the hard flat places of its shape.

"Here now, what's this deviltry. . . ."(116–17)

It is hardly soon enough to engage in summaries. But one thing has become evident this early in John Hawkes' career—that his achievement rests on something more than startling originality of vision. It rests above all, it may be, on his power to render so much uncensored revery, so much significant and violent fantasy, so much of the pullulant underground life, with so much stylistic control.

Notes

*Page references for *The Cannibal* are to the casebound edition of 1949. The novel was reset for the 1962 reissue.

Sensuous Rhetoric: John Hawkes's *Charivari*

GEORGE P. E. MEESE

John Hawkes's novellas and short stories have never been the center of critical attention or acclaim; his novels have eclipsed the startling but minor efforts collected in *Lunar Landscapes,*[1] and those published in literary magazines throughout his career. The short fictions often have appeared as experiments that later became portions of the novels (for example, "The Horse in a London Flat," published in *Accent* in 1960, became part of *The Lime Twig* in 1961), and these instances give us suggestive glimpses of Hawkes's creative method. For my purposes here, however, the short fictions can serve to illustrate how Hawkes's sensuous rhetoric operates. In their brevity, the pieces allow us to focus on just a few aspects of how Hawkes's language works, how his art affects us, and how his aesthetic influences our own moral compass.

During his forty years of creating fiction, Hawkes has assaulted Americans' impulses to repress sensuality, a violence he identifies as puritanism and which he sees as the enemy of imaginative "lyricism." Hawkes has explained his aesthetic: "Reverse sympathy seems essential to the novelistic or fictional experience. If the point is to discover true compassion, true sympathy, then clearly the task is to sympathize with what we ordinarily take to be truly repulsive in life. . . . I enjoy a sense of violation, a criminal resistance to safety, to the security provided by laws or systems."[2] It is important to remember that this position is meant to create art quite separate from daily experience; Hawkes's personal life is conventional: "I'm appalled at violence, opposed to pain, terrified of actual destructiveness. . . . It isn't that I'm advocating that we live by acts of violence; I, myself, don't want to live the nightmare. It's just that our deepest inner lives are largely organized around such impulses, which need to be exposed and understood and used. Even appreciated."[3]

Hawkes's focus on reverse sympathy and his successful enlistment of the imagination's power to expose our potential for violence makes us question our aesthetic values. Hawkes would have readers search themselves for "reverse sympathy" toward his creations, and I believe that most readers would do so in good faith, but often we find our response to be a mixture of wonder and

This essay was expressly written for this volume and is published here for the first time by permission of the author.

revulsion. Two brief examples from Hawkes's short stories will illustrate my point.

"The Traveler" (1962) makes readers wonder what kind of a human being thinks thoughts like "Women have no place in the water. What is the sea if not for the washing of dead relatives and for the swimming of fish and men? . . . My feet cut the water like a killer shark's fins, I breathed deep—Justus Kummerlich—in the world of less-than-blood temperature. The knees float, the head floats, the scrotum is awash; here is a man upon the sea, a rationalist thriving upon the great green spermary of the earth!"[4] As we laugh at Justus's absurd position, both physical and philosophical, we also feel a shock of recognition: rationalism indeed has come to this in our century, and Hawkes has shown us its ugly and perverse misogyny. Hawkes cautions: "Mind you, surface perversity in me always has at its root much deeper, serious concerns for human emotions."[5]

"A Little Bit of the Old Slap and Tickle" (1962) gives readers a prose vision of a post–World War II wasteland every bit as dark as Eliot's. Sparrow, a typically nasty Hawkesian protagonist, comes home on a short leave; the war is over but he is afraid to venture outside the security of the military on his own. Sparrow uses his wife for his own gratification, then muses: "At that moment he took in the swimming woman and paddling dog and sighed. For beyond those two, beyond the [mine] sweeper with its number still faintly stenciled on the bow, there lay in muddy suspension the entire field of ships, encrusted guns, and vehicles. And he thought of the work it would take to set the whole thing afloat again—seeing the splash, the snort of the dog—and knew it could not be done, and smiled, clasping his knees, sucking the sun. All won, all lost, all over. But he had his."[6] Here, Hawkes reveals that the war effort of the British, usually depicted as romanticized heroism, may actually have been more like the efforts of the struggling dog. Sparrow's feeling, "Love, not beauty, was what he wanted," rings as hollow as the rusting hull of the mothballed ship that shelters his impoverished family.

Our enjoyment of Hawkes's brilliant technique, our own complex responsiveness to his created worlds, and our perception of his comically serious but morally equivocal creative acts together constitute a richly sensuous rhetoric. There has been little change in the distinctiveness of these three features of Hawkes's fiction since his first published story, *Charivari*, in 1949.[7] These features are artificial—each permeates the others as we read—but we become focally aware of one or the other as we respond: a well-crafted phrase catches our technical appreciation, we feel a startling affective arousal, we are moved to see life experience in terms of moral fictive analog. Since our focal awareness holds up for us only one feature for consideration at any moment, like the shifting fields of M. C. Escher prints or other optical phenomena, we sense these as separate sources of value. Accordingly, I will now discuss in some detail these acts of valuing, with Hawkes's *Charivari* as my primary example. This exercise should delineate some of the sources of our enjoyment or perplexity and should raise several important questions that bear on our judgments of the value of Hawkes's canon.

TECHNICAL VALUE

Hawkes's most immediate challenge to readers lies in the very structure of his prose. He takes a master's care with the language, but he crafts sentences and phrases that seem diametrically opposite those of other prose masters, such as Henry James, who also place death, sex, and the imagination under intense scrutiny. James is "infinitely syntactical,"[8] while Hawkes appears skeletally simplistic. Higher-order questions about literary art depend on the primary experience of author-determined linguistic structures and narrative techniques; it helps to know how, and how well, Hawkes's language embodies his thought and syntactically controls the range of readers' interpretations.

Charivari defies attempts at plot summary. Part of Hawkes's objective in writing this piece was to destroy conventional plot and temporality. Essentially, the novella is about a modern marriage between Emily and Henry Van, two middle-aged but hopelessly immature and paranoid individuals. Their society has the feel of Gatsby's but none of the sophistication, and the novella's action is the relentless ridicule of the Vans' and their friends' and families' pretentions (hence the title). Here is Hawkes's opening to *Charivari:*

COURTSHIP

I

They slept in separate rooms. A massive dog patrolled the space between. His big eyes glimmered in the darkness, sniffing from doot to door, a weak growl.

Henry curled in one corner of the four-poster. He dreamed fitfully beneath the sagging unwashed curtains overhead.

EXPOSITOR: What time is it, Henry?

HENRY: Four o'clock.

EXPOSITOR: What should you be doing?

HENRY: I should be counting my gold.

EXPOSITOR: Nonsense. You should be out cleaning the stables. Come on; we'll take you to clean the stables.

HENRY: Must I do it with my hands?

EXPOSITOR: Certainly. What do you see lying over there in the hay?

HENRY: A woman.

EXPOSITOR: What is she doing?

HENRY: Making love to the stable boy while I do his work.

EXPOSITOR: Do you notice anything different?

HENRY: Yes, she has a baby in her arms.

EXPOSITOR: What do you have to do now?

HENRY: I have to put it in a bucket of water and keep it there so she can go on making love.

EXPOSITOR: Do you think you can keep it from jumping out and biting you?

HENRY: I can't. It's going to bite. It's going to bite! I'll run away. I'm going to run, run . . .

EXPOSITOR: I'll turn *you* into the drowning baby if you do, Henry . . .

HENRY: I'm drowning. Help me, help me . . .

The dream continued off and on the rest of the night. The dog began to howl. In her room she slept soundly, muffled up to the chin in a fuzzy quilt. A small light burned in a corner of the room as she didn't like the dark. . . . (51–52)

Hawkes's first 250 words are divided into thirty-five sentences or phrases that call up a dream dialogue. His syntax is markedly simple, with a reliance on subject-verb order ("Henry curled in one corner of the four-poster."); there is also extensive use of a deletion transformation (a structurally complete expression, "the big dog was sniffing from door to door," is transformed by deleting words to yield "sniffing from door to door"; likewise, "I see a woman lying over there in the hay" becomes "a woman"), and a feature-change transformation for pronominalization ("Henry and Emily slept in separate rooms" becomes "They slept in separate rooms"). These are easily recognized manipulations; Hawkes's syntactic choices do not retard our reading pace, and they are not the cause of our unusual consciousness of technique. Compare Henry James's opening to *The Ambassadors:* "The same secret principle, however, that had prompted Strether not absolutely to desire Waymarsh's presence at the dock, that had led him thus to postpone for a few hours his enjoyment of it, now operated to make him feel he could still wait without disappointment."[9] This passage exhibits a typical example of late-James self-embedded syntax.

Hawkes's syntax in *Charivari* causes little difficulty for readers, yet the story is by no means easily understood, and Hawkes's use of pronouns is one of several technical sources of difficulty. The first pronoun, "they," is without a partial referent until "she slept soundly" (272 words later), and is without a proper-noun referent until "When Emily," some three hundred words into the piece. This linear-temporal delay is important; Hawkes can use it to stimulate curiosity (who are "they"? are "they" involved in the "courtship"?) while he puts the characters into action through the voice of the narrator. Moreover, since "the woman" in Henry's dream cannot be unequivocally identified as Emily, even after the feminine pronouns outside of the dream have been linked positively to Emily, Hawkes can maintain open possibilities for development of the story at the same time he is giving strongly slanted clues by means of indefinite pronoun associations. It remains possible that the baby threatening Henry in this dream is part of an affair unknown to Emily, or the clues could be a false association designed for a later denouement. As readers struggle to find anchors of conventional recognition, Hawkes resists, and our attention is drawn to the technical ways in which we are being manipulated.

Hawkes's selection of nouns is almost as abstract as his use of pronouns. In one sense, the obscure signification of "gold" or "the stables" or "a baby" or even "Expositor" may be an example of Hawkes's technical solution to the problem of depicting the ethereal world of dreams. But the nouns outside the dream are of the same type: "a massive dog," "sagging unwashed curtains," "separate rooms," "courtship," and even the title itself.[10] With all of the nouns lacking concretization, an equation is drawn with philosophical and moral implications: both the diurnal world and the nightmare world have the same claim upon the characters' and readers' sense of what counts as "reality." This is an efficient way to infuse the story with wonder concerning perceived existence, and is one of Hawkes's staple techniques in every one of his fictions.

Choice of verbal phrases, particularly in Henry's dream, gives the strongest suggestion of the philosophical center of the novella, and helps to provide an initial understanding of Henry and Emily Van's world. The verbs are predominantly intransitive (slept, patrolled, glimmered), obligatory (should, must, have to), and compounds with the auxiliary "be" to express continuation (be counting, be cleaning, [is] making love, is doing) or futurity (is going to bite, going to run). Hawkes sets the mood of the Vans' lives with intransitives that contribute to our sense that the Vans exist but are not in active communication with their surroundings or with each other. This suggestion is borne out in their silent breakfast and the narrator's biting indictment: "If either of these forty-year-old jackdaws had looked up over the crest of the hill and out of the window, they would have seen acres of close-clipped lawn rolling down to the boundaries of the apple country; they might have remarked, of course inwardly, on the beauty of the blossoms, or they might, at least prosaically, by looking at the sky, have determined the costume for the day. Instead, and more prosaically, they seemed irresistibly drawn into the negative contemplation of each other" (53).

The obligatory constructions frame Henry's condition in particular: his anxiety throughout the story is caused by the incumbencies of responsibility on his resisting being; he is terrorized by "should" and "must." Henry knows that Emily's mother and his own father expect him to exhibit competence in financial management ("I should be counting my gold"); he is in fact later berated by his mother-in-law, the "generaless," concerning a failure (64–67). "You should be cleaning out the stables" refers, we subsequently learn, to Henry's need to rid himself of the asinine "dapples, piebalds, grays, and blacks" introduced as the party starts in chapter two (54–55). And the most complex issue in the work, Henry and Emily's rejection of parenthood, is outlined by the necessity here for Henry to drown the baby so "the woman" can go on making love to the stable boy. Continuation of the status quo is signaled in the present participle, "making love," nicely encapsulating the Vans' psychological desire, which has no wish for futurity. Integrating the "stable boy" into this continuum suggests Noel's complicity (what other name could connote a boy in a stable more deftly?); the status quo includes Noel's sexual aggression and even the possibility that he is the source of Emily's pregnancy (62–63). As the auxiliary-future verbs in the dream presage, however, Henry becomes the drowning baby (the water imagery in "The Bachelors" section and the bath scene in chapter fifteen) after he runs to the fishing village where he should have—but failed to—save the pregnant girl (Emily?) from drowning.

Hawkes's command of his medium seems to result in an efficiently compressed presentation of issues to be worked out in the remainder of the story. This efficiency depends in large measure upon verbal phrases capable of denoting mood, tense, and agent. Hawkes's technique also has affective impact, as he provokes curiosity through the use of abstract nominalizations and delayed referents. These techniques would nevertheless fail if Hawkes did not provide an integrating device and a dramatic means for psychological exposition. If he treated its main ideas polemically, his fiction would tend to look more like an anecdote meant to illustrate a doctrine, and he would risk disintegration or at least loss of narrative coherence if he used haphazard or excessively varied points-of-view. Instead, Hawkes invents some of the most fascinating narrative voices in twentieth-century fiction.

Charivari depicts the Vans' perversion of a potentially ideal marriage. They have failed to grow in seriousness, and more damningly, they have failed to grow in mature good humor toward life (we witness this problem again in Hugh's perversion of love in *The Blood Oranges,* and the same consequences threaten Sunny Deauville in *Adventures in the Alaskan Skin Trade* until she becomes Hawkes's single completely redeemed hero). Hawkes needed to establish a narrator aloof enough to attack the target: "And have you heard [addressing the reader], or do you think we are likely to hear what very private shames and resentments and misgivings these people are harboring? May we be cruel enough?" (55). At the same time, the narrator cannot be totally detached, or the ruthlessness of his—and consequently the reader's—indictment of the Vans will militate against any view that their marriage had the potential to succeed. Hawkes does not let the Vans become victims; he sustains the suggestion that they just might be irresponsible monsters who created their own condition. He accomplishes this by having the narrator present details that seem to invite readers' sympathy for the characters, but that actually operate two ways: Henry "longed to go into her room and make it up, to show her all the other things he felt" (54). If Henry were to garner genuine sympathy, readers might react by thinking, poor Henry, but because we've been invited to see him ruthlessly, we conclude, his inaction is his own stupid fault.

The presence of this apparently sympathetic but actually condemning narrator throughout *Charivari* gives the reader a sense of the story's unity. There is much in the story to disorient readers—dream sequences, distortions of time and place, a seamstress who rapes a manikin, a baby aborted by riveters—all of which (and more) might have made the work unintelligible as well as pointlessly unpleasant. Having a dominant voice in charge of telling the story affords consistency and gives direction to the psychological revelations, however painful they may be.

At the same time, Hawkes may have failed to bring the narrator under full authorial control. Hawkes helps the reader to question Emily's maturity by presenting her replete with a fuzzy quilt and "a kewpie doll for every happy party"; Henry's virility is made suspect in the scene with the adventures in green and Henry's spongy celery stalks (52, 72, 58–59). Since these and other integral features already prompt a negative assessment of the Vans, it may be excessive for Hawkes to have the narrator address the reader directly about their private shames, misgivings, and resentments. This story works by keeping the reader in alliance with the narrator. If Hawkes were to use any tactic that brought the narrator into question, the reader might be led to inappropriate judgments. I will return to this problem of authorial and reader distancing in my discussion of the moral dimension of Hawkes's narrative.

The final technique I wish to discuss is Hawkes's dramatization of the dream sequences. An important advantage of the dreams is that Hawkes can, through a method other than stream of consciousness, reveal current pressures of past experiences on the psyches of the characters. Subliminal fears and anxieties can remain unconscious for the characters while being exposed to the reader. The opening passage of *Charivari,* for example, is similar to modern psychological drama in form and tone (I have in mind "The Exorcism" act in Edward Albee's *Who's Afraid of Virginia Woolf?*). Even though naming Henry's interlocutor "Expositor" might be heavy-handed, the dialogue is remarkably powerful as a dramatic representation of a severe anxiety dream.[11] The imaginative extension of the novel into dramatized dreams gives Hawkes the advantage of an alternative perspective on his characters. In addition to the narrator, we gain the Expositor to help depict Emily and Henry, and the Expositor can behave toward the characters in ways different from the narrator without any loss of narrative consistency. The contrast can be seen by comparing Henry's opening dream with the Expositor's far gentler treatment of Emily's dream-visit to her grandmother's funeral at the end of chapter six (75–76).

Charivari demonstrates Hawkes's early facility with technique. The diction, syntax, and narrative formulation embody Hawkes's imaginative expression efficiently. It may be that the language takes over the story's substance, and it is certainly true, as Hawkes himself has admitted, that

Charivari has some moments of whimsy, clumsiness, and self-indulgence.[12] Nevertheless, while noting the flaws in this youthful effort, we have to credit the impressive technique of an emerging prose craftsman and recognize that these elements of his craft remain at the heart of Hawkes's appeal. Only clumsiness disappears as the artist matures.

AFFECTIVE VALUE

Henry and Emily reject parenthood and adult responsibility. While a few contemporary readers might not find this action personally interesting, it is reasonable to assume that procreation and its social context are among the major, common issues of human beings. Thus Hawkes's substantive focus helps readers identify topics in the fiction that are of interest (the theme is one familiar to many). But evaluation of readers' potential identifications does not turn on plot or theme in a simple or direct way; the particular fictional manifestation of topics and actions must be the basis for judgment.

Hawkes chose to present his parenthood/responsibility theme through the actions of "forty-year-old jackdaws," with a heavy reliance upon dream or hallucinatory sequences. His choices entail loss of potential readers, first because many will not subject themselves to experiencing "grotesquely unpleasant people caught by their own emptiness in uneventful situations," and second because part of Hawkes's presentation of the dreams and hallucinations nearly destroys intelligibility.[13] Few would expect that all fiction must make itself interesting to all possible readers (the extreme reading of Henry James's "the writer makes the reader. . . . When he makes him well, that is, makes him interested, then the reader does quite the labor"[14]). It is unreasonable to impose "universal appeal of subject and characterization" as a standard of judgment. The question of intelligibility, however, has more serious ramifications and deserves some examination.

A reader expected to share in the creation of fiction deserves some help from the author, and there are passages in *Charivari* where Hawkes does not give adequate direction. Hawkes's treatment of dream material provides a good example of this shortcoming. John E. Mack describes the conventional understanding of the role of dreams in fiction:

> Dreaming, with its vivid and powerful emotional elements, its rich and flexible use of symbols, its reliance on concrete sense perception, and its access to unconscious mental content, has made use of the very psychological mechanisms that are essential to creative activity. The dream has, in effect, done a part of the job [of imaginative creation]. What remains for the writer or artist is to employ his technique to transform the crude, overly personal, and largely narcissistic dream into shared perception and illusion, to make it into a coherent work in

which larger audiences can find expression, some resolution of their own conflicts, and gratification of their unfulfilled emotions.[15]

Evidence that Hawkes *has* made an effort to accommodate readers' needs is his provision of clear signals to the reader of shifts in consciousness; Hawkes gives his readers transitions that set off the dream-dialogue with the Expositor from the regular narrative: "He dreamed fitfully" (51), "1:30 A.M. Emily's dream" (75). He also provides some overt indications of Henry's passage into and out of sleep in the fourth part of the story, "Rhythm": "Goodnight Henry, goodnight, goodnight" (123), "Click, click, [following a text break] He heard the croquet balls" (125), "Henry twisted again and opened his eyes" (129), "He shut his eyes" (130). Without these rhetorical adjustments, readers might be confronted with a text that resembles a dream researcher's transcription of raw data, or perhaps some of Freud's descriptions of dream material before interpretation.

A problem of unintelligibility occurs when no signals are given and the narrative proceeds, engulfed in hallucination. Hawkes, instead of transforming Henry's anxiety dreams, seems to have transcribed them in all their unshared, personal illusion:

> The door opened and she came out and walked easily into the storm. For a moment she was but thirty feet from him. Miraculously the black hat stayed in place. He could almost see the features of the face, oh, Emily, yes, yes, the howling wind, the shadowed mouth open to gasp for air behind that wind, the eyes covered by a constant veil, the hair beating upon the open throat. Fish were being hammered against the logs, clouds collided with mountains of water, the fishing nets tore loose, and wandering, flying, flung themselves on teakwood ribs, sky and rock.
>
> For one brief moment his hope and desire came together, to walk up to her, hold her, speak to her, hold the blowing hair. The taste of salt was on his lips. Then he turned and was carried off down the street. Once he turned back and saw that she was following. (88)

A careful reconstruction of the details framing this passage fails to reveal exactly how the reader is to interpret them. It is relatively easy to account for Henry's mistaken notion that the girl in the black hat is Emily, but it is not so easy to decide whether the entire fishing village sequence is dream or reality. The girl is later discovered drowned—a scene described in exceptionally realistic detail—and Henry, moved but "calm," decides to "go home"; his father appears in the rooming house and drives Henry back to his home. The ride is described in detail, and the timing neatly dovetails into the clearly wakeful events at the party, yet we are left without a clear motive for the manner of the scene.

Hawkes has remarked (with twenty-five years' hindsight), "By the end of

Charivari this death is revealed to be merely hallucinatory, and Emily lives. Emily Van is the only pseudo-victim in my fiction."[16] But there is no such revelation in the story. The reader can be sure only that the girl who drowns is not Emily; there is no way to know that Henry did not journey on a bus to Madame Mahoney's rooming house in a fishing village swept by a storm, did not share the Sea Horse tavern with the "stags," and did not witness the horrifying drowning of a pregnant young woman. If one argues that the reality of the presentation is inconsequential because we are interested in Henry's reaction to his dream or his real environment, not the status of the stimulus, I must answer that in judging Henry, we need to know how he perceives reality. If he imagines the whole scene, his actions within it do not have to stand the tests of conventional social mores. We are led to believe that Henry is facing the most important choice in his life ("It was his decision" [93]), deciding to face the responsibilities of fatherhood or whatever else might await him in his diurnal life. If this choice is only an unconscious part of a hallucination, then the choice signifies nothing.

    Charivari contains provocative but isolated ideas, caricatures, wonders, and surprises. I think Hawkes is correct in saying that *Charivari* "evokes its share of universal burdens of desire and anxiety framed in the rituals and conditions of married life."[17] If we are not put off by Hawkes's insistence upon staring directly into sources of human anxiety, we can, *with* Henry, feel "a delicate sensation among [the] vertebrae, a macabre delight, an overall, bewildered, ecstatic fear" (60). We can come to know in our own being the situation of a lover reduced to spiteful breakfasts but who still wants to show all his other feelings, who learns the death-risk of those who would create living things, and who responds with one of the most shocking scenes (Emily's "examination") in all of fiction.[18] We can also enjoy Hawkes's clever incorporation of specific literary and historical material (Christabel, Abelard, Jezebel, Susannah, "Ulysses' men with albatrosses hung round their necks" [90]) and his nicely patterned imagery (the black hat, the water-town/ drowning baby/drowning mother, the pins, the extensive bestiary, the kisses, and many others).[19]

    The shortcoming of all these cognitive rewards is that the reader can only relish them atomistically; they do not add up to a holistic sense of fulfilled potential. Donald Greiner suggests the possible cause of *Charivari*'s failure to integrate: "On the one hand the characters are so sterile that we have trouble sympathizing with their problems. Thus the narrator's 'cruel' exposure of their 'private shames and resentments and misgivings' fails to bother us. On the other hand the narrator chooses to have us on his side rather than the characters' so that the partygoers become strawmen. . . . Comic detachment without sympathetic concern negates the attraction-repulsion antithesis which gives Hawkes's later work its complex tone."[20]

    To relish the possible rewards, it becomes necessary to divorce oneself from collusion with the narrator. We want to be able to laugh at Henry and Emily's absurd responses to the challenges of life, but we cannot adopt the ruthlessness of the narrator just to get a cheap laugh. We need a more sympathetic position if only to save our own self-esteem. Since the narrator's overall viewpoint is untenable, the best option for the reader is to glean the respective worth of each individual sequence, structure of images, psychological insight, and joke.

MORAL VALUE

Part of readers' reactions to *Charivari* depends on Hawkes's assault on the reader's moral sensibility. Because readers' responses to the narrative line and their responses to the moral content of the narrative are difficult to separate, I have already touched on matters that some might call moral in my earlier discussion.

There are few justifications for cruelty in the story. If indeed the characters are, as the narrator asserts, "so flimsy, apt at any moment to be blown away forever" (65), what can a reader gain in moral perception by laughing at them? Hawkes tries to implicate the reader by having the narrator claim, "And we too [are flimsy, apt to be blown away], perhaps, with them if we are not careful, over the Via del Rosa, Street of Whores" (65). Unfortunately, the reader tends not to identify with the Vans or their friends, and so is not threatened or challenged by the narrator's ploy. Because the Vans' moral dilemma is not presented in a manner that makes us concerned, our overall impression of the story's power is lessened.

Despite the partial failure of this story to affect us immediately, it is interesting to examine what Hawkes attempted in creating the moral dimension of *Charivari*. Hawkes may have had his own impending marriage on his mind while composing the story. I do not weigh this fact too heavily, and Hawkes himself has warned against "the misleading notion that the ultimate key to the novel lies in the life of the writer, which is untrue."[21] But it is the novel itself, not Hawkes's biography, that contains evidence of its author's concern with the moral implications of irresponsible marriage, of actions appropriate to characters who fear the loss of a loved one, and of participation in vacuous social relationships.

The dreams that reveal the Vans' psyches are caused by some of our deepest anxieties: marital infidelity (the opening dream), death of one's spouse (the fishing village scene and the dreadful hospital dream), one's own death (Emily's grandmother's funeral), and social anomie ("The Wedding"). In the Vans' world, in choices that actually depict the characters' motivations, and that would thereby help to define them, are precluded by impotence, paranoia, and the oppressive incumbency of a cloying history. Henry and Emily seem smothered by their parents, the portraits of ancestors, and an amazing accumulation of dross: "Old college dogs with twenty years of age, and Papal dolls stuffed with cotton . . . a little faded bag of pine scent . . . an ivory god," (54). The vision is morally enigmatic; the characters are trapped by their condition, yet they are free to choose to "play," and I am reasonably certain that Hawkes expects us to condemn as morally irresponsible the way these "jackdaws" play to the exclusion of all other activity.

In other words, it appears to the reader that the Vans really had no viable alternative except their choice to play; they certainly found it impossible to satisfy their parents any other way (or they were incompetent in earlier attempts). The terrifying dreams that the Vans suffer thus seem to be a natural part of an absurd life.

Without any clear possibility for effective, redemptive action, the Vans can hardly be condemned for being irresponsible. At the same time, readers cannot empathize with Henry and Emily because "normal" lives, while full of anxieties and often full of the dreams that anxieties trigger, are perceived as offering at least a few options for responsible adult action as well. Henry and Emily have not been drawn with such options, and it is fair to ask whether this paucity of options does not diminish the moral range of other Hawkes fictions as well.

Hawkes does give readers some grounds for sympathy—perhaps even empathy—in Henry's desire to speak to Emily and his desire to approach the young woman of the fishing-village scene. But Henry's inaction in both cases negates any consideration of his potential to escape into responsible action. In fact, he is not even responsive; the moments simply are noted and pass. Once again, there is too little of substance here for the reader to become seriously engaged.

Hawkes has denied application of conventional morality to *Charivari* by rejecting conventional narration, conventional description, and conventional character portrayal. All of the necessary signs that might invite our contemplation of moral dilemmas in modern interpersonal relations are present in this novel, but our engagement has been forestalled. Hawkes claims, "The work that is deeply and truly moral violates conventional morality. The writer who sets out to create his own world in a sense defies the world around him. He has to become an outcast, an outsider . . . he has an ultimate sympathy with those who have been judged as unfit for conventional society . . . the purpose of imaginative fiction is to generate sympathy for the saved and the damned alike."[22] In later fiction, Hawkes achieves this radically redemptive vision. For example, a self-criticizing sympathy distinguishes our reading of *The Blood Oranges:* we can smile at the characters' foibles and yet see enough of our own tendencies, in both Cyril's eroticism and Hugh's puritanism, to keep us from stereotyping and cheap comic response. Hawkes's command of richly dark comic effect, in which readers find humor in humane recognitions, is absent in *Charivari.*

Sensuous Rhetoric and Value Judgments

Responses of wonder and revulsion seem common among Hawkes's readers; one colleague described his fiction as "disturbing and disturbingly good."[23] In his introduction to a recently published sampler of Hawkes's fictions, William H. Gass candidly discussed the affective-pleasure-versus-moral-aversion dilemma that might drive some readers away. Gass, admitting his own early neglect of Hawkes's works, describes Hawkes's fictive creation as "not a new world so much as a special and very alert awareness of one; and that awareness is so controlled, so precise, so intense, so angular while remaining uncomfortably direct, so comic, too, as if a smile has been sliced by a knife, that many readers have recoiled as though from reality itself, and pretended to be running from a nightmare, from something sur- or un- real, restoring the disguise which Hawkes' prose has torn away."[24] If readers recoil, perhaps they do so not because of squeamishness or lack of sophistication, but because Hawkes has been more precious about his depiction of human circumstances than his formal experiments would necessitate.

Some readers and critics contemporary with the publication of Hawkes's early works, such as *Charivari* and *The Cannibal* (1949), "Death of an Airman" (1950), *The Beetle Leg* (1951), and *The Goose on the Grave* and *The Owl* (1954), indeed recoiled from Hawkes's aggressive experimentation. Eliot Berry has identified their difficulties precisely: "By American fiction standards at the end of the '40s and early '50s, these innovative fictions represent a radical departure, particularly when placed in the context of the Eisenhower years and McCarthyism."[25]

Readers in the 1990s have an altered context in which to experience Hawkes's canon. Most important, the innovations that drew so much attention initially are no longer barriers to most readers' appreciation. Berry observes, "From the beginning Hawkes was different from his American contemporaries, and it has only been in the last fifteen years [between 1964 and 1979] that those recognized as Hawkes's contemporaries—Barth, Barthelme, Coover, Gass, Pynchon and others—have entered, and in some instances surpassed, the territory that Hawkes was occupying a decade before."[26]

In any case, it is no longer Hawkes's formal experimentation with the American romance novel or other fictional constructions that causes readers problems. Those who read fiction today must contend with a resurgence of paternalism masquerading as morality that is as dangerous to art as McCarthyism, and that would prefer to see books like Hawkes's burned rather than read. Hawkes's comically ruthless aesthetic invites us to consider just how far our imaginations, or an author's imagination, can extend into ugliness, violations of innocence, destructive sexuality, and deep psychic conflicts. When Hawkes is at his best, his appeal for our "negative sympathy" works, but we must see, with Eliot Berry, the consequences of failure at such an attempt: "The power of puritanism seems to provoke paradox. In Hawkes' works one encounters both a repulsion and an attraction to the violence that seems inherent in sexuality; but while Hawkes understands Passion as a force in opposition to Home and Security, and while he is able to make his language ring with a certain eroticism, this eroticism, steeped as it is in voyeurism and pain, is essentially sado-masochistic. Though he has profoundly understood both victim and victimization, there is such a complete lack of tenderness that one must really question whether Hawkes has thoroughly explored his territory."[27]

Taking such risks has always been one hallmark of great art, and Hawkes has rarely avoided risk, but the question remains: Is Hawkes's fiction ultimately sympathetic to human predicaments, or does he use sadism, pain, and foolishness primarily as raw material for verbal pyrotechnics?

I believe this question, originally provoked by the problems Hawkes first set for readers in *Charivari,* can help us remain alert to the moral implications of our responses to Hawkes's technique in all his works. For example, in his briefest published fiction, the fourteen sentences that comprise *Island Fire,*[28] we experience the sensuous power of Hawkes's imagination. A couple—unnamed —have lived for twenty years in a clapboard cabin on an island—the Calvinist atmosphere of the New England seaboard is palpable but unspecified—and the pair have survived while sun, salt air, and winter gales have turned the house to warp, peel, curl, and scale. Hawkes packs the sketch with images that recur throughout his fictions: paint that flakes "like dead skin," boards that shrink and pull away "like a lip from teeth," colors that turn "from white to gray to shriveled and porous black," "fish heads" that reek, gales that yank the shingles "out of the roof like rotten teeth." The story's only real action, when the man accidentally throws gasoline instead of kerosene into the lighted wood stove, provides a shocking and horrible closure.

Island Fire has the potential to evoke readers' reverse sympathy, since we might sympathize with the couple's plight even though most could not identify with the couple's circumstances. Even if we regard *Island Fire* as a literary conceit, its vignette of a couple scraping to survive poverty and hostile natural elements shocks us memorably, and this shock might result in a compassionate responsiveness. Such moral concern is forestalled, however, by Hawkes's display of technical brilliance. Experienced Hawkes readers will enjoy the insider's recognition of familiar images and draw their greatest pleasure from the way Hawkes reveals his startling similies: "The chimney collapsed. The grass grew high to weed. The twisted trees began to bear only stillborn apples, nut-red fruity foetuses as small and hard as the knuckle of his stumpy thumb."[29]

Despite its brevity, *Island Fire* is unmistakably John Hawkes's work: the descriptive precision of eyes forced open to the relentlessness of time, similes working like a flamethrower on human presumptions of beauty or grace or immunity, and catastrophe realized in the rhythms of Hawkes's sentences. Any reader who values language, any reader who is willing to be responsive, cannot fail to be rewarded. Nevertheless and, in my opinion, also typically, the destructive act that ends *Island Fire* is equivocal: when the man throws the gasoline, is it an act of human stupidity (allowing us to cluck at the couple's absurdity) or of human inattention (forcing us to recognize our own vulnerability)? Hawkes leaves us hanging; we cannot resolve our moral concern through reference to the story.

While we might testify to Hawkes's virtuosity, we also discover serious problems in our responses to the quality of these literary experiences. Valuing John Hawkes's fiction often places readers, Janus-faced and self-indicted, in the position of the adulterer: we have enjoyed an extraordinary pleasure, we have presumed to transcend conventional knowledge of our place and time, we have styled ourselves artists of the erotic as we completed the loveplay of author and reader, and we have acted out the frottage of fictive imagination, rubbing our senses over each delicious phrase. At the end of our pleasure taking, however, as we return to clarity unfogged by sensuality, our prior commitments to other notions of human value stand waiting to call us to account.

Notes

1. John Hawkes, *Lunar Landscapes: Stories and Short Novels 1949–1963* (New York: New Directions, 1969).
2. John Kuehl, "Interview," in his *John Hawkes and the Craft of Conflict* (New Brunswick, N.J.: Rutgers University Press, 1975), 162.
3. Kuehl, "Interview," 164–165.
4. John Hawkes, "The Traveler," in *Lunar Landscapes* 8–9.
5. Kuehl, "Interview," 163.
6. John Hawkes, "A Little Bit of the Old Slap and Tickle," in *Lunar Landscapes,* 30.
7. John Hawkes, *Charivari,* in *New Directions* 11 (1949) 365–436; reprinted in *Lunar Landscapes,* 51–136. All future references will be to the latter edition and will be cited parenthetically in the text.
8. Ian Watt, "The First Paragraph of *The Ambassadors:* An Explication," reprinted in *The Ambassadors,* Norton Critical Edition (New York: Norton, 1964), 483; and Richard Chase, *The American Novel and Its Tradition* (New York: n.p., 1957), quoted in Watt, 474.
9. Henry James, *The Ambassadors* (1903; reprint, New York: Norton, 1964), 17.
10. *Charivari*'s title is not as problematical as Donald J. Greiner would have it in *Comic Terror: The Novels of John Hawkes* (Memphis: Memphis State University Press, 1973), 30. "Shivaree," the Americanized term, is still in common use, and the noisy taunting of lovers it connotes is still frequently practiced in the west central United States; Hawkes began the story while working in Montana, "waiting with fierce eagerness and fierce anxiety for the moment of [my] marriage" (John Hawkes, "Notes on Writing a Novel," *TriQuarterly* 30, Spring 1974, 112, 115). He was writing for his class under Albert J. Guerard at Harvard, where *Punch, or the London Charivari* could not have been unknown among the post-WWII students recently returned from the European front (*Punch* did not drop the term from its title until 1953, and "Charivari" was part of the lead column title until 1 January 1969).
11. I prefer this term to "nightmare" in this case because of its descriptive accuracy. See John E. Mack, *Nightmares and Human Conflict,* Sentry Edition (Boston: Houghton Mifflin,

1974), for an illuminating synthesis of work done in clinical dream research and psychological theory, contemporary with *Lunar Landscapes*. Severe anxiety dreams are treated in Chapter 1.

12. Webster Schott, "John Hawkes, American Original," *New York Times Book Review*, 29 May 1966; Hawkes, "Notes on Writing a Novel," 115.

13. Donald J. Greiner, *Comic Terror* (Memphis: Memphis State University Press, 1973), 36. I do not agree with Greiner that the Vans' situation is "uneventful." Whether Emily's pregnancy is hysterical or aborted, its ability to produce irrational fears and irresponsible actions in Henry and Emily constitutes "eventfulness," both physical and psychological.

14. Henry James, "The Novels of George Eliot," quoted in James E. Miller, Jr., ed., *Theory of Fiction: Henry James* (Lincoln, Nebr.: University of Nebraska Press, 1972), 321.

15. Mack, *Nightmares*, 93–94. Mack also cites Marie Bonaparte's findings: "The same Mechanisms which in dreams or nightmares govern the manner in which our strongest, though most carefully concealed desires are elaborated, desires which often are the most repugnant to consciousness, also govern the elaboration of the work of art" (from *The Life and Works of Edgar Allan Poe* [London: Imago, 1949], 209.); Mack concludes, "What psychoanalytic writers often fail to stress are the differences in the ego functioning that enable a writer or artist to transform a dream into a creative work," *Nightmares*, 109, n. 24.

16. Hawkes, "Notes on Writing a Novel," 118.

17. Hawkes, "Notes on Writing a Novel," 116.

18. It is telling that the Doc Haines dental scene in Chapter 35 of *Adventures in the Alaskan Skin Trade*, with its outrageously comic confrontation of sadism, sex, medicine, and repression, has its prototype in Emily's examination in *Charivari*. Hawkes achieves a much more integrated vision in his 1985 novel, but its power to shock us comes from the same elemental fears that he tapped in 1949.

19. The use of Coleridge's poem "Christabel" is quite skillful: Hawkes imports Geraldine, the enchantress who appears in the poem as a bird-strangling green snake, into *Charivari* as "Christabel's friend," the "enchantress in green" who torments Henry (59). The howling "mastiff bitch" of the poem howls and prowls as a "massive dog" and the "mastiff" encountered by Beady (51, 74) and, together with the midnight-crowing cock (poem) or "tiny fowl bedraggled in the morning mist" (52), helps to set a surreal mood with archetypal overtones. *Charivari* is rich in these allusions which have not to my knowledge been exhaustively traced.

20. Greiner, *Comic Terror*, 43.

21. Hawkes, "Notes on Writing a Novel," 100.

22. Thomas LeClair, "The Novelists: John Hawkes," interview in *The New Republic*, 10 November 1979, 27.

23. Nancy Corson Carter, personal correspondence, November 1989. I am indebted to Nancy and Howard Carter for their critiques of this essay during its composition.

24. William H. Gass, *Humors of Blood and Skin: A John Hawkes Reader* (New York: New Directions, 1984), xiv.

25. Eliot Berry, *A Poetry of Force and Darkness: The Fiction of John Hawkes* (San Bernardino, Calif.: Borgo, 1979), 9.

26. Berry, *A Poetry of Force and Darkness*, 3.

27. Berry, *A Poetry of Force and Darkness*, 7.

28. John Hawkes, *Island Fire* (Providence, R.I.: Burning Deck, 1988).

29. Hawkes, *Island Fire*, 3.

The Unwinning of the West:
John Hawkes's *The Beetle Leg*

David W. Madden

Throughout his various interviews and essays, John Hawkes has continually insisted on drawing attention to the comic elements in his fiction. By his own admission, one of the most important of these is the use of parody and the many ironic possibilities the mode makes available to him. While critics have acknowledged the use of the parodic mode in *The Lime Twig,* for instance, they have almost completely ignored this important aspect in Hawkes's second novel, *The Beetle Leg.* When they have considered this largely overlooked novel, scholars have stressed its mythic elements and attempted to define the work in terms of numerous fertility sagas.[1] Choosing to consider its parodic dimensions, I will demonstrate the ways in which Hawkes ironically manipulates the conventions of the Western novel in an attempt to question a variety of widely accepted assumptions the form implies about American life and culture.

Although the plot is primarily static, what action there is is set in an arid, Southwestern valley, where inhabitants have constructed an earthen irrigation dam. Camper, a former worker and now tourist, returns to Government City with his wife and child and joins the company of Luke Lampson, the brother of a man accidentally buried in the dam during construction. Paralleling these events is the return of an itinerant quack, Cap Leech, who, as his name implies, searches for patients he can parasitically exploit. He eventually encounters the law in the form of a man known only as the Sheriff, and together with two of the town's other citizens, Harry Bohn and the Finn, the Sheriff, Luke, and Camper track down and ambush a group of marauding motorcyclists. As in most Westerns, *The Beetle Leg*'s most immediately apparent feature is the setting, here a landscape of limitless desert. In a traditional Western such as Owen Wister's *The Virginian,* an equally limitless terrain implies a life of limitless possibilities, a location which John G. Cawelti argues would represent a "social environment in which the American dream could be born again."[2] Cawelti here defines a traditional mystique, one which views success and progress emerging from the conquest of a hostile environment. Hawkes,

Reprinted with permission from *South Dakota Review* 19 (Autumn 1981): 78–91.

however, ironically inverts this process by showing the erosion of the Western life-style and its ideals.

In the western territory of *The Beetle Leg,* man's attempt to transform the desert into a garden has hopelessly failed, with the prevailing image being one of the Garden as Wasteland. Similarly, the dream of progress and development is converted into a nightmare of banality, sterility, and exhaustion, where a dominant sense of barrenness acts both as a backdrop to and as a mirror for the aimless lives struggling through this terrain. Instead of the forces of man and progress conquering and bettering the land as in *The Virginian,* the land is the conqueror in *The Beetle Leg,* and Hawkes clearly demonstrates this in the image of the moving, decaying, and devouring dam.

Early in the story the narrator mentions a breeze that comes from the "funnel of badlands," and the use of this Western cliché hints not only at an ironic narrative attitude but also succinctly describes an area that is evil beyond our customary expectations of the term, "badlands."[3] The location is a town named Government City, where an irrigation dam, which one character proudly refers to as "the cheapest earth filled dam in the western hemisphere," has been erected (26). Ironically, where once there were farms, trees, and grazing areas, there is now only an "infested range," and rather than bringing fertility and life to the area, the dam functions as an agent of destruction and a monument to human futility (28). The one man who has died since the community's founding was swallowed by a chasm in the dam during construction, and although inhabitants assure one another of the structure's security, the audience is fully aware of its instability. Seismographs have "detected a creeping, downstream motion in the dam [as it] eased down the rotting shale a beetle's leg each several anniversaries" (67–68).

Additionally, yellow color imagery is used to emphasize the area's destruction; the earth, buildings, and even characters' teeth are associated with this color of decay. In fact the devastation is so complete that the narrator at one point notes that this is "a country from which the air had been exhausted," producing a "little purgatory" (99, 103).

As the land is destroyed, so it destroys the inhabitants, and the disorders evident in the physical world are mirrored by the psychic disorders in the lives and personalities of the novel's characters. The Sheriff best exemplifies the debilitating effects of the landscape on personality by presenting himself as a rather lop-sided version of the traditional lawman in the work's introductory monologue. Following less the letter of the law than an astrological table, the Sheriff's beliefs spell doom for any living creature. "Aquarius is poor. Sagitarius is poor. Virgo is a Barren Sign, it will produce no growth. The first day the Moon is in a Sign is better than the second and the second is better than the third. Seed planted when the Earth is in Leo, which is a Barren, Fiery Sign, will die, as it is favorable only to the destruction of noxious growth. Trim no trees or vines when the Moon or Earth is in Leo. For they will surely die" (7). His complete faith in the sterility and futility of life dramatically defines the way he functions as the town's chief legal authority.

Obsessed with the suspicion that every man and woman is furtively running off to the nearest bush, car, or bed and "illegally" copulating, the Sheriff is disgusted by "them people too easy found doing things a man can't talk about, things that happened or not depending on whether you arrived five minutes early or five late" (8). Accordingly, he regards his job as one of prevention: "There are other times when you have to step right in, when you are Sheriff or even Deputy, and catch hold of a bare shoulder or head of hair, keeping your face turned back so as it don't get bruised, and drag them off. Maybe you get splashed with a glass of beer or your hand gets bit, but they have to be broke apart. Fast" (11). When called by one of the town's children to investigate a suspicious character who is merely sitting and staring at the river, the Sheriff is disappointed to find nothing illegal taking place. Nevertheless, the seated figure was "something to stare at for an hour or two" (14).

His most extreme attempt to frustrate fertility comes in his confrontation with a wedding party as they enter the neighboring Clare for the nuptials. The scene is an absurdly comic imitation of a high-noon shootout between the hero and the villain. The Sheriff moves with the laconic self-confidence audiences expect of the standard lawman, as he leans against a post, paring his nails and warning the interlopers to leave. When one of the exasperated party members exclaims, "But this here is a wedding," the Sheriff responds, "Don't matter. I don't care if the whole pack aims to rut" (90). After all, he later says, "This town's got a law" (90). The distortion here is monumental, as the principled loner, sworn to foster growth and stability in the town's rage against the wilderness, becomes Hawkes's prime agent for the death and extinction of civilization.

In the wedding party is the brother of the groom, Luke Lampson, who throughout the novel stands as an ironic antithesis to the traditional cowboy-hero. Except for his wardrobe, he is not really a cowboy at all; because the dam has destroyed the grazing lands, herds no longer wander here. Luke's job, like those of the work's other characters, is a purposeless and futile one; he spends his days sowing flower seedlings on the dam that is his brother Mulge's grave. The folly of this activity is especially striking because the dam "took Luke's seeding badly . . . where once bleak needles and spines had popped crookedly from the banks and a few flowers increasingly withered into the plain and disappeared, only the dust from the southward slope, swirling into the air, and a few animal bones and tin cans from a still deeper generation, survived" (66–67).

The particular emptiness of Luke's existence becomes more evident when one compares him with the classic cowboy-hero. Although he has the boots, the slow, silent demeanor, and the patient acceptance of life that characterized the Virginian, Luke is still not the "transcendent hero" that Wister created. Such a figure has always embodied a code of conduct and honor, and Robert Warshaw carefully defines him as a man with "an apparent moral clarity . . . [and] what he defends, at bottom, is the purity of his own image—in fact his honor . . . he fights not for advantage and not for the right, but to state what he is, and he must live in a world which permits that statement. The Westerner is the last gentleman . . . he presents an image of personal nobility that is still real for us."[4] Neither Luke nor anyone else in this work embodies such moral clarity; like the land they inhabit, they are exhausted, lost, defeated.

But like every Western hero, Luke has his moment of violent confrontation with the so-called forces of evil and destruction; however, his moment amounts to a radical reversal of what the traditional hero experiences. Usually the hero is a man who shuns violence; he is a figure of extreme self-restraint. "The most important implication of [the] killing procedure seems to be the qualities of reluctance, control, and elegance which it associates with the hero. Unlike the knight, the cowboy hero does not seek out combat for its own sake and he typically shows an aversion to the wanton shedding of blood. Killing is an act forced upon him and he carries it out with the precision and skill of a surgeon and the careful proportions of an artist."[5] Luke is like the traditional hero in that he does not seek the violence out; it is accidental that he is even a member of the novel's absurd posse. Once the shooting begins, he is also similar to the Western hero in his reluctance to use a gun. However, the similarities end here, for his eventual use of violence is not disciplined or elegant. He is, one must remember, firing buckshot into an unarmed group of cornered motorcyclists. Where the classic cowboy-hero gives "a sense of moral significance and order to violence," this hero and his comrades create only chaos and achieve some motiveless form of revenge.[6] Neither hunters nor victims are in any way ennobled or purified through this senseless use of violence.

Luke's posse, which represents the primarily male relationships of most Westerns, is actually a collection of malignant types. The relaxed camaraderie of a group of equals is replaced in *The Beetle Leg* with a network of coercion and intimidation. Harry Bohn is the nominative leader and his dominance stems less from some moral strength than the magnitude of his physical deformities. Other characters stand in bewildered awe of this man "by miracle born of a dead mother and thereafter in his youth . . . drawn to the expressionless genitals of animals . . ." (108). Bohn is a walking physical grotesque, having "an old man's kidney . . . tumorous girth and thickly dying wind, hardening on the surface of the armpits. Chest and shoulders were solidified against youth, bulged in what he assumed to be the paunch of middle age. . . . A few fingers were broken, snubbed. . . . Bohn argued at, commanded his world and saw it under the pale of bitter years when imaginary friends die off" (55). Only thirty years old, he commands a kind of fear and respect that a middle-aged patriarch might wield.

His hold is especially strong over Finn, "a crippled, ex-bronc rider," who hobbles about on a pair of white canes (54). Throughout the novel, the emaciated, cancerous Finn pleads that he must return home, because "I got things. Lots of things to do, Bohn" (54). But Bohn's control is absolute, and the two wander about the town until they meet Luke and Camper. The four of them then set off on an unsuccessful fishing expedition that culminates in their joining the Sheriff for the midnight attack on the motorcyclists.

Camper, too, is a comic distortion of yet another typical Western figure: the civilized outsider. Often this character is a woman, or failing that, a man who is either a dude or an Easterner, who for one reason or another comes to the West as an initiate to the bluff manners of frontier life. A classic example is the narrator in *The Virginian;* he is an Easterner who journeys periodically to Wyoming and gradually learns the complexities and beauties of the Western way of life from the strong, silent cowboy-hero. The outsider usually represents either an opposing way of life, or by means of his initiation, acts as a bridge between two opposing life-styles.

Though he comes from another way of life, Camper is incapable of learning anything or mediating between opposing forces. He claims that he was once a laborer who worked on the dam and who has now returned to do some fishing and to marvel at the success of the project. He is paunchier than the cowboys, and his apparel of yellow sports shirt, flannel trousers, and yellow "sea-rotted sandals," covering white socks, clearly indicates his alternate life-style. Although he is the quintessential tourist and suburbanite, Camper proudly boasts, "I'm a hunter," but actually "feared through the night the footfall of the hunted" (97, 109).

As a representative of civilization, he brings what are really the worst aspects of the so-called civilized culture. When a rattlesnake bites his child, Camper explodes in anger because he "can't take a leak without kicking up a pack of rattlers" and because his wife cannot find a radio station to his liking. While the child lies stricken and Luke draws the venom from the wound, Camper sits back and swats biting mosquitoes, swearing, "This country's hell on a man" (28). Later, after the child has been put to bed and he accidentally meets Luke again in a bar, Camper confesses, "I've got to have those steerhorn boots of yours. . . . Got to. They've been on my mind ever since you fixed up the kid. . . . You don't need them like I do . . ." (98).

Instead of standing for an alternate way of life that could offer values the West lacks, Camper is as sterile as the landscape he stumbles into. His disregard for his child's injury and for his wife's reluctance to stop in Government City demonstrate a complete lack of concern for those he supposedly loves. He is selfish, foolish, and utterly incapable of any empathetic understanding. Ultimately, it is his callous selfishness which is a reflection of a culture that has emotionally and morally fallen apart and that has created the nightmare that is this West.

Another Western convention is presented in the figure of Ma, widow of the buried Mulge Lampson and a woman who acts as an ironic imitation of the hard-working, unselfish, long-suffering pioneer female. In sharing a shack with Luke and his Indian mistress, Ma taciturnly accepts a life of ministering to others and never to herself. Her obsession with the ghost of her dead husband, a husband who on his wedding night slept with another woman, is grimly ironic. Mulge, one learns, is the focus of attention for a town that ignored him in life; in death, he has become a hero and tourist attraction. The town's barber covets the few relics of Mulge's existence: a straightedge razor with a chipped handle, a shaving mug, "a bottle of tonic and septic [sic] pencil" (71). Dispossessed of his presence in both life and death, Ma guards a handful of pictures that inarticulately record their relationship.

> Ma had all the photographs of his effects. It was the best she could do. She wrote on the backs of them:
> "I remember this one, remember it well."
> "Bought in Clare for twenty-five cents. I didn't take to the color. Right off."
> "Cut 1 lb. fish fresh as it buys to four pieces . . ." (72)

She also honors Mulge's memory by nocturnal vigils at his grave. While the novel's other characters move through the town and around the lake, Ma awkwardly plods her way over the dam's surface, searching with a divining rod for the lost body. Hers is a kind of holy mission; she walks on "sacred ground," and "she sanctified an immane [sic] body of land and depended on the divining rod" (116). But like the other characters, Ma is a lost figure whose efforts are simply futile, futile because she fails to discover Mulge's body and because she has no conclusive evidence of its position in the dam. Donald Grenier aptly describes Ma and the other characters' comic significance when he writes: "The beauty of this grim humor is that it makes us aware of the unbelievable boredom of these people, of the sheer uselessness of their lives. Cut off from larger concerns, they reduce the world to a dirt mound in the middle of the desert so that the center of their reality becomes an unmarked grave."[7] The conditions of boredom and uselessness are especially telling in the context of a Western novel. Boredom is not usually the emotional state of those living on the borders of society and savagery, as *The Virginian* shows. And while uselessness might describe the lives of bandits, thieves, or outlaws, it certainly does not characterize those pioneers who risked everything to advance the cause of civilization and test the American ethic of social progress and personal success.

Travelling into town in a red wagon that is both office and home, Cap Leech stands as the novel's quasi-Indian. Although referred to as a doctor, he is more a corrupted version of the stock Medicine Man. Lacking the qualities of the noble savage, Leech is a grotesque combination of primitive and civilized man, and being neither doctor nor medicine man, he is, as the narrator at one point says, "a midnight vivisectionist in a cat hospital" (146).

Perhaps because of his ambivalent nature, Leech possesses an incredible and sinister omnipotence in this world. He is a figure obsessed with his mortality, living in a twilight world between life and death, "a man who had been anesthetized, against whose chest villagers of forty years had spit their brains" (40). With his sinister powers and ether-permeated clothing, Leech manages anesthetically to overpower and control the Sheriff, in fact, "to put them all to sleep, to look at their women if he wished, to mark their children" (129).

He has learned his craft by "searching coal bins for the ruined," pulling the teeth of unsuspecting children in deserted alleys, and "practicing among those without chance of recovery, doomed, he felt, to submit" (122). Responsible for "fishing" the body of Harry Bohn from his mother's corpse in an operation that "was more abortive than life saving," Leech ultimately practices a decadent skill, one thriving on dominance, victimization, and the creation of new human grotesques such as Bohn.

One of the better examples of his malevolent domination appears in his appointment with Luke's Indian mistress, Maverick. The extraction of an absessed tooth begins slowly as Leech examines, carefully, his tools, then the victim. He steadily applies the ether and finally begins the probing. As the description builds, it grows clear that Hawkes renders this extraction increasingly in sexual terms; this is both a tooth extraction and an obscure form of rape.

> The Indian, in a last bodily defense, slightly bulged some muscles, loosed others, and secreted from licentious scent spots and awakened nodes, a sensation of difference marvelous as anything he had ever seen. The captive, still watching him with unchanged eyes, generated like an octopus the ink of desire. . . . He pulled and the lower half of the Mandan's face followed the swing of his arm, then back again, elastic, cross-eyed, an abnormal craning of the skull to the will of its tormentor, stretched sightless over the shoulder with each plaguing timeless yawl. Leech pulled in waltz-like arcs, now breaking the pressures of motion to apply a series of lesser, sharp tugs which caused the Indian's head to nod obstinately up and down and one knee, wide and soft, to fold slowly backward into the privy bronze stomach. (148–49)

Because of his perverse surgical methods, Leech is a curious combination of Indian and white man, outsider and resident. Although he does lead a nomadic existence, he was at one time a part of this community and still holds considerable influence here. At the close of the work, there is the suggestion he is the father of the Lampson brothers, and whether the relationship is more spiritual than physical, it is clear that Luke and Leech see one another as son and father. In addition to this kinship, Leech is the adoptive parent of Harry Bohn. After performing the gruesome operation that ushers Bohn into the world, Leech abducts the baby and ends any legitimate practice of medicine. Both father and son are human monstrosities, and each exercises a strange and terrifying authority. Grenier sums up Leech's significance by noting: "The good ole "doc" of the standard Western, one of the familiar banalities which Hawkes joyfully turns inside out, becomes the chief instrument of disease and negation. Births turn out to be living abortions, and we begin to suspect that in Hawkes' version of the Western there will be no final triumph of good guys over bad—the characters whose evilness and sterility come naturally will not be punished in the end. It is simply the way things are. Movie-land morals have no place in the nightmare part of reality."[8]

Nonetheless, there is a form of triumph, though a perverse version of the conquest of good over evil. Such a conquest appears in the guise of the customary shootout where the victims are outlaws who have been annoying the townspeople. The renegades are known as the Red Devils, a gang of hoodlums who supplant horses and cowboy attire with motorcycles and black leather uniforms. Their name, Red Devils, invites associations with savage, roving Indian hordes; however, there is nothing to indicate they are red, Indian, or for that matter, even human. One critic suggests that "The Red Devils haunting the men of the novel are ghosts from an American past when the Red Indians were destroyed by men with the technological power of gunfire. Although the Red Devils do not promise a restoration of that past, their motorcycle gang is a comic image of the return to a tribal, nomadic life after the existing culture, obsessed like the sheriff with the stability of law and order, is demolished."[9]

As Camper's wife stares out the hotel window, she falls under the gaze of these voyeurs, and the following passage graphically describes their semi-human condition.

> The creature continued to watch. It was made of leather. Straps, black buckles and breathing hose filled out a face as small as hers, stripped of hair and bound tightly in alligator skin. It was constructed as a baseball, bound about a small core of rubber. The driving goggles poked up from the shiny cork top and a pair of smoked glasses fastened in the leather gave it malevolent and overflowing eyes. There was a snapped flap on one side that hid an orifice drilled for earphones. Its snout was pressed against the screen, pushing a small bulge into the room. (53)

When not found lurking in the shadows of the town's homes and buildings, some of the gang are incarcerated for allegedly "scratching" a dog. At the same time the remaining members disrupt the town dance by driving their cycles in circles through the street. As quickly as they enter, they leave in a tight formation and thundering cloud. In the end it appears that this incident, as much as their physical appearance and their ubiquity, is the cause of their persecution.

However, in this novel the classic moral opposition between the townspeople and the outlaws is neither clear nor absolute. The killings are really a nocturnal hunt in which the Sheriff and his charges set off to redress some unexplained wrong. There is a sense of utter inevitability to these killings, and as they prepare for the battle, the Sheriff explains, "Kill most anything tonight. . . . Bound to. In Saggitarius [sic]" (155). Together the posse and the motorcyclists enact the ritual attack on the wagon-train, as the Devils circle the pickup truck and are fired upon. The orgy of violence ends when Luke pulls the rifle to his chin and either shoots himself or has the gun backfire, though neither is made expressly clear. "He could feel the eruption under his nose before he squeezed; he fell back with the mistake, the searing, double dinosaurian footfall of the twin bores" (158). Because they are "equally full of savagery and death," neither group is elevated by or purged through this use of violence.[10] This is, as Frederick Busch notes, a wild, mass form of suicide, where "people are murdering a part of life because all life is intolerable."[11]

It is a commonplace of the Western that the hero dislikes violence for its own sake and never takes part in gratuitous forms of slaughter. But in Hawkes's Western wasteland, peopled with those who have not moral imperative or justification, violence is a form of empty sport. The force used originally by settlers to tame and shape the land is thoroughly perverted here. Instead, violence becomes a means of ridding the community of a menace that is a threat in appearance only. The Sheriff admits as much before the showdown when he dismisses the Red Devils as "harmless"; they are, he notes, incapable of posing any significant threat.

In terms of its plot, *The Beetle Leg* further imitates the classic Western, presenting the familiar pattern of action as one of flight and pursuit. The most widespread and perhaps least obvious form of pursuit involves the town's worship of and obsession with the dead man, Mulge Lampson. Nearly every character, in one way or another, refers to or ponders the loss of this man and the possible significance his death holds for them. Ma is the most visible of these searchers, but they all seem to share roughly similar motives in their questioning. As we have seen, most of them are concerned with Mulge's death because there is nothing else to do and because their lives are completely sterile. In their boredom they have elevated Mulge to some semi-mythical level and view him as a kind of talisman for their communal fortunes. The search for Mulge is, then, a search for their own significance and for the fortunes the future holds for each of them.

A second group is pursuing Cap Leech. Although it is never certain exactly why they are following him, it appears they fear the outsider and his questionable powers. The Sheriff initiates this pursuit but is overcome when the two figures meet. Later, as Leech extracts the Mandan's tooth, a gang forms outside the medical tinker's wagon and threatens him if he fails to appear. Their threats culminate in the unhitching of Leech's horse from the wagon, upon which they sit the crippled Finn, in a travesty of his former profession as a wild bronc rider.

A third form of pursuit is the most obvious: the chase and eventual showdown with the fleeing invaders. This is a grisly, ironic transformation of the classic confrontation of the forces of good and evil, culminating less in a shootout than in an ambush of unarmed victims. Involving none of the noble characteristics which mark the true Western confrontation, this encounter leaves hero and villain morally and physically victimized by their actions.

A final, common Western convention involves the sense of epic grandeur that surrounds the landscape and the actions of those who inhabit it. There is usually a "special openness of topography of the Great Plains and western desert [that] has made it particularly expressive for the portrayal of movement."[12] The immensity and beauty of the landscape frequently add a sense of majesty to the actions of the characters, and there is a characteristic lyricism often pervading the descriptions of these areas and the action that takes place in them.

Befitting this, *The Beetle Leg* deals with the vastness of an expansive terrain, but once again Hawkes creates an important difference. While there are moments of attack, flight, and pursuit, the novel lacks any vigorous linear action. Instead, there are prevailing senses of repetition, suffocation, and finally paralysis surrounding all actions and lives. Rather than elevating characters and their activities, this landscape debilitates and weakens them; the aridity of the setting strikingly reflects the aridity of character and moral purpose.

It should now be evident that by choosing the parodic mode, Hawkes creates what one critic calls "a wilful distortion of the entire form *and* spirit" of the Western tale, and through the careful exaggeration of various conventions he fashions a new version of the frontier experience.[13] By reexamining and reevaluating the distinctly American myth of cultural and technological progress implicit in most Westerns, Hawkes presents a "vision of America's disintegrating technological culture. [He] imagines the culture as caught in a weird sort of evolutionary process."[14] Consequently, *The Beetle Leg* stands as a kind of fictional post mortem for a dream and ideal that once established and defined a country and its culture. In writing such a novel, Hawkes seems to be asking his audience to look deeper into the myth of the frontier and see that in this case the "Winning of the West" actually represents not only a destruction of the land, but, more importantly, a desperate waste of human spirit and imagination.

For in the world of *The Beetle Leg* man has lost the ability to create anything new or lifegiving; his machines and activities produce only waste and decay. What the novel defines, then, is a cultural "devolution," as Lucy Frost states, that is biologically symbolized by the subhuman forms of the Red Devils, Cap Leech, and Harry Bohn. Thus both man and his culture are running down to states of exhaustion, apathy, and destruction, and the myths and codes of the old West are finally too old to offer anything fresh or invigorating in Hawkes's modern desert wasteland.

Notes

1. Two such approaches are Chapter 3 in Frederick Busch's *Hawkes: A Guide to His Fictions* (1973) and Lucy Frost's "The Drowning of an American Adam: Hawkes' *The Beetle*

Leg," *Critique,* 14, 3, (1972), 63–74. In his treatment in *Comic Terror,* Donald Grenier mentions some of the novel's parodic elements; however, he prefers to discuss the cinematic rather than the literary Western.

2. John G. Cawelti, *Adventure, Mystery, and Romance* (Chicago: Chicago University Press, 1976), p. 225.

3. John Hawkes, *The Beetle Leg* (New York: New Directions Books, 1951), p. 24. Further citations are from this edition and noted parenthetically.

4. Robert Warshaw, "The Westerner," in Sheridan Baker, ed., *The Essayist* (New York: Thomas Y. Crowell Co., 1977), pp. 332–333.

5. John G. Cawelti, *The Six-Gun Mystique* (Bowling Green: Bowling Green University Popular Press, 1972), p. 59.

6. *Ibid.,* p. 61.

7. Donald Grenier, *Comic Terror* (Memphis: Memphis State University Press, 1973), p. 114.

8. *Ibid.,* pp. 109–10.

9. Lucy Frost, "The Drowning of an American Adam: Hawkes' *The Beetle Leg,*" *Critique,* 14, 3 (1972), p. 69.

10. Grenier, p. 118.

11. Frederick Busch, *Hawkes: A Guide to His Fictions* (New York: Syracuse University Press, 1973), p. 57.

12. Cawelti, *The Six-Gun Mystique,* p. 42.

13. J. G. Riewald, "Parody as Criticism," *Neophilologus,* 50 (1967), p. 127.

14. Frost, p. 67.

John Hawkes as Novelist:
The Example of *The Owl*

ROBERT SCHOLES

For over twenty-five years John Hawkes has been a unique voice in American letters. Belonging to no school, following no fashion, he has paid the price exacted of such loners by the literary establishment. He has been reviewed capriciously, embarrassed by unconsidered praise and attacked with ill-tempered venom. His admirers have been mostly his fellow writers, some English teachers, and their students. Recently he has been more honored abroad than at home. For better or worse, he has been taken up by the French, who can see in his writing connections to the surrealists, to Faulkner, and to their own *nouveau roman*. Perhaps they will teach us to appreciate him, as they taught us to appreciate jazz music, Edgar Poe, William Faulkner, and the American films of the studio era.

Meanwhile we must do the best we can to understand him ourselves, which involves measuring his strengths and weaknesses as a writer, and sorting out his best work from his less successful efforts. This discussion is intended as a part of that sorting out. *The Owl* originally appeared in 1954, in a double volume with another short novel, also set in Italy, called *The Goose on the Grave*. That these two works are of unequal quality has become increasingly apparent over the years. *The Goose on the Grave* suffers from a murky atmosphere, a lack of focus and coherence, as if indeed it were written by someone who felt (as Hawkes has claimed to feel) that plot, character, setting, and theme are the worst enemies of the novel. *The Owl* is altogether different. It is tightly organized. It is strong precisely in plot, character, setting, and theme. Which suggests that with Hawkes, as with many other writers, we will do well to take D. H. Lawrence's advice and not trust the teller but the tale. After its first publication, *The Owl* was reprinted in *Lunar Landscapes*, a collection of short novels and stories of which it is fair to say that *The Owl* is its only entirely successful work.

The Owl is one of the very best of Hawkes' fictions, and probably the best introduction to his work. His method has always been to work with strong

Reprinted by permission of the publisher from *Hollins Critic* 14, no. 3 (June 1977): 1–10. Copyright © 1977 by Hollins College. Original publication copyright © New Directions Publishing Corporation.

images that can be developed into scenes of nightmarish power and vividness, and then to seek some means of connecting these scenes in a coherent and developmental way. Because he starts with images rather than with a story, his work *is* different from conventionally plotted fiction, though this is not the same thing as being without plot altogether. Over the years, as his work has developed, he has turned more and more to the unifying voice of a single narrator as a way of giving coherence to the events of his narrative. At the same time, his fiction, which began with an emphasis on terror, violence, and death, has moved from those horrors toward a lush eroticism, initiated in the closing section of *Second Skin* and continued in *The Blood Oranges* and *Death, Sleep and the Traveller.* Even *Travesty,* which moves toward death, draws most of its strength from its slightly over-ripe eroticism—what the French, in speaking of the decadence that brings the grapes of Sauternes to their highest pitch of sweetness, call *la pourriture noble.*

The Owl is about rottenness, also, but there is no suggestion in it of what Walter Pater liked to call "a sweet and comely decadence." Only the narrator of the book finds anything sweet and comely in his world, and he is clearly a monster. He is, in fact, the epitome of fascism, at once hangman and dictator, ruling over a decaying little world with absolute and terrible authority. *The Owl* is an imaginative probe into the heart of Italian fascism, with its deep roots in Imperial Rome and the Roman Catholic church. The novel is localized and historicized, as is much of Hawkes's best work, especially his early novels. The England of *The Lime Twig* (1961), the American West of *The Beetle Leg* (1951), the Germany of *The Cannibal* (1949), and the Italy of *The Owl* (1954) are imaginative settings, to be sure, rather than documentaries of social realities. But they are attempts to reach a kind of depth, a kind of truth about human experience, which is based on historical and cultural processes. The narrator of *The Owl* is as much connected to a particular heritage as the speaker of Browning's "My Last Duchess" though he is not so precisely located in time and space. It is relevant to think of Browning here, for Hawkes has come to specialize in the extended dramatic monologue. Like Browning, he is drawn to the strange and the perverse, and he delights in immersing his readers in the voice and vision of a character whose consciousness is disturbing to "normal" sensibilities. The point of this immersion in the abhorrent is to force readers to acknowledge a kind of complicity, to admit that something in us resonates to all sorts of monstrous measures, even as we recognize and condemn the evil consciousness for what it is. As a literary strategy this requires great delicacy and control. Both the horrible complicity and the shudder of condemnation must be actively aroused by the text and maintained in a precarious balance. In *The Owl* Hawkes manages this feat as well as anywhere in his work.

The narrator, whose voice is our guide to Sasso Fetore (Tomb Stench), is calm, orotund, and self-righteous. Il Gufo (The Owl) has the title of Hangman but is also *de facto* ruler of his village kingdom. Laws were made in the past and they are not to be broken or revised. They mainly take the form of "interdicts, cried or posted, 'Blaspheme no more. Il Gufo.'" In the extremity and consistency of his ruthless complacency, Il Gufo approaches the condition of ridiculousness. He threatens to become a comic figure more than once in the course of his narrative. We read his words with a repressed giggle, a blend of abhorrence and amusement, tempered with fear. This creature is a construct, obviously, a talking fiction—grotesque, macabre, absurd. But such fabrications have stalked our real world all too frequently. Here—in fiction—it is tolerable, but it masks a reality all too like its own false face. And there is a power and an attraction in this evil. The marriageable women in the village are drawn to Il Gufo and their fathers eye him with hope. But he already has his "tall lady," the gallows, and he is forever true to her. As an unknown voice tells one of these fathers in the opening lines of the book, "Him?" Think not of him for your daughter Signore, nor for her sister either. There will be none for him. Not him. He has taken his gallows, the noose and knot, to marry."

The story of *The Owl* is simple and fierce. The town of Sasso Fetore has lost its young men—apparently in a war. As the fathers are reduced to thinking of the Hangman himself as the only candidate for their daughters' hands and dowries, a captured soldier is brought to the town and imprisoned in the Hangman's fortress. The prisoner, who is foreign and never speaks, becomes an object of hope for these fathers and their daughters. But the Hangman has other plans for him. Sasso Fetore is an infertile wasteland; Il Gufo is its king: "Without mass violence, Sasso Fetore was still unmerciful. It was visible in the moonlight, purposeful as an avalanche of rock and snow. Here in the cellars and under roofs as far as the boundary, the old men slept in their stockings and the others, confident wives, warmed wedding bands in their armpits. Politically, historically, Sasso Fetore was an eternal Sabbath."

This lunar landscape reveals a town so gripped by law and order that it is almost dead: "As a prosecuted law with the ashes of suffering and memory carried off on the wind, Sasso Fetore was a judgment passed upon the lava, long out of date, was the more intolerant and severe." Even the "cloud formations over Sasso Fetore were consistent of color, large and geometric, the clear head of a Roman heaven." The Hangman rules here by law: "To the hangman went the souls of death's peasants, to him were bonded the lineage of a few artisans and not least the clarity of such a high place, a long firm line of rule. If there was decay, it was only in the walls falling away from proclamations hundreds of years old, still readable, still clear and binding."

Though the walls may crumble, the proclamations survive and hold the living in their iron grip. The geometry of the sky, the clarity of the view, and the persistence of law shape the village and bind it to the hangman's will. Its history began with "a primitive monastic order whose members worked in strict obedience and were the first inhabitants of the province." As the hangman says, "The immense King's evil of history lay over the territory." He breathes this atmosphere and it refreshes him. He keeps a pet owl of his own, and when it attacks a young woman who had dared disturb its privacy, implanting its claws in her scalp, "circumsizing the brain," the hangman takes it to his arm and comforts it, sending the girl home without a thought for her: "But I wet and smoothed the feathers under the triangle of his beak with my tongue and he regained himself, once more folded into his nocturnal shape, and only the eyes did not relent. I gave him a large rat and slept near him the night."

When the Hangman dreams, he sees his country as a tiny green mountain under three white flags: "The country was no larger than the flags and as perfect. The road was a bright red line winding to the three precipices and the capital of rigid existence. And the flags were moving, fluttering, the motion of life anchored safely to one place." This orderly vision of a country no larger than its flags, of life anchored safely, turns into a nightmare. The flags disintegrate into shreds and the hunchbacked village fisherman's voice comes out of the sky, concealed in the rays of the sun. He says, " 'The fish are running well, Master,' with mockery in his voice." Fertility is the enemy of law and order. The fasces, ancient Roman symbol of justice borne by the Hangman's ward Pucento, symbolizes the power of the law, which is the power of punishment. When the Prisoner arrives, awakening hopes of fertility and fecundation in the hearts of the village's young women and their fathers, the Hangman meets this threat to the eternal Sabbath with the full power of the law and all his authority. He turns the prisoner over to the tender mercies of the prefect, with his live coals and his four hooks of punishment, but he does not concern himself with these "temporary arrangements." He thinks of something more permanent—his gallows:

> The tall lady stood below in the court almost as if she were taking the sun. Now she had no rope. Her place had been appointed by men who with trepidation paced off the earth and tested it upon their knees under her shadow, a shadow taken to earth and remaining there. The scaffold itself, shaped like a tool of castigation, was constructed to support the dead weight of an ox if we came to hang oxen. She was of wood and black as a black ark, calm by nature, conceived by old men with beards and velvet caps, simple and geometric as frescoes of the creation of the world.

The village possesses another landmark, a statue of "the Donna," a different sort of lady, who represents the softer side of the old religion—mercy as opposed to justice. Says the Hangman, "Surely the Donna made the scaffold majestic." The Donna suits the "soft flesh" of the peasants, but the law gives "bony strength to the lover of Donna and legend": "The character and the code, right upon right, crashed into the pale heart when the culprit hanged, her prayers for him so soft as hardly to be heard. She saved none—salvation not being to the purpose. . . ." The statue of the Donna is not given a prominent place in the village. It stands before a cave in the burned forest—"an idol whose nights were spent with a few small deer and speechless animals," says the Hangman. When someone reddens the statue's cheeks with blood, the

Hangman is offended and simply rides past on his donkey and kicks her off her pedestal. After this, the scaffold is the only "lady" in Sasso Fetore.

If the softness of the Donna disturbs the Hangman, the unruly nature of sexuality is even more abhorrent to him. Indeed, when the cheeks of the Donna are reddened, he treats the statue like a painted whore rather than a vandalized icon. Later, one of the most deeply and distressingly imagined scenes in all Hawkes's fiction is based upon the tension between the bodily vigor of sex and the mental power of law. In this scene the villagers hold a pathetic remnant of a fair below the Hangman's ramparts: "The fair was pitched directly below the fortress, in good view, and for the benefit of the prisoner up there." The Hangman doesn't like fairs. As he puts it, "History had forbade the fair, a guise for flirting and the dissatisfaction of a sex—the fair invoked only when the measures of the fathers failed. I listened to the festival, the ribaldry of the viol da gamba, the concert of bushes. How could it be anything but an ill omen, the distraction and the gaiety of woman preceded the fall of man."

The Hangman detests women, seeing in them, as Judeo-Christian tradition has taught him to see it, the source of all human evil, which stems from Eve's breaking of the first law. He watches them coming to the fair: "They stumbled, the swaying shanks of hair, the flaming red scarves binding torso or hips and the cantilevering, the maneuvering of the skirts. Newly shod and gowned, the purple and green of earth and sky became warm in their presence; all that was female, unnatural in congregation, came into the open air walking as geese who know the penalty awaiting the thief who catches them."

This hatred of the feminine, and of the sexuality associated with it, is not a mere aberration of the Hangman's mind. Hawkes is not presenting to us an individual case study in this portrait but the deep mentality of an entire culture. The primitive monastic order that founded the community is the source of this hatred of the female and of the flesh itself. And it is the monks who initiated the grotesque ritual which dominates the fair:

> On their leaning instruments the musicians played the seldom heard 'March of the White Dog." This whole breed had once been deprived and whipped, tied ascetically by the lay brothers on the slopes. The bitches were destroyed. And the rest, heavy of organ and never altered with the knife, day after day were beaten during the brothers' prayers, commanded to be pure unmercifully. The dogs tasted of blood given in mean measure but were not permitted the lather, the howl, the reckless male-letting of their species. Beaten across the quarters, they were taught by the monks the blind, perfectly executed gavotte.

At the fair, the "sole remaining dog" is led in this "devilish dog's fandango" by Pucento, the Hangman's ward and lictor, bearer of the fasces itself. Boy and dog complete geometric figures, "a square and then a circle," all the while "straining to duplicate the measure, the ruthless footstep of the past."

In this scene, which mingles elements of the grotesque and macabre so powerfully, we find that perverse preoccupation with sexuality which character-izes all puritanisms. From the monkish thwarters of canine sexuality to the Hangman himself is only a step. In bending the poor beasts' motions to the mathematical rhythms of the gavotte and the abstract figures of square and circle the monks impose law upon nature—a law which defines itself as the opposite of nature, which becomes "law" by virtue of perverting nature. What the Hangman never tells us, of course, but what comes through his every gesture and word, is the immense and perverse pleasure this fascist takes in the stifling of what is natural and pleasurable in others. And the Hangman's ultimate pleasure is in his ultimate power. The taking of life is his consummation. The gallows is indeed his "lady."

The scene at the fair is followed by the attempt of Antonina, the most eligible young woman in the village, to win the Hangman himself as her husband. He climbs the hill of the fortress with her and she offers herself to him: "Honorable Hangman. Carino. Il Gufo. It is you I love." And this is perhaps the most terrifying thing of all: that the woman should be drawn to that very power, attracted by that very hatred of all things lawless, feminine, and natural, to offer herself to this macabre creature. What happens is grotesque, turning intensity to comedy:

> Antonina rolled stiff on the brown hilltop and the skirts loosened, lifted by the wind. She pushed her fingers into the bent grass and dragged her hair on the silt and stones. Her slender belly thrashed like all cloistered civilization among weed, root, in the wild of the crow's nest. I reached into the sheltered thighs touching this bone and that and felt for what all women carried. High and close to her person, secreted, I found Antonina's purse which she had hid there longer than seven years, that which they fastened to the girls when young. What was there more?

The language reeks of sexuality here, but the deed performed is only a finan-cial transaction or an act of theft. He takes her purse but leaves her person, touches her bones but ignores her flesh. Antonina's father tries to regard this as an act of betrothal. Il Gufo gives him no more satisfaction than he gave the daughter.

It is not my purpose here to examine the entire novel or even to offer a coherent interpretation of it: That is better left to the individual reader in any case, who will find much of interest in scenes involving or concerning the prisoner, such as the extraordinary "judgment supper" in which is enacted the corruption of Christianity, as if its founder had not been a victim but the executioner himself. The prisoner in this novel comes as a potential redeemer, one who might restore fertility to this tomblike and infertile world. But this salvation is not acceptable. The Hangman is in love with death, which constitutes for him the most perfect order of all. He is not a venal sadist. It is the Prefect who plies his hooks and fingers his truncheon. The Hangman is beyond this. He serves the Law and follows the book from which a "hangman knew the terms and directions, the means and methods to destroy a man." He loves not pain but destruction itself. The execution of the prisoner, when it comes, is preceded by a lavish feast, altogether different from the simple meal of fish at the judgment supper—a feast so rare and stimulating that it brings back "the effulgent memory of execution, step by step, dismal, endless, powerful as a beam that transcends our indulgence on the earth, in Sasso Fetore."

To the Hangman, the world itself, the whole earth is Sasso Fetore, a stinking tomb. Behind his hatred of life, of the unruly, the sexual, the natural, is a terrible fastidiousness. Execution cleanses the earth, purifies it. As he rides through his world, or contemplates it from what he calls "the absolute clarity of my vantage above," he sees the men as so many "Garibaldis burning in a cold and wintry piazza"; he sees the hunchback's daughter as "a girl who should have been burned in Sasso Fetore." For whatever appears to threaten order, whether the libertarian politics of a Garibaldi or the apparent sexuality of a girl, Il Gufo has one response: purification by fire. For others, the scaffold will do. But *all* are guilty, *all* must be punished, as they were even "in the time when there were men to hang and those to spare, with clemency for neither." What the Hangman hates is life itself.

This portrayal of repressive fascism is, as I have tried to suggest, at once terrible and comic, bizarre in its extremity but profoundly accurate in probing the philosophical and emotional roots of this mentality as embodied in the Hangman. It is of course an imaginative construct rather than a case study, an emblem rather than a portrait. In saying that plot, character, setting, and theme were the enemies of the novel, Hawkes was hyperbolically and provocatively protesting against certain traditional ways of approaching the construction of fiction. But the only true justification for surrealism in art is that it destroys certain surface plausibilities in order to liberate realities that are habitually concealed by habits of vision attuned only to the surface itself. And this is precisely what Hawkes accomplishes in *The Owl*. It is time to recognize that achievement.

John Hawkes: *The Lime Twig* and Other Tenuous Horrors

In an essay on "Flannery O'Connor's Devil" John Hawkes commented on the work of Flannery O'Connor and Nathanael West in terms that are equally applicable to his own novels. He connects the two writers in their "comic treatment of violence," "their employment of the devil's voice as vehicle for their satire," "their true (or accurate) vision of our godless actuality." Both (Hawkes continues, quoting Flannery O'Connor) "are demolishing 'man's image of himself as a rational creature'"; both "are reversing their artistic sympathies, West committing himself to the creative pleasures of a destructive sexuality, Flannery O'Connor committing herself creatively to the antics of soulless characters . . ."; and both "are remarkably similar in their exploitation of the 'demolishing' syntax of the devil."[1]

Since all committed writers are finally talking about themselves even in their critical writing, it is perhaps obvious that Hawkes is talking as much about his own work as about that of Flannery O'Connor and Nathanael West. And, in fact, Hawkes starts his essay by commenting on the "sudden confluence" of the two in his reading, hence, I would suggest, in his writing.[2] Hawkes' novels and West's, in particular, are comparable in still other ways: in their fantastic landscapes, surreal or antireal, as you will; in their portrayal of a horribly knowing innocence; in their fondness for crossing expectations, so that, for example, the apparently deadly turns out to be harmless and the apparently harmless deadly; in their delighted manipulation of cliché, particularly those fed to the popular imagination, and which perhaps come from the popular imagination, in movies. Possibly most important of all as a common denominator between, for example, West's *The Day of the Locust* and Hawkes' *The Lime Twig* is their insistence that the fantastic events of their novels have at their root sexual fantasy, both the "worst dream, and the best" of their characters.[3]

The "demolishing syntax of the devil," the "comic treatment of violence," the use of "the devil's voice" itself are, in both Hawkes and West, tools for the externalization of the unconscious, an attempt to render substantial

Reprinted with permission from *Massachusetts Review* 7 (Summer 1966): 462–75. © 1966 The Massachusetts Review, Inc.

the phantasmagoric realms behind the commonplace exterior of ordinary people. Hence the temptation to call their work surrealist, and the difficulty in shaking off a sense of the rightness of the term, unsatisfactory as it finally is. Their characters' soullessness does not deprive them of an inner life; on the contrary, the loss of "soul" is more than compensated for in fantasy life, and in the exuberantly serene horror of the fictive worlds which result. Yet, as I hope to show, the fantasy at the heart of all human activity in *The Lime Twig* is itself man's best as well as his worst, and accounts for his creativity as well as his destructiveness.

Taken at its widest in *The Day of the Locust,* fantasy includes not only Tod Hackett's daydreams about sleeping with Faye Greener but also the central image in the novel, Tod's painting "The Burning of Los Angeles." Fantasy in West is not merely illusion, but conception, not only (idle) fancy, but imagination. It is a creative act which *may* turn into fulfilling action, though it usually doesn't. What starts as fantasy may be externalized in violence and "galvanize" an otherwise apathetic Tod, for example, into vital action—*either* throwing Faye down and raping her *or* painting his picture. Either action is a manifestation of power, the power of prophecy which can both conceive an act of destruction and see it carried into actuality. Early in the book Tod conceives himself as a Jeremiah, a prophet with a vision of doom and destruction, and at the end his prophecy is fulfilled as a direct result of Faye, the object of his sex-fantasies. Tod's fantasies of social chaos, though not realized on canvas, are realized in actuality. All sex in *The Day of the Locust* centers on Faye, and though it may seem ridiculous to suggest copulation with a Faye Greener as an alternative to apocalypse, symbolically that is exactly what West does suggest. Sensation, thrills, excitation of the nervous system to climax is exactly what West's characters—and the great American audience which was his concern in all his novels—are seeking, and, of course, exactly what they cannot find.

In the individual lives of West's grotesques—including his "normal" character, Tod Hackett—fantasy does *not* turn into fulfilling action, for West's vision is of sterility, of the frustration of sexual (or spiritual) fulfillment. Tod neither gets Faye nor paints his picture. Yet there is one action in *The Day of the Locust* which is creative, climactic, if you will: the riot itself. The smashing blow which Tod thinks will crush Faye's "egglike self-sufficiency" and give him the satisfaction he needs; the crashing down of tons of water, West's image for Homer Simpson's cresting emotions which dam up, then trickle away like water down a drain—these images of a violent breaking-through are exactly equivalent to the destroying, surging upheaval of the mob in the last chapter. And, in view of the insane world West has created in this book, the act of destruction is clearly a creative act even if the only possible sane response to it is Tod's hysteria on the final page.

The Lime Twig centers on the fantasy of Michael Banks, a completely ordinary lower-middle class Londoner who is lured into a scheme to steal an aged racehorse, Rock Castle, and run him as a ringer in the classic Golden Bowl at Aldington. Michael is introduced to the scheme by his lodger, William Hencher, who acts as go-between for an unearthly archetypal gangster known only as Larry, and Larry's gang. Since Michael's function, unknown to him, is to be a respectable front for Larry, the gangster lures Margaret, Michael's equally ordinary wife, to Aldington and holds her prisoner as a guarantor of her husband's behavior. The lure for Margaret is Michael; that for Michael once the plot is under way is the sexually flamboyant Sybilline Laval. But the overriding lure in *The Lime Twig,* the central image of sexual potency and phallic thrust, is the horse of Michael Banks' imagination which materializes as Rock Castle.

The horse first appears as Michael's fantasy as he is leaving his flat to join Hencher and get the stolen Rock Castle:

> Knowing how much she [Margaret] feared his dreams; knowing that her own worst dream was one day to find him gone, overdue minute by minute some late afternoon until the inexplicable absence of him became a certainty; knowing that his own worst dream, and best, was of a horse which was itself the flesh of all violent dreams; knowing this dream, that the horse was in their sitting room—he had left the flat door open as if he meant to return in a moment or meant never to return—seeing the room empty except for moonlight bright as day and, in the middle of the floor, the tall upright shape of the horse draped from head to tail in an enormous sheet that falls over the eyes and hangs down stiffly from the silver jaw; knowing the horse on sight and listening while it raises one shadowed hoof on the end of a silver thread of foreleg and drives down the hoof to splinter in a single crash one plank of that empty Dreary Station floor. . . . (33)

Here, before Michael Banks so much as sees Rock Castle, is the horse in fantasy, a fantasy that, in typical Hawkes fashion, is so substantial that it takes a second reading to be sure that the horse is *not* in the sitting room. In this passage you have Michael Banks' fantasy of an absolute male potency embodied in a horse, the blow of whose hoof signals, simultaneously, the dream of the smashing triumph of orgasm and the smashing of Banks' whole commonplace existence; the dream of absolute liberty, which is to say, absolute escape fantasy, in his leaving the door ajar; and his dream of absolute mastery over Margaret, whose own "worst dream"—the fulfillment of his—he is toying with. All this is summed up in the horse, Michael's personal symbol; as we shall see, that comes to the ordinary man's dream of himself as angel (or devil): that is, of Michael as Larry.

Larry himself can perhaps be equated with the horse, fantastical and actual, for he is Michael's imago, Michael's "ideal" conception of himself. It is Larry, through his boys, Sparrow and Thick, who literally "smashes" the Banks' flat, cutting up and carting off every last shred of evidence that Michael and Margaret ever lived there, or, indeed, ever existed. It is Larry who leads Michael to the orgiastic fulfillment, in a single evening, of his most incredible fantasies—four times with Sybilline Laval, once each with the widow and the Banks' neighbor, Annie, who magically, if literally, appears, to be taken on the spot. "You can win if you want to," says Syb to Michael, echoing the sign at Aldington station; but perhaps that should read, "You can win if Larry wants you to," for Larry is the dark angel as fairy godmother who makes dreams come true: "Stood straight as he did when predicting, Larry who was an angel if any angel ever had eyes like his or flesh like his"(83).

Why "predicting"? Why Larry "full-of-grace," as Little Dora calls him? In what sense is Larry, like Tod Hackett, a prophet as well as an "angel of Heaven or Hell," as the racing-tout Sidney Slyter says in one of his cryptic newspaper columns which appear as oracular headnotes to each chapter (139). For the same reason that "Sybilline" has the name she does (her peculiar style of prophecy significantly qualified by her last name, probably a reference to Pierre Laval, France's Quisling in World War II); and the three touts with pellet bombs in the Men's are called "soothsayers"; and Sidney Slyter reports the events of each chapter *before* each chapter. In a godless world, who can predict, literally tell before the event, that the event will occur? The killer: Larry, and secondarily, Larry's accomplices and *semblables*. Just so, the agent of terror in any murder thriller is the one man among, say, the dozen at an isolated country house who is *not* in terror, who can toy with the fantasies of his victims—and predict the future. The innocent, of course, cannot. Hawkes, whose prime subject is terror, has William Hencher offer the alternatives of existence on the first page of the novel: in the search for a place "to be a home for the waiting out of dreams" are you the man looking for lodgings who sees the window shade raised an inch and someone peering out? or are you the man with lodgings to let who raises the shade to peer out? In either case, for the Henchers and Bankses of this world the search for the fulfillment of love finds primarily terror; but not for the Larrys.

Larry himself clearly identifies his role in the world of *The Lime Twig* at the wild "party" scene at the widow's. Larry and Jimmy Needles, the jockey, are sitting at, pounding at, the piano, Larry talking over their own noise and that of everyone else in the room (all ellipses are Hawkes'):

. . . And I told the Inspector he was making a horrible botch of it. I said it would never do. Who's pulling the strings I told him and he got huffy, huffy, mind you. I said the killing of the kids was no concern of mine but the hanging of Knifeblade was not acceptable, not in the least acceptable. You'd best not interfere, I said. There's power in this world you never dreamed of, I told him. Why, you don't stand a showing even with a little crowd at the seaside . . . and you'd better not bother with my business or my amusements. . . . (147)

Larry's business and Larry's amusements: "love or money," as Sidney Slyter says. The title of the book itself, though it has referents in several directions, refers first of all to the trap Larry sets for Michael Banks. As W. S. Gilbert has it in *Yeomen of the Guard,*

> If he's made the best use of his time,
> His twig he'll so carefully lime
> That every bird
> Will come down at his word,
> Whatever its plumage or clime.

Larry manipulates the dream of a Hencher or a Banks for his own ends, as the devil would. The twig he limes for Michael is not the only one in the novel, but it is the primal one, for Larry speaks with the devil's voice. Contrary to the blurb on the cover of *The Lime Twig* and the critics who accept the error, Larry and his gang do not "muscle in on" someone else's scheme: it is not a matter of interpretation but of fact that the scheme is Larry's; that Hencher (who has known Larry and Sparrow, "the Captain and his man," during the war) is go-between, in the name of "love" of Banks and Larry, we can only assume from the introductory chapter; and that Michael is the number one bird to be trapped, the front for a plot that can only be Larry's. If Michael Banks could initiate a scheme like this one, he could fulfill his own fantasies as well; he would be Larry, and he clearly is not. It is Larry who beds Michael with his women, fleshes Michael's phallic fantasy in Rock Castle.

Larry's anecdote about the Inspector, a bit of gossip between old friends, one indignant at injustice, the other sympathetic, suggests not only the power at Larry's disposal through the manipulation of the dreams of others, but the impotence of all forces that might stand in his way. (All other forces, that is, except that in his victim that he could not foretell, and that finally defeats him.) The Inspector, Knifeblade, the "killing of the kids"—none of this re-appears in *The Lime Twig,* yet thematically it is all directly relevant. Policemen cross the scene at several points, but their very existence is in vain. *The Lime Twig* ends with the police discovering the body of Hencher, kicked to death in Chapter 1 by Rock Castle and buried in the stable. The last words of the novel present the police driving off "through vacant city streets to uncover the particulars of this crime" (175). But, alas, the death of Hencher is perhaps the only event in the entire book that is *not* a crime, and there is little hope that justice will prevail. The forces of law and order, of civil and military authority, are futile in the face of an evil that is as much internal as external: fantasy cannot be prohibited by law. In one sense Larry (stylistically, if not actually) is an externalization of inner forces, a devil summoned up by Michael himself, and hardly susceptible to legal control.

Moreover, authority in *The Lime Twig* is not only futile but is itself allied with the devil. Police and gangsters alike are prone to the violence that is the working out of dreams. At one point Cowles, Rock Castle's trainer for the race, has his throat cut in the "lower world" of the Baths, but all law and order, in the person of the Constable, can do is peer down into the swirling steam, muttering, "Here now, what's this deviltry?" (117). More important, Banks' orgy ends horribly with Banks running outside upon hearing a shot, to find "the body of a child in a bright-green dress"— ". . . there was smoke still circling out of the belly, smoke and a little blood, and she lay with one knee raised, with palms turned. And the old man [the Constable] crouching with drawn gun, touching the body to see where his shot had gone . . ." (161). Michael attacks him but is in no shape for a fight, and the Constable beats him—"down you go, you little Cheapside gambler!"—kicks him, and walks off.

In typical Hawkes' fashion, the "incident," not after all a trivial one, is never explained. Repellent, apparently arbitrary violence of the sort is often enough used to accuse Hawkes—and West—of sadism, sensationalism, or at least of obscurantist mystification. I would like to suggest that "explanation" of this incident and the like elsewhere in the novel and in all of Hawkes' novels is impossible, that events simply have to be accepted as statements of fact about both the inner and outer worlds. In explanation of the killing of the child—not named but clearly identified as Monica by the green dress and by the fact that Monica when last seen has fled the room where Margaret is being kept prisoner—there are two "logical" possibilities. Either the child in some way attacked the Constable and he kills her in "self-defense"; or, the Constable has killed her for no reason whatever. There are no other alternatives, yet I would suggest that there is no need to choose even one of these. The *facts* are all that is important: that a constable, an old man, shoots and kills a little girl, knocks down a man who runs at him in outrage, and walks off. No motive is necessary—or possible. (And it doesn't matter that constables don't carry guns in England; there is no graveyard of World War II ships off England's coast, either; the "Italian" spoken in *The Owl* and *The Goose on the Grave* is often not Italian at all but almost-Italian; American military overseers do not ride motorcycles and carry Sten guns (*The Cannibal*). The list of "errors" and "anachronisms" in Hawkes is endless.) Is any other explanation needed for the killing of Monica (or the "killing of the kids")? Is it any more possible to explain the appalling details dropped, without comment or expansion, in Hencher's little picture of the boy and his dog: "In one of the alleys off Pinky Road I remember a little boy who wore black stockings, a shirt ripped off the shoulder, a French sailor's hat with a red pompom. The whipping marks were always fresh on his legs and one cheekbone was blue" (8). Hencher's "point" is not in these details, but in the boy's narrow scrutiny of his dog—"the black gums," "the soft wormy little legs," "the nicks in its ears, tiny channels over the dog's brain, pictures he could find on its purple tongue, pearls he could discover between the claws." And in Hencher's one comment, "Love is a long close scrutiny like that. I loved Mother in the same way" (8–9). The boy, once again, never re-appears; the whipping marks are never explained. But are they not enough, as facts? Like Laurence Sterne, Hawkes leaves it to the imagination to fill out the obscenity: just what do *you* make of the French sailor's hat? The burden of understanding must be equally the reader's and the author's: we all participate in the devil's vision.

The brutally handled little boy is introduced, furthermore, as the first detail in the development of a major strand of the novel: the violation of innocence, and the vindication of humanity (primarily Michael's) through that remnant of childhood innocence that remains in him despite everything. The theme develops through the boy; Monica; the cries (certainly not the laughter) of children heard throughout; Margaret's waking vision of children "tied down the length of track" beneath the train to Aldington; and perhaps most telling of all, through Little Dora talking about being "parked" as a child: "But that's past. Now it's my sister leaves her kids with me of a weekend or summer. And I'm at the good end, now" (72). To be a child at all in this world is decidedly not to be "at the good end."

Hawkes' novels are full of unexplained events, untold histories that leave you with questions that cannot be answered. There is no pretense to that verisimilitude which gives you a rounded, completed world; on the contrary, his are angular, elliptical, incomplete worlds which have to leave you unsatisfied if you expect answers to all questions, but which do satisfy you once you realize that there are no answers. Not that there's any coy holding back on Hawkes' part: he could not possibly explain the ritual in the cemetery or that of the iguana on Catalina Kate's back in *Second Skin;* or the sinister priest's ritual at the end of *The Goose on the Grave;* or those of Il Gufo in *The Owl.* Most important of all, he cannot give you the motivations, the psychology of any of his characters. Like West, and perhaps he gets it from West, Hawkes rejects psychological analysis willfully. To turn to his latest book, *Second Skin,* for a moment, consider Skipper and his father; Skipper and his mother; Skipper and his wife; Skipper and his daughter; Skipper and his son-in-law; Skipper and Tremlow; Skipper and Sonny; Skipper and Pixie; Skipper and Kate: explain love. Skipper and his wife, his daughter, Tremlow, Miranda, Captain Red, Jomo: explain hate, or, better still, despair. And certainly the same kinds of permutation and combination hold in *The Lime Twig.* "Freud is your Bullfinch; you cannot learn from him," Nathanael West once wrote. That is, the Greeks had no need for a textbook explicating their mythology; we have no need for one of psycho-sexual behavior. Hawkes can present his comic, violent rituals and the Freudian myths that give rise to them: he cannot explain them, except as Freud would, and that's not the novelist's job, or the critic's. Finally, every one of Hawkes' characters, and every one of those incredibly imagined incidents in all his books stands like a crux in a medieval manuscript: explain as you like, the crux stands, open to innumerable other possibilities, substantial as only a word on paper can be.

But the violence in Hawkes' novels, as in West's, is not merely that of the case-study of purely private aberration. At the heart of his vision of contemporary reality is war, concretely World War II, which takes a central place in five of his novels and short novels. Long after the end of the war, it holds its place at the center of consciousness—and of the unconscious—of his characters (clearly it's at the center of Hawkes' own experience as well). At the Italian restaurant with Syb, promising, and the rest of the gang, Michael remembers nothing, not Margaret, not his flat, not the murder of Cowles, but only "a love note he had written at the age of twelve when the city was on fire" (121). The fantasy of sex and love was already part of him then, and so is the burning city of the past now. Larry's military bearing, his military step, the military march he bangs on the piano are at least in part the heritage of his captaincy and an aspect of the aura of terror which surrounds him. Sparrow's crippled legs—and his addiction—are the result of his having been run over by an armored vehicle (British, not "enemy," just as the plane that crashes in the back yard is British: the enemy of life and reason is not merely a political foe). Most important of all, Hencher establishes the tone and tenor of all human responses in Hawkes' nightmare world: when you hear an echoing military step; when you hear an airplane; when you hear or see or touch or smell anything whatever, the question your nervous system asks is not whether you're going to be killed but how. Hencher cannot smell smoke without wondering whether someone is smoking in the toilet or whether it's coming "from the parlor that would burn like hay" (9). When he merely thinks of a bombing, he thinks, too, "one night wouldn't a cherubim's hand or arm or curly head [from the roof of Dreary Station] come flying down through our roof? Some dislodged ball of saintly brass palm or muscle or jagged neck find its target . . . ?" (10). In the scene when he sees the bomber falling, he wonders whether he will be killed by a "blow of a flying gyroscopic compass or propellor blade," "brushed to death by a wing, caught beneath cold tons of the central fuselage, or surely sprayed by petrol and burned alive . . ." (20). The plane crashes, a "painful missile" hits him in the side—and it's a hard tuft of wool blown loose from the pilot's clothing! (As I suggested earlier, even the apparently innocuous becomes deadly in Hawkes' world.) The point should be clear: in a world of war, all lives, not only Hencher's, are lived in perpetual expectation and calculation of impending destruction: in terror. The mad clarity of Hencher's vision is paranoid, but the word means little when the condition is universal, and when terror does not end on V-E Day. Furthermore, Hencher's fantasies of death, his pre-creation of the exact conditions under which he will get his, are described with a richness of language that suggests desire as well as terror. The conception of his own death, like his assumption of the role of pilot-hero in the cabin of the plane, becomes sexual—the best and worst of him—and it is inevitable that his death come under the hooves of Rock Castle.

Hawkes, then, as he says of West, commits himself in his fiction to "the creative pleasures of a destructive sexuality." Pleasure and Business; sex and sadism; orgasm and power; fantasy and actuality; the angelic and the devilish—these are man's best and worst, two sides of the same coin. Myths expressive of man's deepest dreams externalize themselves as gothic rituals of

Satanic beauty. Hawkes' vision, no less than West's, is no specious cataloguing of personal aberration but a comic vision of what man's fantasies have brought into being. The pure image of urbanized, mechanized violence of *The Lime Twig* is firmly based in the hellish realities of the twentieth century.

However, to say that in *The Lime Twig* whatever is, is a statement of fact, is not to say that both sides of the coin are the same. Finally Hawkes' vision of evil is a moral vision and speech with the devil's voice a literary device. In this novel, more explicitly than in any other of his books but *Second Skin,* redemption (purely secular) is not only a possibility but an actuality. *The Owl* is, I think, Hawkes' blackest book: *The Cannibal* does offer at least the besieged innocence of two children, Selvaggia and her cannibalized brother; *The Goose on the Grave* the perverted innocence of another, Adeppi; *The Beetle Leg* offers the perpetual quest of Cap Leech for a place where he will be recognized, and the perpetual attempt at fertility of a host of eternally defeated Faulknerian women. *The Owl,* however, broaches the end of civilization, copulation and reproduction ritualized out of existence under the aegis of the Tall Lady, the gallows. *The Lime Twig,* like *Second Skin* after it, is relatively cheerful in its affirmation of the possibility of a salvaged decency through an indestructible innocence.

Michael Banks, not Larry, is the norm, the ordinary, to the extent that such exists. He and Margaret are commonplace lower-middle class citizens leading a dull and empty outer existence, though, of course, a rich inner life. Margaret's dreams of "men with numbers wrapped round their fingers [feeling] her legs" (68)—cf. her crostics—and of men having "a go at her with their truncheons" (70) are realized (when Thick beats her) as much as are Michael's dreams of his horse. Perhaps the low point of horror in the book comes after Michael, "screwed silly" (as Leslie Fiedler puts it in his Introduction) with Syb and the widow, comes downstairs where the widow's daughter—a child—tells him that a lady wants to see him outside. Michael's response puts him as close to Larry as he is to come: "I suppose you're not referring to yourself." The girl doesn't understand; the additional sex turns out to be Annie, his long-coveted neighbor, not a child. Michael's decline to devilishness ends that same evening with his instinctive protest against the Constable's murder of Monica. The stage is set for his return to humanity, the child in him coming down a street to meet him to make possible his crossing of Larry's plans and his own victory over himself. He is no Christ; Hawkes' suggestion of Christian sacrifice is only one example of his standing mythic parallels on their heads (see *Second Skin* for the "false suggestiveness" of a dozen mythic analogies). His act does not save humanity; it merely condemns Margaret, in whose name he leaps the track barrier, to Thick's already sweating hands. But Christ or no, through Rock Castle he does defeat the devil: Larry will not fulfill *his* dreams: "A bit of marriage, eh? [he says to Little Dora] And then a ship, trees with limes on the branches . . . the Americas—a proper cruise, plenty of time at the bar, no gunplay or nags. Perhaps a child or two, who knows?" (165). But his twig has been limed, too. Adam has passed the apple—or lime, if you will—back to the devil. Michael Banks' fantasy finally does fulfill itself in a creative act as he runs down the track towards the galloping horses to his death: ". . . at one end the horses bunching in fateful heat and at the other end himself—small, yet beyond elimination, whose single presence purported a toppling of the day, a violation of that scene at Aldington, wreckage to horses and little crouching men" (170).

Despite the more explicitly gothic horrors of *The Lime Twig,* Hawkes' final statement is as unambiguously triumphant as West's is unambiguously futile. At the end of *The Day of the Locust* nothing can withstand destruction; at the end of *The Lime Twig* something remains, "beyond elimination."

Notes

1. *Sewanee Review,* LXX, 3 (Summer, 1962), 395–407.

2. Hawkes says the "confluence" happened ten years earlier, i.e., in about 1952, which would be after *Charivari* (1948), *The Cannibal* (1949), and *The Beetle Leg* (1951); before *The Goose on the Grave* and *The Owl* (1954), *The Lime Twig* (1961), and *Second Skin* (1964). Flannery O'Connor's first volume, *A Good Man Is Hard to Find,* was published in 1953. West's books had, of course, long been on the scene.

3. *The Lime Twig* (New York, 1961), 33. Subsequent references to this book will be given parenthetically after quotation.

Hawkes' *Second Skin*

RICHARD YARBOROUGH,
WITH RESPONSE BY JOHN HAWKES

John Hawkes' novel, *Second Skin,* is difficult to examine in any conventional critical manner. Upon continued examination, the narrative reveals multiple levels of meaning, diverse thematic branches which must be pulled in. A large part of the problem is due to the novel's structure. Narrated by a late-middle-aged character named Skipper, the information the reader receives has been formed by *two* artistic consciousnesses. There is Hawkes, who ultimately retains control over, and responsibility for, the character "Skipper" and Skipper's story; however, the events as the reader sees them have also been shaped and colored by the mind of the narrating character. Skipper himself is very much the creative artist, ordering and manipulating his materials. This is an aspect of *Second Skin* which must be reckoned with if any real understanding of the novel is to be reached.

Several striking analogies between Hawkes' fiction in *Second Skin* and aspects of two other literary forms—poetry and drama—offer valuable insights into just how *Second Skin* works. Regarding the first of these forms, parallels have frequently been drawn between Hawkes' prose style and the poetic use of language; I would like to suggest a relationship between *Second Skin* and an example of modern "confessional" poetry—*The Dream Songs* of John Berryman. The similarity between the situations of Skipper and Henry (the protagonist of *The Dream Songs)* is striking. In each case, the father of the character shot himself; both protagonists were very young when this suicide occurred, and their lives have been greatly affected by the traumatic event. A comparison of selected lines from both Hawkes' and Berryman's works yield very intriguing results:

From "Dream Song #234":

> Mercy! my father; do not pull the trigger
> or all my life I'll suffer from your anger
> killing what you began.[1]

Reprinted with permission from *Mosaic* 8 (Fall 1974): 65–75. John Hawkes's response is reprinted with his permission, © John Hawkes.

From "Dream Song #76—Henry's Confession":

> in a modesty of death I join my father
> who dared so long agone leave me.
> A bullet on a concrete stoop
> close by a smothering southern sea
> spreadeagled on an island, by my knee.[2]

From *Second Skin* (p. 7):

A few years only—yet all my youth—were marked by the folding and unfolding of the wooden chairs and sudden oil changes in the hearse, until that day my peace and excitement ended . . .[3]

From "Dream Song #143":

> I'll sing you now a song
> the like of which may bring your heart to break:
> he's gone! and we don't know where. When he began
> taking the pistol out & along,
>
> you was just a little; but gross fears
> accompanied us along the beaches, pal.
> My mother was scared almost to death.
>
> He was going to swim out, with me, forevers,
> and a swimmer strong he was in the phosphorescent Gulf,
> but he decided on lead.
> That mad drive wiped out my childhood . . .[4]

From *Second Skin* (p. 2–3):

. . . these then are my dreams, the once-living or hardly living members of my adored and dreadful family, . . . the figures cut loose so terribly by that first explosion which occurred in my father's private lavatory. I know it was meant for me, his deliberate shot.

From "Dream Song #83—Op. posth. no. 6":

> For I have much to open, I know immense
> troubles & wonders to their secret curse.[5]

From *Second Skin* (p. 49):

> I will be fifty-nine years old and father to innumerable bright living dreams and vanquished memories.

The overwhelming influence of the paternal suicide is evident in the words of these two narrators. The violent loss of the father is a force which destroys innocence, a force which has filled their lives with guilt and pain and the desperate need to slow the spiritually-inherited "mad drive" toward death.

Another facet of Berryman's *Dream Songs* is extremely helpful in looking at *Second Skin:* the intensely lyrical vision of the narrator which informs the textual symbols and patterns. Both Henry and Skipper, as first person speakers, are not only actors in the events which they are discussing, but are also very involved with the telling itself. In *Second Skin,* Skipper relates his "naked history" and the reader's task is to determine the credibility of his rendering of events. By the end of the first chapter, the high-blown rhetoric and melodrama of Skipper's rendition forces us to cut through the superficial layer of speech in an attempt to learn what Skipper *isn't* saying. While the events do not appear to have been altered substantially in Skipper's version, the sense conveyed, the fine points of emphasis are subject to change at his discretion—in order to protect himself from the distress of harsh emotional realities. The tone of Skipper's speech also works to convey the impression that he stands alone, oppressed by the people and things around him. Indeed, language is Skipper's primary weapon against the pain and fear he has to overcome.

Skipper is a self-dramatizing, self-proclaimed (though at times, humble) hero. Witnessing Skipper tell his tale however, the reader sees him as selfish, short-sighted, timid, arrogant, and helpless. The term which seems to best characterize Skipper is "immature." Like Henry in Berryman's *Dream Songs,* Skipper never fully grew up; the intense trauma of the paternal suicide and the resulting guilt and resentment are never fully resolved. Part of his emotional self has been stunted by this experience and he relives over and over again the death of his father.

The child-like side to Skipper's personality is referred to frequently. Early in the book, Cassandra, his daughter, admonishes him, "don't be a child" (p. 15), and sees him as one of the "high-school boys in uniform" (p. 31). Skipper refers to himself once as "an old child of the moon" (p. 29) and again as a "traveling child" (p. 29). He is, in fact, writing his "history" in his "schoolboy's copybook with its boyish valor and its antiquity" (p. 45). In his verbal exchanges with his daughter, with Miranda, with Jomo, he is the petulant, hard-headed, attention-seeking youngster; and it is this emotional immaturity which is his most damning weakness. Seldom do we see this large, soft man openly express true feelings of caring in his first world—even for those about whom he purports to care most. His strongest term of commiseration is "poor"—"poor Sonny," "poor Gertrude," "poor Jomo," "poor Pizie"—an easy token of emotion used as a child might, a child who has not yet developed the ability to deal with his own complex emotional responses. This sense is strengthened by the pervasive use of the word "poor" throughout *Second Skin,* either as an adjective or as a proper noun—to the point of parody.

Skipper's feelings toward intricate interpersonal relationships are often inchoate and confused. At times, he seems to frantically want some response from Cassandra, some show of affection; nevertheless, he vacillates from describing her as "poor Cassandra" (p. 70), to "my little bride at last" (p. 116), to "my daughter, my museum piece" (p. 29), to "heartless" (p. 15). Similar confusion arises when he attempts to verbalize his feelings for Miranda and Gertrude. Skipper is simply not mature enough to meet the sexual demands involved in the roles of father, husband, or lover. Coming to terms with his own masculinity is a major problem for him; in an attempt to sever any connection with his father and the self-destruction his father represents, Skipper has also disowned the influence of the dominant male-figure in his own maturation—undercutting the development of his sexual ego in the process. Discussing his father's suicide, Skipper says that "The shot, after all, killed everything . . . except my love" (p. 161). Believing that if he meets threats with this "love" they will be eventually smothered under its weight, Skipper makes "love" his cushion, his protection. That his "love" can be a destructive force occurs to him at times—for example, upon his daughter's death, he asks, ". . . as in the case of my poor father, was I myself the unwitting tinder that started the blaze?" (p. 197); however, he ultimately decides, "I won't ask why, Cassandra" (p. 199), realizing the hopeless damnation implicit in the answer.

Skipper is the lens through which we view the other characters, and because Skipper does not (as we must finally acknowledge) have the ability to deal responsibly with the emotional content of his story, these characters often seem either excessively flat—for example, Captain Red, Jomo, Tremlow (who can be seen to embody respectively: Skipper's own incestual urge toward Cassandra, a villainous "Captain Hook," and the Devil)—or else very melodramatic—for example, the picture of his mother "who more and more grew to resemble a gifted angel in a dreamer's cemetery . . ." (p. 6–7).

In total control of the story, Skipper tried to raise his "history" to mythic proportions; as a result, details of place and time and the particular roles that his characters fill become then simple components in a straightforward narrative. The recurrent images, details and tones in *Second Skin* are the keys to Skipper's "truth." A look at the more important images will lead to a deeper comprehension of the purposeful complexity of Skipper's mental machinations.

From the beginning of Skipper's "history," sexual roles and order seem to have been scrambled by his father's suicide. Skipper sees his father's death as an attempt to hurt him and, subsequently, almost every male character in his narrative is threatening to him. Only two major male characters are not. The first is Mac, the priest whose religious role implies a security for Skipper. Indeed, Mac seems to be a father-figure for him—one, however, who arrives too late to rescue Skipper from Tremlow's assault.

The other male is, of course, Sonny. It is interesting to note here the somewhat analogous roles played by Sonny in *Second Skin* and by the "Black-face" character in portions of *Dream Songs*. Whereas the character in Berryman's work is primarily an extension of Henry's consciousness while Sonny is quite definitely an independent being in Skipper's story, both serve as contrasting, balancing forces for the main characters. If the "Black-face" speaker in *Dream Songs* can often be seen as a countering element of Henry's self, prodding and prying at Henry's fears from within, Sonny can be viewed as Skipper's alter ego. Where Skipper is slow, passive, gentle, impotent in the face of violence and pain, soft and pale and fat, Sonny is slim, dark and solid; he is warm, aggressive, honest, caring, insightful, loyal, and helpful in a skilled way. He is everything Skipper would like to be. By the end of Skipper's narrative, a spiritual union between the two has taken place on the tropical island. While Sonny has changed little, Skipper notes that the sun has burnt his own skin "so brown that the green name ["Fernandez"] tattooed on my breast has all but disappeared in a tangle of hair and in my darkening skin" (p. 47). The sharing of Catalina Kate by the two men further exemplifies this union. Indeed, it seems that it is Skipper who is changing the most in order to reach this joining. It is he who is darkening under the sunlight, not Sonny (the pun, doubtless, is intentional). Sonny seems to already have possessed the saving vision which Skipper attains only after Cassandra's death. When bidding Skipper farewell at the bus station early in the narrative, Sonny tells him, "Take your ladies on off to your island—I'm going to be on mine—no unfaithful lovers on my island, Skipper, just me, now you keeps your island the same" (p. 26). Skipper does not, however, keep his first island (Miranda's) the "same" and there is the strong indication that his contentment on the second island is due, to a great extent, to the presence of a "fellow victim" (p. 1)—Sonny—for it is just as much Sonny's island as it is Skipper's.

It is significant that there are no adult males prominent on the island other than Sonny and Skipper (there is but slight mention of some "squatting men" [p. 207] at the celebration in the graveyard). Thus, all potential sexual confrontations are precluded by Skipper.

Contrasts and polarities are also manifest in the images of women in Skipper's story. The women on his tropical island are warm, loving, docile, obedient, and, above all, accepting of his love (which has not grown any less ponderous). The female figures of his earlier world are either tremendous threats—like Miranda—or beyond the reach of his fumbling expressions of affection—like Gertrude and Cassandra. On his island, however, instead of the castrating, imposing figure of the witch-like Miranda leading Cassandra ever further out of his grasp, there is the tiny, harmless Sister Josie (this nun-like "lady of the cloth" [p. 169] is but one manifestation of a strong religious strain which underlies this novel). While on the cold, Atlantic island, Miranda accompanied Skipper to the abandoned tower—the site of Cassandra's fall after her encounter with the steel-taloned Jomo—on the tropical island, Sister Josie leads him to the pregnant Kate lying in the swamp bestridden by the hook-clawed iguana. While Skipper's attempt to rescue his daughter contributes to her suicide, his wrestling with the iguana (while just as misguided) does no substantial harm to Kate. Contrasting with the sexual threat of Miranda and her massive thighs encased in the bright, yellow slacks, on the southern island, a playful steer called Edward (Skipper's real name) momentarily mounts the "soft, yellow flanks" (p. 168) of the cow Sweet Phyllis under the calabash tree.

The two islands themselves are juxtaposed: the chill, rocky, desolate, crumbling northern island versus the warm, smooth, soft, fertile southern island teeming with life—"the ants were racing through the holes in my tennis shoes" (p. 105). In the last view Skipper gives us of himself in his "old" world, he is with Pixie who is covered with the gore of strawberry jam; Skipper has just buried the dead fetus of Cassandra's child. This is balanced by the scene of the cleansing of blood from Kate's newborn offspring.

Like classical tragedy, there is a starkness, a tension in the style through which we gain access to the striking dramatic narration of Skipper. Skipper's fears and anguish are pointedly stylized in the rich pattern of symbolism woven into his "naked history" and the characters clearly take on mythical roles in his mind. Further, "fate" (that is, the unstoppable course of events) plays an important role in Skipper's narrative. The ruthless treatment of violence—often grotesque sexual violence—also seems to find some of its origins in Greek tragedy. Gertrude's horrifying self-mutilation after her husband's suicide is possibly the most understated and yet the most striking of these. The evocation of characters from Greek tragedy at the beginning of Skipper's story—Antigone, Iphigenia, Clytemnestra—further affects the tone of the narrative, imparting a swirling sense of chaotic, confused, and torn sexual roles. While, on one level, Skipper—like Oedipus Rex—is the traditional flawed hero who bears the seeds of his own downfall within, Hawkes manipulates his novel to entirely different ends.

In classical tragedy, the resolution often lies in the hero's final recognition of his own role in carrying out the dictates of Fate. This recognition is often accompanied by the tragic hero's destruction or at least his paying retribution for an earlier sin (or ancestral taint). Indeed, Skipper feels the obligation to "make up" for his inheritance of death. In his role as artificial inseminator, he asks, referring to his father (a mortician), "And haven't I redeemed his profession, his occupation, with my own?" (p. 47).

Fate, in the classical tradition, is portrayed as a controlling, avenging destiny—a force essentially located outside the individual. In *Second Skin*,

Skipper frequently expresses an implicit belief in some external force. He complains early in the narrative, "I am convinced that in my case I should have been spared" (p. 2), and he often refers to himself as a "victim" (p. 19). It is in these pained expressions of persecution that Skipper most strikingly fits into the mold of the "tragic hero." As Richard B. Sewell writes in his essay, "The Tragic Form," ". . . above all, the source of tragic suffering is the sense, in the consciousness of tragic man, of simultaneous guilt and guiltlessness."[6] Skipper sees himself as "harmless and sanguine" (p. 1), a "six feet and two hundred pounds of expectant and fearful snowshoe rabbit" (p. 86), and, after his rape, as "my poor self" (p. 146). It is Skipper's sense of his own innocence which motivates his awkward defense of Cassandra; his actions are directed outward, toward some external enemy. Firmly convinced that his behavior is based on a protective love for his daughter, his failure to save her is doubly painful to him. As the events leading up to her suicide run their course, we see that Skipper is forced to abandon any belief in the rationality of existence. What is finally implied by the fact that Skipper can tell us his "history" at all is his recognition that he can control, can re-order that flow of events. If Fate shows itself to be a blind, slashing fury from which spring those incomprehensible motivations behind the happenings in each man's life, Skipper's manipulation of his narrative is grounded in the awareness that the source of these "incomprehensible motivations" is the individual himself.

Skipper, in an attempt to live up to his name, to be the "skipper" of his world, is struggling to mold the dried skin of his fears and repressed guilt, struggling to get outside of his memories by relating them to us as his "history." In the development of this narration, the reader has the sense of watching layer after layer of Skipper's life pulled back and sloughed off. Finally, we see him on his wandering tropical island where he finds refuge. Some of what he feared in himself earlier he can now face: his heavy, sensuous, large-hipped feminine walk, for example. While he is unable to remove the iguana from Kate's back, he accepts his incestual relationship with her—Kate is everything he might want in a daughter (with Sonny as the ideal son-in-law). In his role as artificial inseminator on his island, Skipper now controls the sexual order—probably the most threatening aspect of his earlier world.

One of the most difficult things about examining *Second Skin* is evaluating what exactly Skipper has finally achieved by the end of the novel. He seems to have merely survived; his personality hasn't grown perceptibly, and his success on the island seems due more to the situation as he describes it than to his own actions. Another character, after all of the trials Skipper has undergone, might have finally come to some larger realization of the human condition. However, what may obstruct a full acknowledgment of Skipper's "viction" is the strength of the Puritan ethic, the legacy of the strong, hard attitude toward life which Western culture possesses. Part of this attitude is the belief that in order to overcome what can be called an "agonized conscience," one must stay and suffer and finally prevail. From that point of view, Skipper's life on the tropical island is a flight from a reality which he can't handle—a flight like that of the young man who turns to the seminary to avoid sexual crises. Skipper himself is an exceedingly religious figure at times. From his vomiting in times of stress, noting ironically that "anyone who has gotten down on his knees to vomit has discovered, if only by accident, the position of prayer" (p. 127), through his serving as altarboy for Mac on the *Starfish* and his accepting the cross from Uncle Billy after the belly-bumping contest, to his role as god-ruler on the tropical island, Skipper is the self-canonized martyr who happily exclaims, "how satisfying that virtue always wins" (p. 98). In western culture, however, martyr figures are often least attractive in their passivity in the face of a harsh reality. Norman Lavers, in an article on Hawkes' work, puts it this way: "It is clear enough that not the meek Christian, but the heroic Greek part of our cultural heritage has the greatest hold on us still. . . ."[7]

One's first reaction to Skipper's story might be to protest that a vision of life as a self-contained, wandering, invisible island is not maintainable. However, if the goal in life is seen as being simply to endure, to survive, to live in spite of all the pain and hurt and fear driving you toward death, then Skipper *has* achieved something—just by being alive. While he has gone through no great psychological metamorphosis to reach his island, one must recognize that the trip to the cemetery (near the end of the narrative) by Skipper and his entourage—not to mourn but to accept—is a confrontation with death he could not have made earlier.

In Skipper's ability to relate his "naked history," one can see a hope which, if the opposite is the despair underlying the suicidal urge, then, in fact, forms the basis for some sort of affirmation. This hope springs from the resolution of Skipper's childhood trauma and it is a resolution which he significantly attains through the child's greatest tool with which to handle a painful reality—the vivid, desperate use of the imagination. On the bus ride across the desert, Skipper tells us "for the rest of the day the emotions and the problems of this intensive fantasy saved me from the oppressive desert" (p. 32). This escape through "intensive fantasy" is the foundation for Skipper's new life.

Skipper and Henry (from *Dream Songs*) are two tragic artists manipulating their memories in a passionate attempt to face death and truth, to find an order, a good in the evil and fear which their fathers' bullets made a permanent part of their lives. Michael Berryhill, in the wake of John Berryman's suicide, asks the question, "How to survive?" He answers his own query using two of Berryman's phrases—"with 'courage and Kindness,' and 'children and high art.' "[8] It is Skipper's "high art" which, while no permanent resolution has been reached, has saved him. In the same sense that Wallace Stevens writes, "poetry is the supreme fiction," we can see Skipper's survival as dependent upon a desperate reordering of reality through the saving process of his narrative, his "naked history." Perhaps these lines from Berryman's "Dream Song #325" best characterize just what Skipper has come to:

> Our dead frisk up, and later they get better at it,
> our wits are stung astray
> till all we can do is groan, bereft:
> tears fall: and then we reckon what is
> left, not what was lost.[9]

John Hawkes: Response to Richard Yarborough

While you were talking I began to worry about *Second Skin* and possibly about Skipper in terms of mythologizing death. You referred to Skipper's inability to acknowledge meaninglessness. It seems to me that in actuality, of course, death does not deserve mythologizing. We should not poeticize it, all those dark shadows, the waiting grave, the tree limb with the noose hanging from it, the axe blade that's going to fall, the skeleton with his scythe, and so on. All of this is perhaps a way of heightening life, but it is probably not a very good way to react to death. I was appalled a few weeks ago when I visited an art class in which an artist was using some of my fiction as a basis for students to create works of art. I started talking about the novel that I have just finished, *Death, Sleep & the Traveler,* which does mythologize death. The novel mixes the night sea journey with a real descent into the realm of death; the narrator is accused of murder and suffers his own psychic death. One student said to me, "I don't know why you're talking about death all the time. Why are you so preoccupied with all this heavy darkness; it doesn't mean a thing to me." I said, "Well, maybe I'm older than you are." He said. "That's not the point. I was thrown off a motorcycle once and nearly killed." I said that I had been nearly killed too. He said, "It's just not this big thing, it's just a stopping." I said, "Well, I admire your extraordinary ability to imagine that cessation, the ability to think of the self as non-existent." It is hard for me at least to imagine not existing and perhaps that inability causes me to try to monumentalize death.

Of course I suppose the mythologizing of death would force us into romanticizing the opposite. I mean a kind of multiple gargantuan total sexuality which may be nothing more than eroticizing the landscape. Well, if it's not a good idea to mythologize death, let us at least eroticize the landscape.

I'm deeply moved by almost all you said, Richard, but I am puzzled by your mentioning the religious elements in *Second Skin*. I met a young man in New York, he was about 30, on the brink of maturity, and he was deeply concerned with religion (I think that he might have been a seminary student) and he said, "You know, the one thing about your fiction that interests me is the fact that it is religious." I said, "But, look, the only thing I care about is the fact that there is no basis for religion in anything beyond the world and beyond ourselves. I don't understand religion and my art has nothing to do with it." He said, "You misunderstand. I only mean that your fiction deals with the deepest of human concerns." I think you are saying the same thing and I'm grateful to you as I was to the man in New York. In this sense my fiction is deeply religious.

When Skipper gives up the cross he becomes God, if we're going to use the word. In *Second Skin* I was trying to make Skipper a god-like figure, an androgynous figure. I had a vague notion that throughout mythology the gods have been bisexual or multi-sexual so I thought of a man who, on a literal level, would be male, female, impotent. I meant him by the end of the fiction to be a very powerful, all-fulfilled, all-fulfilling, totally self-sufficient human being. He, to me, in all his weakness is supposed to embody the strength of knowing that there is nothing else in the world except what he creates and the figures he discovers in his creation.

I guess that I had very mixed feelings about Mack, the Catholic chaplain. I was concerned with him as a potential father figure and I think that he was in some sense a spiritual supporter. He is called Mack the Catholic Chaplain, a comic designation. He could not prevent Skipper's rape. His presence perhaps had something to do with that star-shaped hole in the canvas over the life-boat in which Skipper is raped. I suppose that's a cheap religious symbol. I would hate to think that Skipper is a Christ figure when he's lying in his stateroom before the moment of his rape, anticipating his rape. I do not know the Bible well. I was thinking of Christ in the Garden of Gethsemane, trying to gird himself to accept the deepest possible pain. His acceptance of the violence did not really depend on his moment of contemplation; I could not forebear echoing in Skipper that other vast and terrifying moment.

You mentioned language. You talked about the child as a sort of poet and that's an extraordinary idea. I want to be a mature person and I want to be detached. I've had an amazing correspondence recently with a cousin of mine, a woman who suffers from being accused of immaturity. In her own terms she wants to be "immature." We've had a lengthy argument about detachment by mail. When we were children she took me into a deserted house by the sea; it was this moment that resulted in the lighthouse in *Second Skin*. It's perhaps the source of all of the penitential constructions that permeate my fiction. I thought of her as very old at the time but she was only a year or two older than I was. Together we visited the abandoned house that was being destroyed by the sea. It was on the edge of the ocean and the floor was open to the ocean which spewed up as we stood there, terrified and in awe. It was a fabulous moment, and in some way sexual. But now we are arguing about detachment. She says that detachment is an abomination in the lives we lead, and I insist that detachment is the only way that we're able to live or create anything. She says that one must be committed and that detachment means indifference. I write back, "You're quite wrong, detachment does not mean indifference, detachment is a psychic state that one learns in the face of the most overwhelming emotional destructiveness. You can live and create only when you manage to control, to keep at a distance the terrors that exist within the human being." All of this has to do with the psychic cesspool that I talked about earlier. I don't think that the task is to deny it but to expose it and make something out of it which I guess I was trying to do in *Second Skin*. At any rate, artists all depend on detachment.

Notes

1. John Berryman, *The Dream Songs* (New York: Farrar, Straus and Giroux, 1969), p. 254.

2. *Ibid.*, p. 83.

3. John Hawkes, *Second Skin* (New York: New Directions, 1964), p. 7. All subsequent page references are to this edition.

4. Berryman, p. 160.

5. *Ibid.*, p. 98.

6. Richard B. Sewell, "The Tragic Form," in *Commentaries in Doctor Faustus by Christopher Marlowe*, ed. Sylvan Barnet (New York: New American Library, Inc., 1969), p. 171.

7. Norman Lavers, "The Structure of *Second Skin*," *Novel: A Forum of Fiction*, V (Spring 1972), p. 213.

8. Michael Berryhill, "Introduction: The Epistomology of Loss," in *John Berryman: A Checklist,* compiled by Richard J. Kelley (Metuchen, New Jersey: Metuchen Press, 1972), p. xxxi.

9. Berryman, p. 347.

John Hawkes's Plays: Innocence on a Limb

Carol MacCurdy

In 1964 when the Ford Foundation awarded John Hawkes a fellowship in drama, the foundation wanted to entice gifted writers like Hawkes into using their talents in the theater. As a result, Hawkes devoted 1964–65 to writing plays and being playwright-in-residence at the Actor's Workshop in San Francisco. Although his venture into drama proved brief, it resulted in four one-act plays, all of which received limited productions at various theaters, and in 1967 New Directions published the plays in a collection entitled *The Innocent Party*. The plays have never received much critical attention, however.[1] Hawkes's literary reputation rests firmly on his thirteen books of fiction; in comparison, the plays are minor works. Nevertheless, they reward further examination because they provide insights into the theme of innocence central to Hawkes's work at a particularly significant time in his career.

The period from 1964 to 1968 marked an important crossroads in Hawkes's writing. The year *Second Skin* was published and nominated for the National Book Award (1964) was the year Hawkes began writing plays. Four years later he was working on *The Blood Oranges,* the first novel of his triad on aesthetics and the imagination that includes *Death, Sleep, and The Traveler* and *Travesty.* Critics generally consider the novels prior to *Second Skin* as Hawkes's early work (dark, deterministic novels set in entropic environments), and the novels following *Second Skin,* his later work (for the most part, first-person narratives told from psychic landscapes). In the plays, written in the intervening years, Hawkes works out in dramatic form one of his central preoccupations, before going forward with his next phase of fiction—the triad. All four of the plays in *The Innocent Party,* are concerned with what Hawkes once called "the terrible theme of innocence."[2]

Hawkes himself has frequently referred to his "preoccupation with innocence" maintaining, "Idealism and innocence lie behind everything that I write."[3] In his early fiction, innocence is always damned: a child is cannibalized (*The Cannibal*), a fetus is fished from the river (*The Beetle Leg*), an orphan roams helplessly through the warscape of Italy (*The Goose on the Grave*), an innocent

This essay was expressly written for this volume and is published here for the first time by permission of the author.

prisoner crashes in his futile escape (*The Owl*), and the children of wartime, Michael and Margaret Banks and Hencher, all die violent deaths (*The Lime Twig*). No one escapes, learns, or gains experience and survives, until Skipper in *Second Skin*. In that pivotal novel, Hawkes's innocent is his first artist-figure as first-person narrator. Skipper's memoirs testify to the profound innocence required of the artist who embraces his worst nightmare and imaginatively transforms it into a better dream, a "second skin." For the first time in his fiction, Hawkes shows the correlation between innocence and the artistic act of creation—a relationship he pursues further in *The Blood Oranges* and the following novels.

Written shortly after the publication of *Second Skin,* the plays continue to explore the innocent's conflict: the naïveté that represses fears, thus causing inevitable nightmares, and the naïveté that creates artistic visions in the face of the nightmare. In *Second Skin* Hawkes depicts through alternating landscapes the opposing forces at work in Skipper (Skipper's black island versus his floating island). In the plays, Hawkes uses dialogue to dramatize this paradox inherent in innocence. To emphasize the dialogue he strips the stage, transforming it into a psychic never-never land—an abandoned motel, a wax museum, a lavatory, and a vacant, white room. Most often only two characters inhabit the nearly bare stage. Like an exercise in counterpoint, the pair, with one conventionally stronger than the other, engage in a dialectic that mounts in intensity. Meaning comes primarily from the language as Hawkes uses dialogue to express the tension inherent in the innocent party's conflict. At each play's conclusion the innocent party is uncovered with often ambiguous results: violence erupts, roles are exchanged, dreams are realized, or reality is improvised.

The play that most obviously looks back to *Second Skin* is *The Undertaker*. The shortest and most compact of the plays, it reworks the suicide scene of Skipper's father. Although Hawkes devotes only four pages of *Second Skin* to the father's death, the scene remains one of the most poignant and comic in the entire novel. *The Undertaker* begins with a reenactment of the fatal moment: the father, sitting "bolt upright on the toilet lid and holding an old-fashioned silver revolver at right angles to his temple," is suddenly "caught in a burst of light."[4] The opening shocks the audience into identifying with the agony of the innocent son, Edward, who is standing outside the lavatory door.[5]

In the play Edward is in his mid-forties, the same age as the father at the time of the suicide. Since a middle-aged man plays the part of a twelve-year-old, the audience realizes that the scene just witnessed exists only in Edward's memory. He is reliving his father's death, presumably one of countless times, in a ritualistic effort to come to terms with it. Having a grown man recreate a scene from his youth not only suggests the torment he has carried through time but also introduces a comic element into the play. Hawkes himself has referred to *The Undertaker* as a "farcical melodrama."[6] At one point the large, middle-aged Edward begs his father to allow him to sit on his lap and play with his beard.

The father resists such pleas and tells Edward that he has done nothing wrong: "You're innocent. You're just the innocent son of a middle-aged small-town undertaker" (142).

Even given his innocence, Edward feels no consolation. Thirty years later he is still reliving his father's suicide, a scene that Hawkes repeats at the play's beginning, middle, and end. At the conclusion Edward, now assuming his father's place in the lavatory, utters the final lines, "So come on, old man—I'm waiting. Let's get it over with" (167–68). The past has a tight grip on Edward's present and causes him to recreate the moment over and over again in a paradoxical attempt to forget and destroy it.

The continual reiteration of this moment suggests stasis. Although Edward is an innocent (like the pathetic black dog his father loves), he remains implicated in his father's death. No movement into experience has taken place, no rite of passage or initiation, only stasis. His father remains a "rusty fishhook lodged inside his brain" (167), and every time Edward tries to fish it out, he only recreates the horror rather than achieving a peaceful resolution.

The Undertaker uses race metaphorically to suggest the collective nightmare that civilization has repressed. Edward's father tells him that for twenty years he has "embalmed the corpses of penniless Negroes" (140). Because he spent his life burying "dead Negroes," he is afraid they will "rise up out of the ground like a mob of raving minstrels and try to stop me" (141). He also knows that his son is "afraid of the dead Negroes." The father has clearly passed on to his son what he has buried and denied; therefore, despite innocence, has inherited the nightmare. The father even tells him to "give a little thought to all those dead Negroes coming after you in the night" (143).

Innocence based on inherited denial is often dangerous in Hawkes. Especially in his early fiction, for example *The Cannibal,* history is destined to repeat itself. *The Undertaker* suggests that same horrifying reiteration of the past when at the close of the play, Edward looks like his father, shaving in the lavatory.

The audience sees little hope of absolution through the retelling of the story (the absolution Skipper achieves in *Second Skin).* The only creative vision that offers Edward any solace is his dream of his mother (Skipper has the same dream). Edward tells his father that his mother told him never to be afraid. Her legacy is Edward's dream, in which death offers her a serene yet speedy drive in a yellow roadster. Described as a "royal lady," his mother leaves a "big, white house on a hill" to ride away with "some prince or maybe an executioner" (147). Her departure is a scene of tranquility and beauty: "The tires are rolling, the truck swaying, [his] muffler beating the air, and suddenly [his] white coat is brown with the dust of the road and the little auto, severe and shiny like a golden insect, is gaining speed, and I see that you are serene, Mama, serene and unshaken as the downward ride commences, and are merely touching your fingers to the crown of your hat and raising a soft white arm as if to wave to me, and . . ." (148).

In response to the darkness of his father's psyche, Edward has created a dream of innocence about his mother, which he tells to his father (all the while his father is dressed like his mother to offer comfort to Edward). But instead the dream angers his father, provoking him to shed the mother's clothes and castigate Edward for desecrating the memory of his mother: "I'll tell you something, Edward. She died in bed, with blood all over the sheets. Blood. Do you hear? . . . I'll destroy this nonsense once and for all" (149). In the dream (reminiscent of the Emily Dickinson poem "Because I Could Not Stop for Death") Edward has made his father the driver and has him "kindly stop," all in an effort to transmute the pain, violence, and blood into a lovely tableau of death passing by.

Artistic creation is not enough to stop his father, however; in fact, it seems to provoke him. His father experiences Edward's artistry as resistance, and it is. The son uses the dream as well as his cello playing not only to thwart the impending horror but also to transmute it into something that allows him to cope. In doing this, Edward draws on his profound innocence. To counter the forces of death or to believe that such an assault is possible requires incredible naïveté, thus the man in his mid-forties who has remained twelve. Yet this view of the artist is exactly what Hawkes implies in *Second Skin* and in *The Undertaker.* Both Skipper's and Edward's artistic attempts to transform pain create a balance at least, as Hawkes says, between the "life-force versus death."[7] In *Second Skin* Skipper achieves the balance from the perspective of his floating island. For Edward no such distance exists; he continues to talk to his father in the lavatory. Ironically, Edward is trying to ward off "the seeds of death" (142), the very things he carries with him. In this play, as in *Second Skin,* Hawkes begins to explore the paradoxical plight of the artist: his guilt and his innocence.

In the title play of the collection, *The Innocent Party,* a young girl named Jane is the innocent one. Unlike Edward, who confronts death, Jane, as a virginal nymphet, confronts her sexuality. Coveted by a rich, seductive aunt and stifled by prim, impoverished parents, Jane and her virginity are the source of the dramatic conflict. Phoebe, the wealthy, carnal aunt, arrives in a white Cadillac to visit her Prufrockian brother and remains there in an attempt to gain control over Jane. The play depicts the struggle between the parents and Phoebe to shape Jane's future. For her part in the drama, Jane primarily dreams and pantomimes.

The play begins with Jane seated by an empty pool, revealing her narcissistic fantasy to Phoebe. Every morning Jane comes out to the dried-up pool, touches herself, listens, imagines she hears water filling the pool, leans over, and sees her own reflection. Admitting that the pool "went dry before I was born" (19), Jane asks her aunt what's wrong with it. An overt symbol for the collective unconscious, the pool partially filled with debris is the locale of Jane's upbringing as well as for the entire play. While her mother dumps ashes into it every day, Jane imagines her own reflection in its waters. Because her legacy is a dried-up pool, Jane has to rely on an imagination that is already corrupted.

The Innocent Party is set on the patio of "an abandoned motel in a subtropical area of the United States" (14). Doomed to live in this fallen Eden, Edward and Beatrix, the father and mother, bemoan their impoverished fate and try to convince Phoebe to offer help.

BEATRIX: It's not paradise. Believe me.

PHOEBE: You think it's not? Orchids, bougainvillea, acacia trees, all these doves and the swamp moss like frozen mist—lots of people would call it paradise. . . .

BEATRIX: An abandoned motel on the edge of the universe. It smells of obsolescence and rank decay, it smells of the tears of uncouth strangers and the refuse of their sordid pleasures. It smells of death. Is this any kind of home for me? Is this any kind of home for a growing girl? (62–63)

Fearing the loss of Jane's innocence in this unredeemed environment, Edward and Beatrix reveal two long-held nightmares to Phoebe. The first is the ritualistic reappearance of a centipede that jumps out of the basin every morning as Edward shaves. Shooting out of the rusty sink drainhole, the "slick wriggling monster" (68) terrorizes the helpless couple each morning until Beatrix catches it in a can and flings it into "the festering swamp" (68). Their concern is that it will come out one night and poison Jane in her sleep. The tale of "degradation" (70) leaves Phoebe unimpressed.

PHOEBE: It's all in your head. You've got a head full of degradation, that's the trouble. It flows like sap from a dead tree. . . .

BEATRIX: So it's all in my head. All this collapse and ruin and ignominy is my invention, is that it? (70)

Phoebe is the experienced world traveler; all the tropical growth seems part of paradise to her. Not an innocent party, she has no repressed nightmares; she lives out her demons and thus mocks the comic impotence of her brother and sister-in-law. She has just disembarked from a worldwide tour on the *Santa Maria*. Like Columbus recently arrived in the New World, she sees no fallen Eden and believes Beatrix has made it one in her mind.

The other secret, besides the centipede, is the sign that Jane discovers on her arrival at the motel. Half buried at the edge of the swamp, it reads COLORED ONLY. VACANCY. Expecting Phoebe to react to the horror, Beatrix asks triumphantly: "Now do you believe me? Will you take my word for it that this place is cursed and rotten and filthy? Is it what we deserve, Phoebe?" (73). Again using racism as a metaphor, Hawkes suggests that the formerly segregated motel hints at the collective guilt of a once buried past. The previously all-Negro lodging is an image of the past's impingement on the present. Like the centipede, the motel's history is a reminder of repressed terrors that inevitably return in the form of a curse. Phoebe knows that such recurring nightmares are the price of repression; she wishes to save Jane from her parents' fate and accuses them of crippling their daughter.

Jane's innocence is, however, already perverted. A victim of her parents' "pee-pot morality" (93), she now victimizes others and has become the predator. She steals not only "from the Negro children down the road" (45), subsequently destroying whatever she brings home, but also from Phoebe. Even Beatrix, who fears for Jane, says, "Someday our Jane is going to do something horrible. She is dangerous" (45).

The climax of the play is a wild scene in which an intoxicated Phoebe tries to seduce Jane into dancing with her. No longer the victim, Jane resists Phoebe's seductive overtures, feigning ignorance. Only after Phoebe collapses in a drunken stupor does Jane begin to dance wildly. At the height of Jane's frenzied dance, "the overpowering sound of water rushing into the swimming pool fills the stage" (95). The sound of rushing water seems more apocalyptic than it does life-giving; furthermore, the pool fills up only in Jane's imagination.

Both *The Undertaker* and *The Innocent Party* end much as they begin. In the last scene of *The Innocent Party,* Jane ritualistically reenacts her dream, much like Edward at the end of *The Undertaker.* Touching herself and kneeling down at the pool's edge, Jane looks at her own reflection. This time, however, she looks out at the audience and says, "I look into the swimming pool and try to see our faces in the water" (96). The audience and Jane have become synonymous. The innocent party is not able to create a new, life-giving vision but is destined to reiterate the past. Because of the pool's corruption, Jane must use her own imagination to envision her reflection. At the very end, by associating the audience with Jane, Hawkes implies that Jane represents all of us trying to "see our faces in the water." Even though the ending is ominous, it also suggests the power of Jane's reckless innocence to maintain itself amid impending doom.

Written in the same year (1964) as *The Innocent Party, The Wax Museum,* a shorter play and smaller in scope, also renders the effects of repressed sexuality on a naïve young woman. The innocent in this play is Sally Ann, a tourist visiting a Canadian wax museum with her fiancé, Frank. While he is downstairs visiting the Chamber of Horrors, she encounters Bingo, a female attendant who is caressing a wax figure named George, dressed as a Royal Canadian Mounted Policeman. By the play's end the two women exchange roles. Bingo convinces Sally Ann that Frank will return from the Chamber of Horrors "a different man" (121). Knowing that she should have gone with him, Sally Ann is nevertheless terrified of the atrocities below. The seductive Bingo simultaneously titillates and frightens Sally Ann with her knowledge of what resides there. During the provocative dialogue, Bingo exchanges clothes with Sally Ann; all the while the young virgin insists on her ignorance and normality: "I've always been just a thin girl with stringy hair, packed in a community swimming pool with other thin girls with stringy hair. My life has always been—disinfected. I'm not—glamorous" (125). Sally Ann's fear of losing her innocence prompts her to choose to stay with the waxen George and allow Bingo to have the real-life Frank.

Even though the play ends with Sally Ann embracing the dummy George, Hawkes suggests the power of her virginity, much as he does Jane's in *The Innocent Party*. At one point Sally Ann boasts that Frank will be "sorry he left me up here all alone . . . he'll find out something about the power of my virginity. He'll see . . ." (127). Although the fruition of her sexual dreams is impossible in the wax museum, she is now free to indulge in her imaginings, and these, after all, are the source of her power. Like Jane at the end of *The Innocent Party*, who chooses her own masturbatory fantasy, Sally Ann embraces her sexual dream, in the form of George. She muses: "I've always wanted a big man in a bright coat to take me within full view of kings and queens and school children in a wax museum—at noon!" (131). Both virgins' sexual potency comes from the strength of their imagination.

These two plays particularly anticipate the thematic connection Hawkes makes in *The Blood Oranges* between sexuality and the imagination. Whereas *Second Skin* is a testament to the imagination's power to transform death or at least to achieve a balance with it, *The Blood Oranges* suggests an underside to the narrator, Cyril and his sex-singing. While Skipper's artistry seems life affirming, Cyril's passionate endeavors become authoritarian and painful to others. By the end he realizes that he was not the antithesis of his friend Hugh, but his "accomplice."[8] Drawn to Hugh's dark imagination, Cyril acknowledges the genuine eroticism of the chastity belt that Hugh places on his wife Catherine. Incredible sexuality comes from both Hugh and Sally Ann as a result of such repression. Sally Ann is able to express her sexuality at the play's end because she is in the safe confines of an imaginary world. Like Sally Ann, Cyril desires a still-life tapestry, void of time and change, in his Illyria where "there are no seasons" (271). In a way, Cyril wants his world to be as virginal as Sally Ann does when she opts for a place frozen in time and preserved in art. In the wax museum, Sally Ann hopes to maintain her innocent stasis and remain amid a permanent collection, rendered virginal for eternity. The danger of such visionary innocence (also evident in *The Innocent Party* and *The Blood Oranges*) is suggested in *The Wax Museum* when Bingo tells Sally Ann that the wax is poisonous to the touch. In the museum, Sally Ann is relegated to the confines of the world of art—a world poisonous to human touch yet preserved in history.

The final play of the collection, the last play Hawkes has written, and the best, presents an innocent party who is finally able to move beyond stasis. *The Questions* focuses on a young girl's confrontation with death and sexuality and, more important, the role that art plays in the process. Appearing on a setless stage, the only two characters, "The Man" and "The Girl," engage in a dialogue marked by questions. The isolated voices of these two in the "pure space of psychic activity" (170) generate the play's considerable dramatic tension. The adolescent girl remains seated in a wooden armchair throughout the play, while the man interrogates her and paces the stage. A ceiling fan hypnotically hums over "a white setting so neutral and shadowed that it might be courtroom, doctor's office, sun parlor . . ." (170). The pattern of dialogue suggests psychoanalysis, yet the hint of mystery and unresolved antagonism evokes an air of courtroom cross-examination. Hawkes places his characters in the unidentifiable space of pure artistic imagination. In this no-man's-land, which resembles Skipper's floating island or Cyril's Illyria, the drama intensifies in the void. The relentless crescendo of suggestive questions builds to a final desperate truth that emerges from fiction.

The Questions is clearly a verbal play and, as Hawkes says, "the most interesting of the plays" (Kuehl, 167). Hawkes has also commented that it "was an effort to see how much narrative I could get into drama, not the other way around" (Kuehl, 167). In this play he relies on language not only to tell the story but also to create the dramatis personae. Three central characters—a father, a mother, and Adrian, a live-in houseguest—never appear on the stage but are made real through the dialogue of the young girl and the man. The closer the narrative moves to the climax, the more the two characters lose themselves until they become what they are relating. They make the story their own and act out the parts.

When the girl opens by telling her father's embarrassing dream regarding her mother, the man's questions are loaded with moral innuendo and judgment. Although the girl answers him, she is clearly defending her father, evading the questioner's implications, and trying to maintain an innocent picture:

MAN: And all this time they were living together—your mother and father and Adrian—without rupture or regret or antagonism. Is that correct?

GIRL: Well, heavens, they weren't living together. Adrian was a person of independent means. He just came and went, that's all.

MAN: You know what I intended by the phrase, do you not?

GIRL: OK—living together. What's the difference? Your words don't mean any more or less than mine. (201)

Indeed they don't, for both of their interpretations of events suggest relative perceptions. Nevertheless, the man asserts a superior, authoritarian position throughout the play and alludes to undisclosed but severe ramifications: "How can you consider the possible consequences of all this—consequences such as death, grief, anguish, a life of emotional oblivion—and not cooperate?" (202). His moral stance is designed to penetrate the girl's defenses.

For the most part the girl adheres to her own version of the "story." Occasionally she titillates the man by seeming to assign guilt or shame. For example, when she tells him about the secret tryst between her mother and father, she taunts, "It was full of indiscretion—really. It was the worst moment in my life. OK?" (203). Of course, the shame she feels is ironic because she stumbles on a secret meeting between her mother and father, not between her mother and Adrian. The Freudian implications are obvious; the girl would prefer her mother to be with Adrian so that she can be with her father. Wishing her to acknowledge her father's malicious innocence, the man assaults the girl's manufactured reality with one of his own:

MAN: The point is that your father may simply have wanted Adrian to be his rival, that's all.
GIRL: Then he wasn't trying to win back Mama?
MAN: (smiling) Win back your mother and lose your mother—both. It's been done before.
GIRL: Well, heavens. I mean, I just don't know what you're driving at, unless you're trying to say they were all pretty awful and that Papa was the nigger in the woodpile. You know—the real cause of the trouble, the worst offender. (219)

Because of the girl's insistence on her father's purity ("Papa was just pure" [215]), the man suggests a close identification between the two of them: ". . . you are rather like your father. You and your father had rather similar ways of thinking" (216). Pointing out the close (even incestuous) relationship between them, the man is simultaneously implicating the father and the daughter through his questioning.

The conflict between the man's moral assessment and the girl's innocent denial culminates in the climactic retelling of a fox hunt. Previously, the girl has commented on her father's aversion to fox hunting and his incompetence at horseback riding. In her recounting of the hunt, however, she describes her father as she wants him to be—"fiendish," "cold-blooded" (225), carrying a whip, and riding Gunpowder hard. She, her mother, and father are united, "laughing and riding three abreast across the green" (228). Abrasively interrupting her idyllic portrait, the man reminds her that her mother and Adrian "set out together for the kill" (230) on a brutally cold morning, leaving the father behind. Her version negated, the girl protests: "I hope you enjoy tearing up the *fabric* of everything. I hope you like using tooth and claw to just rip the veil" (229–30). The man, beginning as the questioner desiring answers, finishes as the teller of the tale.

During the final recitation of the fox hunt, both the girl and the man become artist-figures at work. Because the man orders, directs, controls, and judges, he suggests Hawkes's dark authoritarian artists. He not only looks back to Hawkes's early fascist artist-figures like Zizendorf (*The Cannibal*) and Il Gufo

(The Owl), but he also looks forward to Hugh *(The Blood Oranges)* and his puritanical repression. With authorial detachment, the man wishes to snare the girl's deepest fears and desires and then preside over her loss of innocence. She, on the other hand, is the artist as victim, the one who must innocently and cold-bloodedly defy the man's control. In rebellion her creative spirit flies much like the prisoner with wings in *The Owl,* like Skipper, the "lover of the hummingbird" in *Second Skin,* or like Cyril and his "sylvan sources" in *The Blood Oranges.* At one point in the play she says, "I guess I'm like the girl who gets turned into a bird and has to sing forever just because of the messy life she was mixed up in" (204). As such, she resorts to song, to dream, to artifice.

Ultimately the girl ends up participating in the man's rendition of the kill, a scene meant to represent the death of both her innocence and her father's. The man purposely uses language to heighten the brutality of the event: "So the clouds grew darker and colder while your father and his rival wallowed in the greasy pit, stripping the white fat from the slender bones and cracking joints and squeezing small elastic viscous bulbs and yanking on cold tufts of fur and stabbing, slitting, slicing, poking until between them they opened up the animal's little dripping coat and posed grinning together" (236).

This bloody scene in the pit suggests many of Hawkes's set pieces in which the stillness of art heightens the appalling disorder of life. The power of this controlled chaos works on the girl until the entire scene suggests a psychic rape. The brutal description is reminiscent of the Duke's dismembering of the young boy in *The Cannibal.* In both scenes the innocent subject is stalked and the carcass cut up with destructive precision. Just as Hawkes the artist tracks down his subject, so the interrogator psychically rends the girl. He then dismisses her from the chair and closes: "You may still give way to—shame" (237).

As in the other three plays, however, the innocent party has the last word. Still defending her father, herself, and her story, she says: "Listen—don't you think he was sorry for what he did to that fox? I mean, Papa was cold-blooded sometimes, but he wasn't a criminal. (She tries to lure the man from the darkness with her smile.) Anyhow, whoever heard of being pure without being cold-blooded? You know. (Pause) Listen—my story was just as good as yours. I mean, they were the same, weren't they?" (238–39). On one level the stories are the same; they both are works of art, or verbally created tableaux. Even though the man has dramatically delineated the breakdown of her father, he has clearly not defeated the girl. His moral judgment ends up being meaningless. While he stands in the darkness of the stage, she concludes: "Papa said we were all virgins under the skin, and I guess that includes him too. (Pause) But listen—according to Papa the silly virgins always beat the moral barbarians at their own game, so I guess we won" (239).

Of course, the irony is that there is nothing to win. Nevertheless, the girl seems to have bested the man, leaving him alone in the dark with his authoritarian construct of events disregarded. Throughout the play he thought he was in control, using his questions to capture what was in the girl's mind; at the end he is ensnared himself by the girl's naïveté.

Despite being threatened by sex, time, and death, the innocent parties in all four plays maintain their innocence through artistry. In the first three plays, however, the innocent parties are not able to use their artistic vision to move beyond stasis. In fact, Jane in *The Innocent Party* and Edward in *The Undertaker* seem destined to reenact their same imaginary ritual, for their imaginations have been corrupted by inherited guilt and repression. In *The Wax Museum,* Sally Ann does not repeat the past, but she remains sealed in a timeless museum. Free to explore her sexuality in this imaginary world, she is nevertheless relegated to the static world of art. Only the girl in *The Questions* moves on while simultaneously maintaining her innocence. Rather than denying the past and its incumbent guilt or repeating it in an effort to forget it, she spins stories from it and designs it in a new way. Her artistic ability both to order and disorder enables her to survive the interrogation into her past. She shuns the imprisoning confines of the man's moral judgment and creates her own moments of poetic song. In fact, her creative and destructive approach to life suggests Hawkes's own paradoxical view of the artist at work.

The Questions clearly looks to Hawkes's next novel, *The Blood Oranges,* in both theme and technique. The novel's contrasting artist-figures, Hugh and Cyril, (suggestive of the man and the girl) provide greater dramatic conflict than is present in the earlier, more deterministic novels or in *Second Skin* and its alternating landscapes. The evolution of Hawkes's dramatic form and the presence of more dialogue in *The Blood Oranges* suggest that his play writing did influence his fiction. In 1971, the year *The Blood Oranges* was published, Hawkes acknowledged that "perhaps the writing of dialogue relates to the plays; I suppose there is an increasing use of dialogue in *The Blood Oranges*" (Kuehl, 167). Hawkes also had much to say on his "preoccupation with innocence," the theme of the plays and of *The Blood Oranges:* "I now want to challenge concepts like guilt, retribution, atonement, etc., since I no longer believe that the pursuit of the dream, say in sexual terms—such as Cyril's efforts to destroy monogamy—is necessarily evil or destructive" (Kuehl, 166). In fact, Hawkes goes on to say that once the characters are "freed of the question of guilt in their sexual lives . . . they are all pure, all innocent, no matter what they are doing—which is my own view" (Kuehl, 166). This sentiment expresses exactly the girl's desires at the end to be free from the "moral barbarians" and to recognize that "we were all virgins under the skin" (239).

A radical innocence triumphs, especially in the last play. Hawkes reverses the traditional expectation that innocence is a liability, a quality of naïveté or helplessness that must be overcome. Instead, in Hawkes's view, what needs to be overcome are the conventional notions of morality. All of Hawkes's innocent parties end up more "pure" than the seeming goodness of the "moral barbarians." To underscore this point, Hawkes makes his characters children, and states: "In a sense, the children can be taken as authorial innocence, purity, and are the victims of our corrupt, conventional, apparently moral, but actually destructive world" (Kuehl, 170). This comment again suggests the paradox Hawkes finds in innocence: the power of innocence in its capacity to create, even in the face of nightmare, and also the powerlessness of innocence because of its victimization by the "moral barbarians."

In the plays, Hawkes overturns the audience's conventional perceptions of innocence and corruption. Initially, the innocent parties seem perverted or disturbed: Jane has her ritual by the pool, Edward reenacts his father's suicide, Sally Ann has her timid virginity, and the girl is unwilling to cooperate. By the plays' conclusions, however, the characters who seem the most corrupted are those like Jane's parents, with their "pee-pot morality," and the man who serves as inquisitor. For Hawkes, what is truly nightmarish is the conventional morality brandished by society, and what is truly pure lies in the imagination, which only the innocent values.

Notes

1. Frederick Busch's *Hawkes: A Guide to His Fictions* (Syracuse, N.Y.: Syracuse University Press, 1973) remains the only critical book on Hawkes to devote a chapter to the plays.
2. John Hawkes, *Humors of Blood and Skin: A John Hawkes Reader* (New York: New Directions, 1984), 256.
3. John Kuehl, "Interview," in his *John Hawkes and the Craft of Conflict* (New Brunswick, N.J.: Rutgers University Press, 1975), 171, 158. All subsequent references will be noted parenthetically in the text.
4. John Hawkes, *The Innocent Party* (New York: New Directions, 1966), 137. All subsequent references to the plays will be noted parenthetically in the text.
5. In the *New York Review of Books* (13 July 1967) Nigel Dennis claims that "nobody has ever started a play like this before" (p. 6).
6. John Hawkes, Preface to *The Innocent Party*, 12.
7. John Graham, "John Hawkes on His Novels: An Interview with John Graham," *Massachusetts Review* 7, Summer 1966, 32.
8. John Hawkes, *The Blood Oranges* (New York: New Directions, 1971), 256.

Desire, Design, and Debris:
The Submerged Narrative of
John Hawkes' Recent Trilogy

C. J. ALLEN

Almost thirty years after the publication of his first novel, John Hawkes remains one of our best under-read fiction writers. Despite fine, even proselytizing commentaries from such critics as Tony Tanner and Albert Guerard, he is unknown to all but a coterie of devoted readers. Although he has given several interviews about his work, he does not provide many helpful entrances to his fiction; he seems to treat interviewers with a kind of mock seriousness, conceding all interpretations and preferring to let the novels stand on their own. Similarly, his own public readings are tour-de-force performances delightful as those of any good stand-up comic, but misleading for the uninitiated who then turn with anticipation to the novels only to be surprised by their inaccessability and sometimes to be put off by their concentration on sex, death, and violence. But if Hawkes is at first confusing, he is also powerful as he records the strange dreams and obsessions of his narrators in lucid lyrical prose.

Hawkes' three recent novels, *The Blood Oranges, Death, Sleep & The Traveler,* and *Travesty,* are certainly "about" sex, particularly about what he calls sexual extension or sexual multiplicity—relationships involving more than two people. And in all three, characters either die violently or imagine doing so. But what makes the three a trilogy is a submerged narrative in which the power of the conscious mind to create idyllic visions is gradually undermined by unconscious needs and fears. Earlier Hawkes novels also emphasize these tensions; in the trilogy, however, there is an overall design that emerges only after the completion of *Travesty.* Implicit ideas about imagination in *The Blood Oranges* are explicitly parodied in *Travesty* as a result of the threatening portrayal of the unconscious in the middle volume, *Death, Sleep & The Traveler. The Blood Oranges* celebrates an imagined world of sexual multiplicity only to have it end when one character's autoeroticism leads to his death and the end of the celebration. *Death, Sleep & The Traveler* shifts away from conscious image-

Reprinted with permission from *Modern Fiction Studies* 25 (Winter 1979/80):579–92. © 1979 Purdue Research Foundation, West Lafayette, IN 47907.

making to explore the way that sexual repression is lived out in the unconscious. Though the narrator is a murderer at heart, he leaves that part of himself unacknowledged. It remains for *Travesty* to take the murderer within and make him literally a killer. The trilogy begins with a vision of sexual multiplicity and ends with one of cataclysmic destruction. Both are creative acts; how Hawkes gets from one to the other is the subject of this essay.

The Blood Oranges begins the trilogy by setting up an opposition between the narrator Cyril, who wishes to recreate his vision of idyllic love in reality, and his friend Hugh, who resists his efforts because he cannot free himself from his inhibiting jealousy and sexual constraint. Cyril calls himself a "sex-singer": his "song" recalls the relationships between himself and his wife Fiona, and Hugh and Catherine who live in the next villa. When the book opens Hugh is dead, Cyril's mistress Catherine is confined to a sanitarium, and Fiona, lover to Hugh after lengthy reluctance on his part, has departed, taking Hugh and Catherine's children with her. Cyril remains; in his narrative he reconstructs the past for Catherine as a partially successful attempt to free her from the cataleptic state into which she froze following Hugh's death.

For purposes of the trilogy as a whole, the most important emphases in a reading of *The Blood Oranges* are the exuberant sexual freedom that Cyril experiences with Fiona and Catherine, the opposition between Cyril and Hugh, and the thread of references to Cyril's orderly imagination and to his implicit desire to live out his private vision of love in Illyria. The first of these is the primary focus of the book, both of its plot and of its fictional argument. Cyril the sex-singer, the white bull in the tapestry of love, celebrates sexual multiplicity, disdains monogamy as the "only enemy of the mature marriage" *(BO,* p. 209), and proclaims himself a match "for the hatred of conventional enemies wherever they are" *(BO,* p. 36).[1] Critical commentators have dwelt at length on the novel as a paean to sexual extension, a celebration of paradisal openness, however temporary, and I mention it here only because it is the most obvious, perhaps least interesting link among the three novels. The second emphasis, the opposition between Cyril and Hugh, has also had some attention and is important because in the other two volumes of the trilogy the narrators grow increasingly more like Hugh. Cyril is all self-confidence and consciousness. His life is filled with sensuous and sensual pleasures; he is absolutely sure of himself as a husband and a lover. There would be no cracks in his armor if he wore any (most often he wears pajamas), no repressed guilts, no signs of a dark unconscious about to well up. Though he is "two or three long leaps beyond middle age" *(BO,* p. 16) and in a period of sexual dormancy, he remains confident that Catherine and his wife are both soon to return to him.

Cyril is the striking blond "headless god"; Hugh, the dark, repressed, angular St. Peter. While Cyril is a heavy, dreamless sleeper, Hugh says he has "spent all the nights of his life in sleepless writhing" *(BO,* p. 95). Cyril describes Hugh's face in its first appearance as "so weathered and pebbled, so grained in darkness and cold rain that it resembled stone" *(BO,* p. 31). Throughout the novel Hugh exhibits a puritanical repression of his own sexual feeling. Nor in his jealousy does he allow Cyril's affair with Catherine to go unnoticed. His cruelest act is to imprison his wife in an ancient rusted chastity belt to prevent her liaison with Cyril. Like his own withered arm, Hugh is crippled by his refusal to partake fully and openly of the sexual nourishment Fiona offers him. Instead he is a voyeur, a photographer of peasant nudes, an autoerotic actor who dies while attempting to stimulate himself in a mock hanging. In a more traditional novel, Hugh might be simply the aggrieved husband or the comic cuckold. But in *The Blood Oranges* there is no world except the one Cyril describes for us; its values are Cyril's, and there are no suggestions that we are to view Cyril as anything other than the champion of a free, loving sexual temperament and Hugh as his repressed opposite, an unhealthy tormented puritan; the novel is nearly over before he becomes Fiona's lover. Cyril describes him: "He was capable of greed and shame and jealousy. When at last he allowed the true artistic nature of our design to sleep into consciousness, for instance, he persecuted himself and begrudged me Catherine, tried to deny me Catherine at a time when I knew full well that, thanks to my unseen helping hand, he himself was finally about to lurch down his own peculiar road with Fiona. And yet Hugh was also a sex-singer of sorts. But in Hugh's dry mouth our lovely song became a shriek" *(BO,* p. 58).

This same passage touches on something of Cyril's nature even as it describes Hugh's. In referring to "the nature of our design" and to "my unseen helping hand," Cyril alludes to the need for pattern and the desire to actualize it that permeate his imagination. It is this third thread that Hawkes takes up and makes central in *Travesty.* The "design" that Cyril refers to here has as its emblem "Love's tapestry," Cyril's metaphor for his own imagined vision of ideal love. The opening sentences of the book introduce it: "Love weaves its own tapestry, spins its own golden thread, with its own sweet breath breathes into being its mysteries—bucolic, lusty, gentle as the eyes of daisies or thick with pain. And out of its own music creates the flesh of our lives." He goes on to describe himself as a servant of the gods, a fortunate victim of Love's will, but Love's whole "pink panorama" is, of course, of his own imagination's making. He is the mental spinner, the verbal weaver, his credits to the gods notwithstanding, and it is his own imagined vision of idyllic sexual openness he tries to bring to life in Illyria.

References to Love's tapestry appear several times, most tellingly as Cyril recalls an afternoon when their foursome is sun-bathing on a beach. A small goat dances nearby, and Cyril muses on the synapse between the imagined and the real:

> Was it dream, change, coincidence, or was my state of mind a menagerie of desire from which real animals might spring? Could it be that one of my speechless creatures of joy and sentiment had torn itself loose from the tapestry that only I could see? Was it now bearing down upon us with blue eyes and the wind in its

hair? Was the little goat that had danced among us in my mind now going to leave its little hoofprints in the center of Fiona's blanket or come rushing and butting between her legs? It did not seem possible. But of course it was. *(BO, pp. 92–93)*

Cyril's mental tapestry provides tableaux and patterns that count heavily in his view of actual events. Not only do creatures from his "menagerie of desire" seem to materialize, but the actors in his physical life must also be made to fit his imagined design. And while still casting himself as the passive servant of Love, he works actively with his "unseen helping hand" to weave Hugh and Catherine into the tapestry his mind has created for them. He attempts to make that metaphoric vision come alive, to bring it into being and thus live out his imagined design in actual events.

    Cyril's love of pattern shows up in other figures of speech besides the tapestry metaphor. He describes their quartet as "a four-pointed human starfish" *(BO,* p. 37), "the four-pointed constellation of our adulthood" *(BO,* p. 157), "a sacred circle" *(BO,* p. 118), and "the four major points of the compass" *(BO,* p. 135). They "fit together like the shapely pieces of a perfectly understandable puzzle" *(BO,* p. 88). He notes their symbolic positions: "I . . . was well aware that Fiona stood on my left and Catherine on my right and that Hugh was doomed forever to the extreme left and could never share my privilege of standing, so to speak, between two opposite and yet equally desirable women" *(BO,* p. 118) as well as the "symmetry of orange sky" *(BO,* p. 130), the complementary grape arbor and lemon grove, the twin villas in which they live, and the opposition of altars in a chapel. Thus, he rejects the conventional pattern of monogamy, in order to adopt other designs, creations of a mind that has an unacknowledged need for pattern to control the chaos released by his breaking of traditional sexual restraints.

    Cyril's imagination is apparent not only in the repeated references to Love's tapestry and other designs, but also in his narrative recreation of events. Here, too, control is important. Like the novelist who creates his own stories for an audience of readers, Cyril reconstructs for Catherine the events in Illyria according to his own predispositions. In so doing he both calls forth from his memory incidents as he thinks of them and makes up what his "characters"— Fiona, Catherine, Hugh, and other less prominent figures—must have been thinking and feeling. He can then, at least in retrospect, have control over them. He is especially prone to imagining Catherine's thoughts: "Catherine was no doubt thinking of nothing more than the possibility of turning and placing a gentle hand on my bare chest" *(BO,* p. 137). He also construes comically what one of Illyria's natives thinks: "At least there was a pleasing moisture in my cheek and mouth, at least the goat-girl considered herself loved by the unattainable man whose name she would always try to remember and say aloud to her goats" *(BO,* p. 146). He can, in the retelling, have a power he did not have in the events themselves. For although he has an eye for the sex tableau, for the imagined tapestry of love, he is unable to escape the fact that for most of the novel Hugh refuses to fit the pattern Cyril designs for him. For some time nothing that Cyril says or does can get Hugh to overcome his repression, become Fiona's lover, and thus complete Cyril's intended design. Cyril's retelling makes clear the pattern he desires. When he kisses Catherine, he imagines that Hugh must be kissing Fiona on another hilltop. Or he imagines Hugh to be making love with Fiona only to find him masturbating asleep alone in a field.

Hugh's death brings to an end the playing-out of Cyril's mental vision of sexual extension. Whether his hanging is a suicide as most commentators have understood, or an accident in an act of autoeroticism as Hawkes claims he intended,[2] is less important than its destruction of Cyril's tapestry. Though the novel emphasizes Cyril's delight in overturning conventional sexual mores, it also suggests implicitly that the tapestry of his imagination's weaving cannot be made to come alive for long, even in idyllic Illyria. Other people cannot be fitted so easily into the design.

In *Death, Sleep & The Traveler,* the adventurous quaternion of *The Blood Oranges* becomes a seemingly amiable triad. Non-monogamy is now the established norm, so the radical vision of sexual extension gives way to an examination of the narrator's confusions as he tries to understand his complex relations with his wife and his best friend. The converse of Cyril, who is highly conscious of the patterns he creates, Allert, the bumbling Dutchman, who is the protagonist of *Death, Sleep & The Traveler,* is never quite able to bring his perceptions out of his unconscious. Hawkes' interest in conscious image-making in *The Blood Oranges* becomes in the trilogy's central volume a portrayal of dreams and mental projections the import of which is never fully grasped by their creator. Allert has none of Cyril's interest in making a vision into reality because he has no conscious awareness of what he would like his life to be like. Unlike Cyril, the dreamless sleeper, Allert dreams, although he has little understanding of his nighttime images. At least he acknowledges his dreams; he also presents fictions of his unconscious that we try to understand but that he does not. What we see in them is not Cyril's sexual idyll, but something resembling Hugh's repressed desires and violent actions. In the submerged narrative of the trilogy Cyril's vision seems to have been realized in *Death, Sleep & The Traveler* and, in its incarnation, made commonplace; what follows it is an uncomprehended vision of interior agonies.

There are two distinct geographical settings in the novel, each with its own triad; it soon becomes clear, however, that the scenes at sea are somehow extensions of the scenes on land. The novel moves between the two geographies in short sections, some only a paragraph or two long. The rapid juxtapositions emphasize the not-quite-conscious connection between the two in Allert's mind. The novel opens in the wintry land world, and Allert tells us that his wife

Ursula is leaving him three years after the death of her lover, his best friend, Peter. On land Allert is a passive voyeur who successfully sublimates his attraction to Peter and invites him to share Ursula's sexual favors. Governed as it is by an overlay of social amenities, his land world does not permit him to understand even his own motivations, let alone his wife's departure. On land he recounts a series of dreams in which his obsession with sexuality is apparent, but he never permits himself to meditate on them. Instead he turns them over to Ursula who does a short, cruel analysis, thus vitiating any need for him to think about them himself and perhaps to come to a fuller understanding of his feelings. Peter, a psychiatrist, also believes he has Allert carefully analyzed and frequently expands on the clinical facts of Allert's personality. Allert spends his days smoking cigars, drinking endless glasses of water and schnapps, and looking at his extensive pornography collection, an interest he shares both with Hugh and with the narrator of *Travesty*. He observes Ursula and Peter's sexual play but only occasionally participates. Sometimes Peter's presence stirs old childhood memories whose import is never quite clear to him. Finally Ursula tires of his presence and of his continual recital of dreams and sends him away on a summer cruise ship. She even points out to him a woman whom he might meet for sexual pleasure.

Geography and climate are always significant in Hawkes' novels, so it is not surprising that Allert's second world, free from the constraints placed on him by Ursula's and Peter's presence, is marked not only by snow but by high temperatures, shimmering light, and a disturbing whiteness, all import- ant to the atmosphere of psychological extremity on board the ship. It is as if the temperature of Illyria had been raised twenty degrees, so that what was lushly tropical in *The Blood Oranges* becomes unbearably overheated for the traveler. As he cruises among barren islands, Allert is freer to exercise his imagination, to project his unconscious desires in a way he never could while Ursula was squashing his dreams and Peter was labeling him with clinical precision. On board ship Allert is part of a second triangle which re- plicates the first, but which is free from its veneer of politeness. Young Ariane seduces Allert early in the voyage, much to the displeasure of Olaf, a wire- less radio operator on the ship's crew. On the cruise Allert experiences directly the sexual pleasure that comes largely from voyeurism on land. Near the end of the cruise, on the night of a masquerade ball, Ariane disappears and Allert is accused of drowning her. Olaf is sedated and Allert imprisoned in his cabin. When he returns to land he is tried and acquitted of murder. Like Cyril he gets what he wants, but his success is more tenuous. Cyril's foursome is temporary, but consciously created. Allert's sexual fulfillment comes in un- conscious wanderings. His final isolation is without Cyril's hope for future idylls.

The absence of Ursula and Peter from the ship is a necessary condition for Allert's fantasies. On land they dominate his life. Ursula is both sensual and rather tawdrily promiscuous; for Allert her power is engendered in her name:

"uterine, ugly, odorous, earthen, vulval, convolvulaceous, saline, mutable, seductive" *(DST,* p. 61). Despite her physicality, she most often challenges Allert verbally, through dream interpretations. Her commentaries are brief and stinging. He dreams of grapes filled with fetuses; she wonders how anyone "could be so afraid of life as to dream such a disgusting dream" *(DST,* p. 15). Or he dreams of being endowed with great potency, and she speaks of his "explicit sexual insecurity" *(DST,* p. 17). Ursula herself does not figure in the directly sexual dreams since they are autoerotic. When she does appear, it is negatively (e.g., crushing the fetus-filled grapes). Though Allert makes passing references to a distant past in their marriage when mutual sexuality was important, they now show no direct sexual interest in one another.

Instead Ursula seems to be primarily a socially acceptable medium through which Allert effects his erotic feeling for Peter. Allert's longings are especially poignant in the scene in which he comes to Peter and Ursula's bed to have sex with Ursula while Peter sleeps. When Ursula protests that his arrival makes no sense, he replies that it makes sense to him and that he wants it so *(DST,* p. 82), but he never says more than that. He never makes love to Ursula alone; Peter is always present. His homoerotic attraction to Peter remains a repressed part of himself that he never directly recognizes.

Peter is consistently linked to fleeting impressions from Allert's childhood, and as Allert's recollections of his early life accumulate, he moves toward making a connection between Peter's triggering of these memories and their erotic content. But the recognition is gradual and never fully explicit. Peter's tobacco reminds him of when he was a "helpless boy" *(DST,* p. 36). An evening with Peter and Ursula, filled with "a slow and unmistakable drift toward sensuality," recalls a childhood trip *(DST,* p. 91). As the evening becomes increasingly sexual, he thinks of the white chateau where he lived as a boy, is "too awakened" to remain in the room with Peter and Ursula, leaves the house, and outside in the snow remembers himself as a child riding in a sleigh driven by a man in heavy gloves *(DST,* pp. 93–94). Later in his narrative he remembers riding behind his family's old pipe-smoking coachman and experiencing his first ejaculation *(DST,* pp. 146–147). The chain of memories is finally completed; Peter's presence helps him recall his early sexual pleasure. The smell of Peter's pipe is specifically linked to Allert's boyhood coachman and his first erotic experience.

Allert makes no new acquaintances aboard ship, for Ariane and Olaf are simply purer, more mythic versions of Ursula and Peter. Ariane is pure promiscuity; stripped of titles like wife and mistress, she is Ursula's opposite and essence. Small, rather than large like Ursula, boyish, not buxom, air, not earth, she is Ariadne trying to lead a bumbling Theseus out of the labyrinth of his sexual confusion. She extends her favors to whoever wants them—to Olaf, to other crew members, and to passengers and crews on previous voyages. She is Pan as well. She owns an island of unreal goats and plays her hypnotic flute for

Allert, wearing only a rose. On the night of her death, she seduces him wearing a goat's skull to mask her sex. Androgynous, she is the boyish lover that Peter never could be and the unrecriminating woman that Ursula is not.

Just as Ariane is pure promiscuity, so Olaf is pure sexual threat, the arch-rival both threatening and sinisterly attractive. He taunts Allert with pornographic pictures; the sex of the participants in them is never stated. He jeers at him for his clumsiness and his aging physique. He is coarse, leering, even lewd, totally without Peter's suave charm and sophistication. On board ship where Allert's imagination need not be restrained, they compete openly for Ariane. Still, near the end of the trip as Allert sits in chains accused of the murder of Ariane, he makes a telling comment, its significance increased because it stands alone as a separate section:

> The islands became more numerous. They were small and golden, each one a perfect bright sphere for exploring. But I was confined and he was heavily sedated.
>
> Even inside my cabin I could hear the rumors. And a few dumpy women with wooden sticks and pucks. (*DST*, p. 172)

The "he" here could refer only to Olaf; the suggestion, never made more overt, is that it is Allert and Olaf who should be exploring those golden islands.

Ariane and Olaf are Allert's versions of Ursula and Peter stripped to their essences. On the ship Allert gives way to his desire to be seduced, his anger at his rival, and, momentarily, his attraction to him. Thus, at sea he does what Ursula accuses him of doing on land: he mythologizes their sexual lives (*DST*, p. 176). In moving toward myth he follows Peter's earlier description of an archaic asylum cure in which the patient is subjected to deeper and deeper states of coma, but always at the risk of death. Peter maintains that true myth can be experienced only in coma, and Allert's sea voyage is an enacting of that state.

If, however, in his coma state he experiences "true myth" in the figures of Ariane and Olaf, he also fails to recover from the experience and instead sees himself as a victim of interior forces he does not understand. Two juxtaposed sections near the end of the novel touch on these forces; in them Allert meditates on "psychic wounds," then recalls his sensations at the time of Ariane's murder. In the first of the two, he wonders "who is safe" from his own unexpected actions:

> We . . . hope to catch a glimpse of ourselves, and in this furtive pursuit we hope for courage. But on the brink of success, precisely when a moment of understanding seems nearest at hand, and even if the moment is a small thing and not particularly consequential, it is then that the eyes close, the head turns away, the voice dies, the surface of the bright ocean becomes a sea of lead, and from the very shape we know to be our own there leaps a mansized batlike shadow that flees or crouches to attack, to drive us away. Who is safe? Who knows what he will do next? (*DST*, p. 164)

This passage describes the self protecting itself against the shadows of the unconscious. Even in retrospect Allert is not able to examine precisely what has happened to him.

Nor does the subsequent recounting of Ariane's death include an explanation for the murder. As Allert stands with her in his arms, then throws her overboard, he detaches himself from his actions:

> I could not feel her weight. I heard a shout. I turned. I heard a splash. The deck was a hard crust of salt. The night was cold. I heard the splash. I could not feel her weight. And then along the entire length of that bitter ship I saw the lights sliding and blurring beneath the waves. Clumsily, insanely, I wrestled with a white life ring that bore the name of the ship and that refused to come free. I saw the ship's fading lighted silhouette beneath the waves. Who is safe? (*DST*, pp. 165–166)

In the first part of the passage the short sentences and the lexical and syntactic repetition have a hypnotic effect that underlines his coma state. He perceives with his senses but not with his intellect. He hears sounds, notes the temperature, describes the deck's texture but at the moment of the murder negates Ariane: "I could not feel her weight." His closing "who is safe?" links the moment with the preceding meditation on the fear of the unconscious. Allert is not safe from his own complicated and unacknowledged motives. He leaves them unexplored though there are several possibilities. At the time of Ariane's death she is dressed in an officer's cap and tunic. Perhaps the cap identifies her as a "sailor's whore" as it does earlier on a brief, brutal off-ship adventure when she and Olaf grope on the floor of a zoo reptile house. Such an identification is reminiscent of Ursula's promiscuity. Or perhaps since Ariane is "impersonating a wireless operator" (*DST*, p. 166) Allert thinks of Olaf, literal operator of the ship's wireless and of Peter, metaphoric "wireless operator" in his probings of the psyche. They, too, are Allert's tormentors. Or Allert may be following Peter's suggestion that one must commit murder to lose one's virginity, that is, to prove his manhood requires an act of violence rather than of sex.

Whatever his motives, he never consciously recognizes them. The freedom to cruise on ships of the unconscious does not mean one reaches a destination. At the end of the novel Allert feels no benefits from Peter's cure; he has no profound and joyous recovery from his life-coma as Peter's patients are supposed to. He does not acknowledge his murderous act or the anger from which it comes. Instead, he sees himself as passive victim and has no plans for doing much of anything except sitting. His final words are "I am not guilty." So although the cruise allows his repressed version of himself and those around him to rise momentarily to the surface in a freeing of unconscious desires not possible in the confines of his life on land, he learns nothing from them. In his projections we see how life expands to myth and how myth moves out of the unconscious, but Allert himself never sees. Back on land he is content to "think and dream," to proclaim himself not guilty, to go on being the obtuse Dutchman unable to incorporate into himself the rich possibilities of his time at sea.

As the central novel of the trilogy, *Death, Sleep & The Traveler* is important not so much as an expansion of the ideas in *The Blood Oranges* as a temporary backing off from them. Cyril's vision of sexual extension has been made real, although the configurations are different. Allert's patterning, which recasts Ursula and Peter as Ariane and Olaf, is an escape from the social realities of multisexuality, not a design for its implementation. Allert with his repressed sexual feeling resembles Hugh more than he does Cyril. Perhaps because Cyril's vision cannot be sustained, the novel turns from his conscious artistry to Allert's unconscious voyaging. It is the unacknowledged discoveries of his cruise that give rise to the parody of *Travesty*.

An odd little book barely more than 100 pages long, *Travesty* often reads more like an essay on the imagination than a novel. It brings the submerged narrative of the trilogy full circle by seeming to return to the highly conscious artistry of Cyril. Like him, the unnamed narrator of *Travesty* creates an artistic design in his imagination and wants to bring it to life. He, too, has a fascination with pattern and is part of a sexual foursome. But the resemblances are purposefully superficial as the title suggests. *Travesty* completes the trilogy by parodying both *The Blood Oranges* and *Death, Sleep & The Traveler*. In this final volume the narrator imagines a totally destructive car wreck rather than a paradise of sexual openness; his patterns not only repeat but burlesque each other; his foursome includes his daughter as well as his best friend and his wife. The narrator, who combines Cyril's creative power with Hugh's unreleased feelings, envisions not an idyll but a holocaust.

The parody starts with Allert's unacknowledged discoveries in *Death, Sleep & The Traveler*. On board ship Allert is a murderer despite his claims of innocence. He is capable of violent action and sexual jealousy even if, as he says, at the moment of understanding "the eyes close, the head turns away, the voice dies, the surface of the bright ocean becomes a sea of lead" (*DST*, p. 164). Hawkes makes the narrator of *Travesty* the literal murderer whom Allert fails to recognize within his own psyche. The self-described "privileged man" is a burlesque of Allert's unconscious version of himself. Hawkes returns to the ideas of *The Blood Oranges* by way of *Death, Sleep & The Traveler*, and it is difficult not to read his exaggeration of Cyril's obsessions as a judgment of them.

Cyril tries to use an "unseen helping hand" to unite Hugh and Fiona and make his design complete. The privileged man of *Travesty* simply seizes control by imprisoning in his car his daughter Chantal and his best friend Henri who is lover to both his daughter and his wife; the three of them careen at high speed down back roads, past his chateau where his wife Honorine lies sleeping, then toward a stone wall into which he plans to slam the car in a double-murder and suicide. We hear only the voice of the narrator as he lays out his plans for his captive audience. He does not bother to present direct dialogue of other characters as Cyril and Allert do. We have almost no sense of "characters" at all; they have been so swallowed up by the privileged man's design that they never really exist as separate entities. His fictional monologue rambles between past events and the coming smash-up as the narrator taunts them with possible motives for his actions. Cyril's "unseen helping hand" is here writ large by the narrator's complete control over his victims.

The monologue begins with the narrator establishing his control: "No, no Henri. Hand off the wheel . . . As for you, Chantal, you must be brave. You must obey your Papa." In his subsequent recounting of his past, it is evident that the privileged man has had little control over his life. Honorine and Chantal picked out a woman of pleasure for him, his mistress Monique beat him into impotency just when he was expecting his greatest happiness, his wife and daughter turned to Henri with their affection. By locking Henri and Chantal in his car, he gains the power necessary to complete the one moment in his past when he had a modicum of control. He speaks early in his monologue of "a travesty involving a car, an old poet, and a little girl" (*T*, p. 47) and later tells of the formative event of his early manhood—running down an old man and a girl with his car, uncertain whether or not he killed them. In the present circumstances, he imagines a fiery wreck designed to finish the job.

This recollection is one of several in the novel in which the narrator's love of symmetry is apparent, and in it he again resembles Cyril. The privileged man has a "theory of likenesses," a desire toward total coherence that leads him "to see in one face the configurations of . . . another" (*T*, p. 75), just as Cyril observes patterns everywhere. Narratively the effect of the privileged man's theory, however, is to create, in his monologue, travesties, figures who resemble and parody each other. His mistress Monique physically resembles Chantal and in her sexual experiences deserves the nickname given to the daughter, "porno brat." The narrator finds a version of himself in a one-legged doctor whose wife has left him. His greatest travesty is of Henri the poet. Like the privileged man, Henri has lung problems and already shares his wife and daughter. The narrator intends the wreck, his "tableau of chaos," to be a work of art just as Henri's poems and Cyril's tapestry are. Henri is famous for "some kind of *mythos* of cruel detachment" (*T*, p. 43), and his attitude is parodied by the narrator's entire monologue with its pose of rational examination of an irrational act. Henri himself has told audiences "that the poet is always a betrayer, a murderer, and that the writing of poetry is like a descent into death" (*T*, p. 80). The privileged man's design will make the poet's metaphors a reality. In becoming a murderer he becomes a poet. And just as Henri has had a lifetime of audiences, so now the privileged man has a captive one with whom to share his design.

Like a poet he knows "imagined life is more exhilarating than remembered life" (*T*, p. 127), and much of his monologue is given to visions of what might be or in the case of their coming death what is to be. He imagines what Henri will do in the course of the trip: "You are determined to hide your trembling, achieve a few moments of silence, begin smoking one of your delightful cigarettes . . . then you will attempt to dissuade me, to talk me back to sanity" (T, p. 12). He pictures the local curate hearing the car's explosion and sees their bodies being brought through the kitchen of the small rural hospital. But his clearest vision is of the wreck itself; his description of it is his essay on the imagination: "Nothing is more important than the existence of what does not exist. . . . I would rather see two shadows flickering inside the head than all your flaming sunrises set end to end. There you have it, the theory to which I hold as does the wasp to his dart. . . . My theory tells us that ours is the power to invent the very world we are quitting. . . . The unseen vision is not to be improved upon" (T, pp. 57–58). He would prefer that the wreck go undiscovered and undestroyed by fire. He imagines the aftermath as "bits of metal expanding, contracting, tufts of upholstery exposed to the air, an unsocketed dial impossibly squeaking in a clump of thorns—though this same baffling tangle of springs, jagged edges of steel, curves of aluminum, has already received its first coating of white frost" (T, pp. 58–59). Thus the artist desires an impossible permanency for his creations.

All of this—the desire to control, the theory of likenesses, the murderer as artist, the pleasure in imagining the wreck, the drive toward making the vision a permanent reality—takes us back to Cyril and his mental weaving of patterns, but with a difference. Hawkes' parodic treatment of these ideas in Travesty suggests that Cyril's attempts to reify his vision are maniacal and destructive. The world does not belong to Cyril the visionary but to Hugh and to Allert. In his motives the privileged man is clearly aligned with them and their unacknowledged jealousies.

The privileged man protests too much that jealousy is not his motive for us to believe him. Though he denies being jealous of Henri's attention from Honorine, he also attacks him as a bad poet, an unknowledgeable lover, and an emotional parasite. Above all he wants to make Honorine the source of his private apocalypse just as she is the Muse for Henri's poetry. As she sleeps in their chateau Tara, its name a comic reminder of that romantic southern mansion where private possession is all, the narrator, still denying his jealousy, moves toward creating a travesty of art. He designs a death in which imagined tapestries and visual poems go up in flames, taking tormentor and tormented, author and audience with them.

In The Blood Oranges there are no breaks in Cyril's portrayal of himself as a "sex-singer" and artistic servant of Love. Hawkes provides no ironies, no clues to the reader that suggest Cyril is to be viewed in any way other than he presents himself. Even the reader who pauses at Cyril's hyperbolic description of himself as a "great white creature horned and mounted on a trim little golden sheep" (BO, p. 2) can only admire the lyricism and keep going. In Travesty the narrator is not only crazy but self-deceived as well. Hawkes' choice of Tara, for example, or his countering of the man's denials of jealousy by juxtaposing them with attacks on Henri suggests that he wants us to see the destructive quality in the narrator's psyche as well as in his intended violent act. By making him a travesty of Cyril, Hawkes comments on the earlier novel by completing his trilogy with a mad vision created out of unexpressed hatred and contempt.

The concluding words of *Travesty,* set against the endings of the two earlier novels, suggest the movement of the submerged narrative. *The Blood Oranges* ends on Cyril's hopeful observation that his relics are circular, that "everything coheres, moves forward." He expects the return of his idyll, for in Illyria because "there are no seasons," the lovely life will continue. The conclusion of *Death, Sleep & The Traveler* is considerably darker; Cyril's pensive optimism gives way to Allert's feeble protest. The Dutchman is "not guilty" because, unlike Cyril, he is not conscious of what he desires and cannot be responsible for or even cognizant of his actions. The idyll never really happens for Allert. *Travesty*'s narrator blots out Cyril's vision altogether by using reminiscent talents of vision to imagine not a tapestry but a holocaust. "There shall be no survivors. None," the narrator promises. With that final negation, Hawkes' lyric rendering of passionate life in Illyria and mythic recreation at sea speeds toward a black abyss where there also are no seasons.

Notes

1. John Hawkes, *The Blood Oranges* (New York: New Directions, 1971). Further citations, identified *BO,* will be placed parenthetically in the text. Other Hawkes novels cited are *Death, Sleep & The Traveler* (New York: New Directions, 1976)—*DST; Travesty* (New York: New Directions, 1976)—*T.*

2. In a talk at the University of Washington, Seattle, May 1976.

Postmodernism as Autobiographical Commentary: *The Blood Oranges* and *Virginie*

HEIDE ZIEGLER

The relationship—the similarities as well as the differences—between modernism and postmodernism has been all but too widely discussed. The usefulness of the terms themselves, particularly of the term "postmodernism," has often been called into question, even when postmodernism is restricted to mean little more than an American reaction to literary modernism in Europe. And almost no contemporary writer, whether American or European, would wholeheartedly describe himself as a postmodernist writer. Still, the terms "modern" and "postmodern" serve a purpose and are not merely validated by the fact that they have been in circulation long enough to preclude the possibility of their abolition. Contrasting the terms modernism and postmodernism invokes the question of intertextuality that mirrors the concerns of many contemporary writers. Gérard Genette, especially in his latest study *Palimpsestes,*[1] defines intertextuality as the ability of a text to comment upon another text, either through the imitation or through the transformation of an earlier literary model. Also, the later literary text will affect our reading of the earlier one. Postmodernism, as the term says, reflects on modernism: either on modernist texts or on modernist ideas. It presents a running commentary on modernism, and a postmodernist author formerly of modernist leanings would be bound to reflect in the same manner upon his former self; that is, he would have to write his later texts in light of and as commentaries on his own earlier ones. In a sense, therefore, the postmodernist writer needs to be autobiographical; but autobiography, for him, has changed its meaning. It no longer requires that he write about his *life,* or even that *he*—an unalterable identity—write about his life; instead, autobiography comes to mean the process of narration itself as the author relates to it. Not only may a fiction text contain the seeds for subsequent variants of the same text, but it has a direct impact on the further life of the author, making it, in a sense, also fictional. Especially the "marginal" problems of the text acquire autobiographical importance: editorial questions, publication procedures, and the intellectual and emotional feedback offered by

Reprinted from *Review of Contemporary Fiction* 3 (Fall 1983): 207–13. Copyright © 1983 Heide Ziegler.

literary reviews shape the author's life and become part of his further fictional endeavors.

It is in this "autobiographical" sense that John Hawkes can be considered a postmodern writer. Ever since he started to write fiction after World War II, he has been concerned with the relationship between his narrators and himself in the role of author in the text.[2] However, since Hawkes believes in poetic language as the expression of the life of the imagination, which for him is an absolute entity, the text has ultimately always been more than its narrator or, by implication, its author. If Hawkes's narrators have been noted for their unreliability, this feature always served to direct the reader *and* the author towards poetic language and the workings of the imagination as such. The unreliable narrator relentlessly calls for a reading between the lines, for a subtext that validates the role of interpreter of the text. In this role, however, as the reader of his own text, the author is faced with a special problem: since he wrote it, he needs not to interpret, but to re-interpret the text, which means that he must first forget his own text in order to regain the innocence necessary for a second interpretation. This forgetting of the text can be obtained through the device of narrative unreliability. Reliability would veil innocence, because it does not allow for spontaneity, for the choice of the contingent over the predictable.

Innocence is the main theme of two of Hawkes's novels, one of which is representative of what might be called his earlier modernist and the other of his recent postmodernist stance: *The Blood Oranges,* published in 1971, and *Virginie: Her Two Lives,* published in 1982. If the force of the innocent imagination has not changed for Hawkes in the intertextual space created by the decade between the publication of the two novels, its forms of narrative expression have changed to a degree that gives rise to the proposition, advanced at the end of this essay, that the course of Hawkes's fictional life parallels that of the development of the novel at large; yet, this development ought to be regarded less as a chronological progression than an exfoliation of intertextual interdependence. *Virginie* comments on *The Blood Oranges,* while *The Blood Oranges* contains the seeds of the later novel. The relationship between these two novels is dependent upon the weaving of a narrative tapestry that progresses and unravels in turns, and that, as a tapestry of love, becomes a metaphor for the two novels as well as for Hawkes's fictional life.

Innocence for Hawkes means either the non-existence or the dissolution of any power resulting from sexual dominance. One of the symbols in *The Blood Oranges* which embodies innocence is the statue of a hermaphrodite, whose ambivalent appearance is supposed to represent, and to propel into the mode of timelessness, the changing sexual interrelations among the four main characters of the novel. The statue, dating from antiquity, carries the characters back into a realm of mythical virginity: "There was a time when all our days were only memories of hours that had not yet passed and each one of us was in some way virginal."[3] The narrative precondition for such a state of innocence is the conception of space as pastoral landscape. But the imaginary landscape of Illyria becomes an ironic Arcadia that cannot exist without the memory of death. Associated with the Golden Age, Illyria at first seems to mean an indestructible present, but hints referring to the past and to the future—"memories of hours that had not yet passed"—constantly encircle that present and threaten its self-sufficiency. Innocence in *The Blood Oranges* does not mean a virginal Not Yet, but a paradoxical Again and Again that attempts to repress the idea of recent or imminent loss—a loss, however, that appears inevitable as soon as innocence is seen against the foil of passing time and of age. The last sentence of the novel, "In Illyria there are no seasons" (271), is not a description, but a prayer.

Cyril, the unreliable narrator, incorporates both the serene Apollonian will to form and the festive languidness of the Dionysian cult, asceticism as well as self-indulgence. He regards himself as a heroic figure in the context of a timeless myth, as Love's emissary, allegorically represented on a medieval tapestry: "Throughout my life I have simply appeared at Love's will. See me as a small white porcelain bull lost in the lower left-hand corner of that vast tapestry, see me as a great white creature horned and mounted on a trim little golden sheep in the very center of Love's most explosive field. . . . I was there always. I completed the picture" (2). As narrator, Cyril indeed appears to be privileged. He appears to hold the strands of the story like the threads of a vast tapestry in his mind's hands and to weave them into an intricate narrative design. But his power is ironic: he is not the author and he mistakes Love's will for his own. Like the intrigue of Penelope, who unraveled at night what she had accomplished during the day, his design consists in a constant conjuring up of the appearance of timelessness. Since Cyril, in his double role as narrator and character, creates both a story and an intrigue, the process of narration saves and at the same time threatens this paradoxical design; for it assures the continuity of the story while threatening its success as intrigue.

Cyril's adversary Hugh, a Christ-like figure, represents the beginning of historical time which dissolves Cyril's pagan timelessness. However, Hugh would be capable only of disturbing Cyril's design, not of disrupting it, if the tapestry of love—like the tapestry of narrative—were not defined by its own inherent limits. Cyril divines that he may disregard these limits if he succeeds in establishing a harmonious balance of relationships *within* the intrigue. Therefore, he strives, for a time successfully, to persuade Hugh to overcome his "greed and shame and jealousy" (58) by acknowledging his repressed desire for Fiona and by satisfying her needs. In making love both to his own wife Fiona and to Hugh's wife Catherine, Cyril thus establishes a pattern of correspondences which validates his concept of idyllic timelessness. But then Hugh dies through what only appears to be an absurd accident: holding the photograph of a nude peasant girl, he dies when he undergoes a partial hanging in order to experience sexual release. Hugh's death represents a perversion of the narrative concept of poetic justice; it is not the result of the interference of an authorial *deus ex machina*.[4] Instead it is the result of a mistake within the tapestry of love as such: Hugh's death is an example of the limits imposed upon the life of the senses. Cyril's "guilt" regarding Hugh's death originates in the imperfection of his design. Cyril as character, as the figure "in the very center of Love's most explosive field," confuses self-sufficiency and self-indulgence and indirectly forces Hugh to locate himself at the edge of the tapestry of love. This is symbolized by the fact that Hugh has but one arm; whenever the four characters attempt to form a chain of sympathy by holding one another's hands, he can never be a link between them. Hugh's erotic deficiency creates a tension between the two male characters which eventually leads to the catastrophe that threatens to destroy Cyril along with Hugh: "Why, after more than eighteen years, does the soft medieval fabric of my tapestry now hang in shreds—here the head of a rose, there the amputated hoof of some infant goat? Is it possible that in purging her field of Hugh's sick innocence Love (impatient Love) purged me as well? Eliminated even her own faithful sex-singer from the joyous field? It is possible" (3). Cyril is the troubadour who serves a personified Fortuna who is omnipresent, but always ready to withdraw her favors. Cyril's tapestry is not his own; it is not even that of the author. The intrigue is not identical with the story and the story is not identical with the myth whose presence reaches beyond the limits of the text and informs the life of the author. "I was there always. I completed the picture," says Cyril without realizing that his constant presence, his constant performance, always implies absence as its precondition: Hugh's regression and ultimate death; Love's impatient rejection of Cyril's services; the end of the novel.

However, narration cannot exist except as constant presence. Hugh, although the representative of history and death and thus the destroyer of the harmony of Cyril's erotic world, cannot invalidate Cyril's role as narrator. Cyril hopes that through patience he may regain Love's favors. He hopes that his relationship with Catherine, who has suffered a breakdown after Hugh's death, will eventually be restored; that Fiona, who has left Illyria with Hugh and Catherine's children, will return; that the peasant girl whose photograph awakened the impulse that sent Hugh to his death will become his mistress. And his hopes are not unfounded. But his patience functions only as narrative patience. The segments of the novel can be considered as expressions of rhetorical strategies, as verbal images of the past, evoked to regain the confidence of Catherine, to whom they are addressed. As spoken words, they easily seem to fill the void created by Hugh's death and the simultaneous end of Cyril and Catherine's sexual relationship, and they seem to link past and present. But Cyril's implied and at times explicit pleading at the end of each narrative segment, "Remember?" (55, 187, 229), alerts the reader to the fact that the presence of the past is always ironic, that it always retains the mark of the past. Cyril is caught in his own rhetoric: he must recreate for Catherine their lost, former landscape of timelessness which is then supposed to cover any consciousness of the time that has intervened.[5] This is an impossible task, and Cyril could only execute it if he succeeded both in supplanting Catherine's feeling of guilt about Hugh's death with another innocence and in purging his narrative of his own "guilt" as well. He nevertheless tries to fulfill this task by proposing the paradoxical ideal of "sexless matrimony" (81) as a way of life for himself and Catherine and by disrupting the time sequence of the novel's events. But the ideal of sexless matrimony undermines Cyril's belief that innocence cannot be regained through the renunciation of sex, but only through renovation; and the deconstruction of the plot cannot create timelessness, but only a consciousness of the interdependence of past and present. Thus the price Cyril must pay for the role of narrator is too high: sexual impotence and narrative unreliability.

Only the author, by writing another text which constitutes a comment on *The Blood Oranges,* can regain the innocence that Cyril has irrevocably lost. Cyril had learned to interpret objects and events as subjective signs, and he had learned to use language to reobjectify these signs. But in the process, innocence was supplanted by consciousness, and consciousness implies remembrance. Memory, however, causes desire, and it causes the past to be supplemented by the future. Through memory, the values of absence, of those time categories that defy the present, gradually dissolve the values of presence. Innocence, it appears, only exists as a forgetting of time, but for Cyril innocence has become a phenomenon of the past, an unconscious mode of being, lost again and again through memory; while for the author, once he has marked the narrator as unreliable, innocence can become a conscious mode of being that asks to be regained again and again through a series of innovative, and at the same time renovative, texts. Textual innovation thus defines itself, not in opposition to renovation, but as another commentary on an archetype.

In *The Blood Oranges* the innocent imagination reveals its paradoxical nature as memory that does not exclude the erotics of forgetting. The author, by creating a series of fiction texts, can create an independent memory, stored in those texts, which permits him to practice simultaneous forgetfulness—a forgetfulness that implies the possibility of new beginnings. However, there is always the danger that memory stored will become death and no longer allow for further commentaries. For Hawkes, therefore, each new novel must be a "re-vision" of his earlier ones—beginning with his first novel, *The Cannibal*— without becoming too self-conscious a commentary. The resulting textual dilemma has induced many critics of Hawkes's work to accuse him of an increasing lack of innovativeness. Yet Hawkes must follow the inner logic of his fictional autobiography; he can only attempt to give voice to it.

In *Virginie: Her Two Lives,* paradox becomes the sole mode of being. Innocence and consciousness are established as opposite poles—only to become ultimately indistinguishable. As an epigraph for his novel, Hawkes uses a travestied quote from Samuel Beckett: "Birth was the death of her." Like many a postmodern fiction, *Virginie* is about the impossibility of storytelling, but here this impossibility results from, and in turn engenders, the impossibility of true womanhood. *Virginie* is about the loss of narrative innocence as defined through the loss of female innocence. Female innocence is an absolute value since it cannot become experience without losing its essence, while narrative innocence, through self-reflectiveness, can always be invoked as an ironic possibility, but never possessed without compromise. Thus the form of female innocence causes the uncompromising character of the female spirit which Hawkes claims he believes in, while the form of narrative innocence leads to either shame over its tentative loss or exultation at its subsequent recapture. Narrative innocence has the fluidity of time which may, however, lead to growth; female innocence can present an unalterable vantage point, yet as a result, it can only be destroyed.

The paradox of female plus narrative innocence is incorporated in the eleven-year-old heroine of the novel: Virginie. In each of her two lives, which take place in the eighteenth and twentieth centuries respectively, her identical psychic and physical innocence meets with the same fate: destruction by fire. As the novel consists of Virginie's journals, which are consumed by the same fire, she also represents narrative innocence that is lost and preserved at the same time, since there is still the novel. Virginie passes her first life as the companion of Seigneur, a member of the *ancien régime* who "creates" women as erotic artifacts and who can be understood as the image of the omniscient author of the eighteenth-century novel. In her second life, Virginie becomes the little sister of the taxi driver Bocage, who in 1945 likewise "creates" a brothel in Paris after his mother has suffered a stroke. Virginie and Bocage die during a fire begun by their mother while Bocage attempts to make love to his little sister. Bocage is the twentieth-century author who, after having lost his former narrative power, can no longer prevail over the vindictive female spirit as represented by the mother. Only Virginie, the as yet innocent female, would still yield to his embrace. Virginie, the incestuously desired Other, is the author's own text: "Thus I am only the child before the woman, the insubstantial voice of the page that burns."[6]

Virginie's virginity is the special twist of Hawkes's postmodern novel. Virginie is constantly exposed to the art of eroticism in her first and to the art of sexuality in her second life, yet the value of her innocence is only heightened by the contrast. Her journals—in keeping with Hawkes's unwavering conviction that pornography is, or should be, the highest form of art—constitute a genre that could be called the "pornographic sublime," a genre that strives to preserve the sanctum of the soul through a precarious balance of paradoxes. Virginie observes whatever happens around her with devout eyes; her journals thus render experience as innocence. The beauty of language, Hawkes seems to imply, cannot be defiled, since language does not partake in experience. Like language, Virginie, by remaining aloof, can come to express everything, since no personal experience will foreshorten her perspective or clutter her senses.

Virginie is the Virgin before the Immaculate Conception, the page before it is read, the text before interpretation—worthy of every form of regard, but incapable of receiving it into her mind or body. Like the text, she fascinates the beholder through her constant readiness, which nevertheless resists any "real" embrace. Like the text, Virginie is the unattainable Other.

The virginity of the text thus presents a problem for the author. What seems to have become *the* distinguishing mark of the postmodern text is that it strives to become as self-sufficient as female innocence, but self-sufficiency engenders the paradox of simultaneous presence and absence. As soon as the fiction text begins to lose its mediating function between the author and the reader and begins to become an independent object in the sense in which, for instance, William Gass would have it, it tends to become a barrier between author and reader—its very presence creating an absence of communication. *Virginie,* the text and the heroine, are conscious of this dilemma. They try to face it by effacing themselves. Virginie spends both her lives voluntarily serving everyone in her environment until she reaches the stage when her virginity becomes endangered. She then yields to the entreaties of the author to offer up her innocence, but she dies in the process, bringing her life as text to a close in order to insure the possibility of its interpretation.

Virginie ends her first life by throwing herself into the flames that already consume Seigneur. Seigneur dies at the stake, sacrificed by the very women he has raised to become incarnations of erotic art. He dies because he has enraged his beautiful pupils by denying himself to them sexually, by treating them as living objects of art. Like God, like the omniscient author, Seigneur was always present and absent at the same time. He is sacrificed in order to dissolve this existential paradox. But the death of God affects His creation just as the death of the omniscient author affects his characters, for the memory of him will perpetuate his paradoxical influence and make it indelible. Virginie, therefore, is giving up her role as character altogether, defining herself as the mirror image of the author. She will not survive his death, but will become his "autobiography." In other words: the death of the omniscient author confines him to the role of author within the limits of the text and postulates the text's self-sacrifice. Self-sufficiency as the ontological status of the postmodern text can only be understood as the condition for its self-dissolution. "Writing would never be man's writing, which is to say it would never be God's writing either," says Maurice Blanchot in "The Absence of the Book" ("L'Absence du livre"); "at most it would be the writing of the other, of dying itself."[7]

Fire, which consumes Virginie's journals and the two worlds they contain, is the dominant metaphor in Hawkes's *Virginie: Her Two Lives.* It represents the imagination as it purges the author's self in the struggle between the unconscious and the conscious. The nature of fire is paradoxical: as one of the four elements, it is an archetypal force; at the same time, fire is the most inconstant of the elements, the least reliable. In order to put it to use, man has to employ his wit, that is, consciousness. Prometheus, in presenting the fire of the gods to man, is usually seen as the saviour of mankind; however, his gift is always associated with culture, not with nature. And Loki, the old German demon of fire, whose cult was later identified with that of Prometheus, is an even more ambivalent figure. Although representative—as "Logi" ("Lohe")—of an element that can also be life-sustaining, he kills Baldur, the god of light. The Germans believed that the world would end in fire and thus Loki came to represent destruction and death. He is the herald of the "Götterdämmerung," the twilight of the gods; he is the negative force of civilization, of consciousness become destructive in its struggle to overcome the unconscious. Yet the repression of the unconscious entails its own revenge: life becomes a task and a responsibility.

Seigneur represents an historical period that still knew that all art was supposed to serve God as its great Origin. The omniscient author was but a secularized version of His omnipotence; he still tacitly presupposed a stable reality as was formerly guaranteed by divine law. Because of this hypocrisy, Seigneur's art, like the eighteenth-century novel, unwittingly created a tradition of guilt which had its source in the unacknowledged tension between God and man and which would finally result in man's decision to proclaim the death of God, not in order to gain an advantage over an absent God, but in order to find a way of suppressing his own inferiority complex. For Hawkes, therefore, the history of the novel is an exfoliation of repressed guilt that is displaced into metaphor. When Seigneur dies, his last words are a command: " 'Virginie!' " he shouts. " 'Destroy your innocence!' " (212). Her options in fulfilling this command are either to live and become a woman or to die and destroy, not her innocence, but her body which represents that innocence. Out of love for Seigneur, Virginie chooses the metaphorical solution to his demand. Living would have implied the will to independence, the negation of everything Seigneur had come to mean. Virginie sacrifices her life in order not to destroy meaning. Hence her reincarnation as text: life-in-death that results from death-in-life. Virginie's deed expiates Seigneur's guilt since she sacrifices her title to the same kind of experience he had denied his pupils; however, her journals, which carry the memory of this guilt, serve to prolong it. The reincarnated version of Virginie thus inherits the burden of Seigneur's guilt as well as its metaphoricality. Her presence forces the twentieth-century author, that is, the author of her second life, to become nothing but an ironic repetition of a former self.

In her second life, Virginie is less radically innocent than in her first, since female innocence and narrative innocence have become intertwined. The memory of her former death is both present and absent in Virginie's mind as a form of erotic consummation which requires, as well as forbids, repetition: "Consummation prompts prior passion. Thus I both know and do not know that in the most secret recess of my spirit my prior life exists" (18). The unconscious memory of her former commitment to Seigneur renders Virginie incapable of expiating the guilt of Bocage, which is the guilt of civilization. Her female innocence thus only serves to set off the depravity of her second environment: Bocage's brothel becomes a degraded version of Seigneur's *école des femmes*. On the other hand, Virginie's narrative innocence draws her closer to Bocage in the role of author; together they achieve the consummation that was denied the omniscient author and his text. But this closeness paradoxically only serves to underline their ultimate difference: the biological difference between male and female, and the ontological difference between author and text: "Thus he is heaviness itself while I am weightless; thus his great body gives solidity to the sounds of his passion, while my own small breaths of sweetness are mine alone and toneless" (9).

Seigneur's characters were as incapable of receiving his gifts as they were of becoming independent. They could not overcome the feeling of humiliation resulting from the fact that their erotic curriculum was not a matter of their own free choice. Their historically necessary reaction was revolt. In 1945, Bocage no longer attempts to educate the women he gathers into his brothel; but still their erotic experiences are not a result of free choice, but of random sexual encounters. Thus, they cannot even rebel, since they don't know what to rebel against; they can only suffer. The difference between a text in which the character can still rebel against his or her author's intention by developing, in the course of a changing historical context, an independent, even opposing intentionality, and a postmodern text, in which the character becomes the language of the text itself, is that the latter cannot develop a distinctive voice that is not the author's. This in turn implies that none of his own texts will help the author to overcome his rising sense of personal shame over his historical guilt, unless he manages to regain his narrative innocence again and again through an ever more conscious effort.

The intertextuality of Hawkes's novels, that is, the way they comment on one another, mirrors such a development between unconscious guilt and conscious innocence, and thus parallels the development of the novel between the eighteenth and the twentieth centuries as it is imaginatively rendered in *Virginie*. At the beginning of Hawkes's fictional autobiography stand two unselfconscious novels, *The Cannibal* and *The Beetle Leg*, which reveal his ability to eroticize poetic language in order to woo, and as a tribute to, the power of the imagination. With *The Lime Twig* the author reached the apex of his narrative omniscience which, turning into self-consciousness, called for the first-person narrator of his next novel, *Second Skin*. But in striving to write himself into the text, the author found that he attempted to deal with a narrative tradition of repressed guilt which, as soon as it was raised to the level of his own consciousness, endangered his narrative innocence. Therefore, Hawkes's first-person narrators became more and more unreliable, throughout the triad of *The Blood Oranges, Death, Sleep & The Traveler,* and *Travesty.* Thus the author could always hope to recuperate from his identification with his narrators, who had developed into artist-narrators. Still it became increasingly difficult for him to regain his narrative innocence since the rising degree of the narrator's unreliability could no longer veil the unfolding of an artistic consciousness within the text. After *Travesty,* Hawkes believed that he had exhausted his imaginative resources. But in *The Passion Artist* he began to face his dilemma by turning the struggle between the protagonist's unconscious and his consciousness into the struggle of an everyman. And in *Virginie: Her Two Lives* the paradoxical fusion of guilt and innocence has found its expression in an allegory that generalizes even more the necessity of fictional autobiography. Hawkes's next novel, whose working title is *Adventures in the Alaskan Skin Trade,* may demonstrate how his personal life has become a mirror for the life of the novel.

Notes

1. Gérard Genette, *Palimpsestes: La littérature au second degré* (Paris: Editions du Seuil, 1982).

2. Cf. "John Hawkes and Albert Guerard in Dialogue," in *A John Hawkes Symposium: Design and Debris,* eds. Anthony C. Santore and Michael Pocalyko, *Insights-I: Working Papers in Contemporary Criticism* (New York: New Directions, 1977), p. 23.

3. John Hawkes, *The Blood Oranges* (New York: New Directions, 1971), p. 269. All further references will be in parentheses.

4. John Hawkes's own attitude towards Hugh's (his alter ego's?) death is ambivalent: "I meant the death of Hugh in a sense to trick the reader into thinking of it as a moral judgment on the multiple relationships—but to me it is not. Hugh's death is thoroughly absurd" (John Kuehl, *John Hawkes and the Craft of Conflict* [New Brunswick: Rutgers University Press, 1975], p. 169). Steven Abrams regards the "difficulty of coming upon Hawkes's solution without his help" as reason for "a serious criticism of the novel" (Steven Abrams, "*The Blood Oranges* as a Visionary Fiction," *The Journal of Narrative Technique,* 8 [1978], 108).

5. Cf. Frederick Busch, *Hawkes: A Guide to His Fictions* (Syracuse: Syracuse University Press, 1973), p. 147.

6. John Hawkes, *Virginie: Her Two Lives* (New York: Harper & Row, 1982), p. 11. All further references will be in parentheses.

7. Maurice Blanchot, *The Gaze of Orpheus and Other Literary Essays,* trans. Lydia Davis, ed. P. Adams Sitney, introduction, Geoffrey Hartman (Barrytown, NY: Station Hill, 1981), p. 151.

The Cannibal to The Passion Artist: Hawkes' Journey toward the Depths of the Unconscious

PAUL J. EMMETT

In 1948 with the publication of John Hawkes' second novel *The Cannibal*, his most important critic Albert Guerard stated that this novel was less surrealistic than Hawkes' first novel *Charivari* and predicted that Hawkes would continue to move toward realism. Guerard stressed that this movement toward realism was essential to Hawkes' progress as a writer, which "most obviously depends on how far he consents to impose some page-by-page and chapter-by-chapter consecutive understanding on his astonishing creative energy." In 1962 after Hawkes had produced *The Beetle Leg*, "The Goose on the Grave," "The Owl," and *The Lime Twig*, Guerard claimed that "The predicted movement toward realism has occurred, but chiefly in the sense that the later novels are much more orderly and more even in pace, and distinctly less difficult to read." In 1977, after *Second Skin*, *The Blood Oranges*, *Death, Sleep and the Traveler*, and *Travesty*, Guerard suggested that Hawkes had continued his progression toward realism, moving away from unconscious understanding toward "a more conscious and a more suave psychology and art." But now Hawkes has produced *The Passion Artist*, and Guerard sees this novel as a movement back to Hawkes' early work, rather than a logical progression from his most recent novels. ". . . the new novel [*The Passion Artist*] has little of [*Blood Oranges'*; *Death, Sleep and the Traveler's*; and *Travesty's*] sinuous, suave playful sophistication . . . It represents rather . . . a powerful return, after thirty years, to the bleak devastated fictive world and the psychic cripplings of *The Cannibal*."[1] Guerard's assertion that Hawkes has returned to the unrealistic world of *The Cannibal*—a novel Hawkes himself considers "a hallucinatory vision"[2]—emphasizes what Guerard leaves unsaid in his review of *The Passion Artist*. He is disappointed with Hawkes' movement away from realism. To Guerard *The Passion Artist* is not as "suave" as Hawkes' recent novels because it represents Hawkes' "astonishing creative energy" more than the "page-by-page consecutive understanding" of realism. Hence, even Guerard's plaudits—like "powerful" above—are severely qualified. "*The Passion Artist* is, whatever its deficiencies, a

Reprinted with permission from the *Chicago Review* 32, no. 1 (Summer 1980):135–52. © *Chicago Review* 1980.

serious work of art."[3] Guerard's reaction is representative of recent Hawkes criticism: Hawkes is becoming known as the creator of nightmare visions, which are both intense and chaotic.

But Hawkes is not a chaotic visionary, and *The Passion Artist* is nothing less than Hawkes' most challenging and most rewarding novel. To see this we must take a closer look at the "realism" of Hawkes' fiction, the progressions Guerard has discovered in the Hawkes' canon, and *The Passion Artist* itself. Indeed, *The Passion Artist* will help us to see that Hawkes' career has not been a direct progression toward realism, and we will find that we cannot fully appreciate this work until we realize that it is not a return to the fictive world of *The Cannibal.* The subject matter of the two novels is similar, but this should not be surprising since Hawkes is, as he himself notes, an obsessive artist[4]; hence, what does not change throughout his work is his subject matter. Hawkes maintains that: "[significant literature dramatizes] elemental fears and desires, which are constants in the inner lives of men. Fear of the unknown, fear of sexual destruction at the hands of the father, fear of annihilation at the hands of absolute authority, infantile desire for the security and sublimity of the mother's love—these components of the familiar Oedipal situation as defined by Freud are to be found in significant literature through the ages."[5]

And over the past thirty years Hawkes has repeatedly stressed that the subject matter of his own fiction is the inner lives of men—the unconscious fears and desires of mankind. Since each of Hawkes' fictions deals with elements from what he calls "the psychic cesspool,"[6] it has been suggested—all too frequently—that Hawkes is more the hallucinatory visionary than the controlled artist, more the surrealist than the realist. But Hawkes insists that he is not a surrealist and while he tends to agree with Guerard's theory concerning his movement toward realism, Hawkes is quick to note that "it's only a surface realism."[7] Hawkes uses the term "surface realism" to suggest that his work has both a surface coherency that is not found in surrealism, as well as depth of meaning that is not found in realism. Indeed, "surface realism" is just one of Hawkes' frequent references to the different levels of his fictions, and these references suggest what a careful reading of these fictions confirms: all of Hawkes' works have both a surface reality *and* an underlying exploration of the psychic cesspool. Like dreams, Hawkes' fictions have both a manifest content and a latent content; like dreams, the manifest content is a distortion of the latent content. And the techniques that Hawkes uses to achieve this distortion are, in fact, the very ones that Freud refers to as "techniques of dream distortion": condensation, displacement, overdetermination, juxtaposition, verbal ambiguity, symbolism, complex patterns and imagery, contradiction, fragmentation, bisexuality, merging of characters, allusion . . . Hawkes' "surface realism" is, in fact, the tenuous "realism" of well-constructed dreams. Hawkes asserts that "two constructions—dream, nightmare—are the core of my own writing,"[8] and this statement is true for all of Hawkes' writing: each of his own dream-like constructions has a surface reality that is a distorted form of materials from the psychic cesspool.

In all of Hawkes' fiction manifest content—surface realism—is the distorted form of latent content—psychic depths—but Hawkes' progress as a writer stems from his movement toward more conscious use of distortion. Consider some of Hawkes' own comments on his craft.

> As a writer I'm committed to innovation in the novel, and obviously I'm committed to nightmare, violence, meaningful distortion . . .

> My own imagination is a kind of hall of "whippers" in which the materials of the unconscious are beaten, transformed into fictional landscape itself.

> You can live and create only when you manage to control, to keep at a distance the terrors that exist within the human being. All this has to do with the psychic cesspool. I don't think the task is to deny it, but to expose it.

> I write out of a series of pictures that literally and actually do come to mind, but I've never seen them before. It is perfectly true that I don't know what they mean, but I feel and know that they have meaning. *The Cannibal* is probably the clearest example of this kind of absolute coherence of vision of anything I have written, when all the photographs do add together or come right out of the same black pit.[9]

The recurring concern here is distortion—*The Cannibal* is a series of pictures that came from Hawkes' unconscious, distorted to the point that at times he himself doesn't know what they mean. The distortion, spontaneous and unconscious, is never penetrated by Hawkes. But from *The Cannibal* Hawkes has moved from unconscious distortion to *conscious* distortion, which is "meaningful distortion": he has used his creative imagination to transform these visions from the unconscious into fictional landscape. He has thought about, shaped, and rewritten unconscious terrors to control and distance them by providing them with a surface realism. And he has done so by *consciously* employing the techniques of dream distortion to transform latent content into manifest content. So, as Hawkes moves on from *Charivari* and *The Cannibal*, his fictions become more ordered, more coherent, more plotted and, hence, as Guerard suggests, distinctly less difficult to read. But it must be stressed that contrary to popular opinion, Hawkes' well-told stories like *The Lime Twig*, *Second Skin*, and *The Blood Oranges* are not less difficult to understand. Since story, plot, coherency, order, surface realism are in one sense only manifest veils for latent content, the well-constructed novel is problematic in the same sense that Freud finds the well-constructed dream to be problematic. "From the point of view of analysis, however, a dream that resembles a disordered heap of disconnected fragments is just as valuable as one that has been beautifully polished and provided with a surface. In the former case, indeed, we are saved the trouble of demolishing what has been superimposed upon the dream content."[10] From the point of view of literary analysis, Hawkes' "disconnected" earlier works are *not* as "valuable" as his later, well-polished novels; these later works, consciously and maximally distorted, are more interesting, more artistic, and, as this passage suggests, more difficult to deal with.

Indeed, the fragmentation and lack of order in *Charivari* imply that there must be more going on than meets the eye, whereas the fully polished surface realism of *The Lime Twig* tempts the reader to linger on the surface. Consider one passage from each work. *Charivari* begins with two paragraphs of narration and then shifts to dream dialogue.

EXPOSITOR: What time is it, Henry?

HENRY: Four o'clock.

EXPOSITOR: What should you be doing?

HENRY: I should be counting my gold.

EXPOSITOR: Nonsense. You should be out cleaning the stables. Come on; we'll take you to clean the stables.

HENRY: Must I do it with my hands?

EXPOSITOR: Certainly. What do you see lying over there in the hay?

HENRY: A woman.

EXPOSITOR: What is she doing?

HENRY: Making love to the stable boy while I do his work.[11]

In *The Lime Twig* William Hencher describes his nighttime visits to the lavatory. "Sometimes I wake in the night, very late in the still night, and go sit in the lavatory and run the water and smoke half a thin cigar until there is nothing to feel, nothing to hear except Margaret turning over. . . ."[12] Once we note that Margaret is in bed with her husband Michael, who is at least twenty years younger than Hencher, we can see that these passages deal with similar latent content: an older man who associates sex and excrement and who is left with masturbation, longings to be clean, and feelings of inadequacy because the younger "man" has the girl and the sexuality he himself craves. But in *Charivari* the suddenness of the dialogue shocks us to attention; the abrupt juxtaposition of gold, filth and sex enhances the Freudian association of gold and excrement and forces us to associate these three things in our heads; the illogic of "Must I do it with my hands?" helps us see the sexual implications of the phrasing. In *The Lime Twig,* however, it is harder to discover latent content. First of all, this passage is just one in a long series of descriptions of Hencher's life; hence, the reader might well read right over it. And even when the reader does pay close attention, he must penetrate Hencher's distortions: he must penetrate the surface coherency to find the displacement from phallus to cigar, the inadequacy implicit in "thin" and the incompletion implicit in "half"; he must realize the symbolism of water and discover the subtleties in "nothing to feel, nothing to hear except Margaret turning over."

It is important that these are Hencher's unconscious distortions, not Hawkes'. Hencher's narration in *The Lime Twig* is the crucial turning point in Hawkes' movement toward realism because as Hawkes notes, Hencher is both his first "individualized character" and the source of the first-person narration of his next four novels.[13] Prior to *The Lime Twig*, Hawkes' characters might well be considered as just parts of his nightmare landscape—two-dimensional displacements in Hawkes' own visions from the unconscious. But with Hencher come "realistic" characters, characters individualized from Hawkes himself, with their own unconscious distortions. Also, the use of first-person narration in *The Lime Twig* allows Hawkes to distance himself from his own hallucinatory visions, and the rough drafts of this pivotal novel show exactly how Hawkes achieves this distance. The first of the four drafts, which were written over a period of four years, is fragmented and frequently chaotic: much like *The Cannibal,* it is a series of primal visions right out of the black pit. But the revisions show Hawkes penetrating his distortions and transforming his visions into Hencher's unconscious obsessions by creating a world—his surface realism—which is Hencher's own distorted form of his obsessions. The latent content of the final draft is the same as the latent content of the first draft, but the manifest contents are radically different because Hawkes has consciously constructed Hencher's unconscious distortions. Hencher tells his own story and by the final version of *The Lime Twig,* it is nearly polished surface realism because Hencher is not aware that his story of his own "surface" conscious existence is really the projection of his own inner unconscious existence.

Still, even the final version of Hencher's narration is only *nearly* polished realism because for brief instants Hencher has insights into his unconscious and then his distortions fade and surface reality gives way to inner compulsion. At one point, for example, he intuits that his obsessions are concerned with being a pilot, so he walks outside "flinging an end of [his] shawl aside flier fashion,"[14] and then magically, prophetically, unrealistically, a huge bomber with no crew floats down to him. However, this scene is not typical of *The Lime Twig* since for the most part the characters cannot penetrate into their unconscious; hence, their distortions remain effective and latent content cannot overtly intrude upon manifest content. But as Hawkes moves from *The Lime Twig* to *Second Skin* to *The Blood Oranges* to *Death, Sleep and the Traveler* and to *Travesty,* the narrators become more aware of the realm of the unconscious. Indeed, Hawkes has noted that each narrator is "the source" of each succeeding narrator, and upon the publication of *Travesty,* he noted that the narrator of this novel goes further into the unconscious by doing consciously what the narrator of *Death, Sleep and the Traveler* did unconsciously.[15] These two comments suggest an important progression found in Hawkes' later novels: from Hencher to Skipper, to Cyril, to Allert, to the nameless narrator of *Travesty,* each successive narrator moves further into the unconscious; each successive narrator is, in one sense, the *same* person with progressively more self-knowledge. Hencher and Skipper, for example, have the same obsessions, but Skipper is conscious of obsessions that remained in Hencher's unconscious. And as we watch each successive narrator learn more about his own unconscious, we ourselves learn more about the unconscious of mankind.

Once we see that Hawkes' narrators move further into the unconscious, we can begin to see why some of Hawkes' latent concerns become more evident and why Hawkes' movement toward surface realism is not a direct progression. Let us consider each of these separately. Guerard suggests that certain displacements and condensations are no longer present in *Travesty,* that finally in this novel Hawkes can directly refer to the phallus as a "great bird" and talk directly about the tensions of the Oedipal triangle.[16] And, of course, what allows Hawkes to be more direct is the increasing self-knowledge of his narrators. Both Freud and Hawkes are aware of the unconscious association of bird and phallus, but in *The Lime Twig* Hencher was not far enough into his own unconscious to realize this association, so when he talks of birds, his displacements still transform latent content into surface realism. "I hold my *head* awhile and then I rub my thighs until the sleep goes out of them and the *blood* returns. In my own dark room I hear a *little* bird trying to sing . . ."[17] (my italics). Even Allert (in *Death, Sleep and the Traveler,* the novel just before *Travesty*) does not understand the phallic implications of birds, just as he does not understand his cravings for "Peter"; hence, he cannot tell us why the only time he remembers himself alone with Peter is when the two go duck hunting. But the narrator of *Travesty* has moved beyond Hencher and Allert, so when he is aroused by Monique, he can say, "my great bird was soaring in flight," and after Monique beats him into submission, he can say, "my great bird was dead." However, one wonders if he fully understands the transcendent, spiritual associations of the bird and the destructive, earthbound, maternal associations of the cat since in this same scene he twice refers to Monique as "a cat in a sack"[18] without realizing the symbolism, projection, and verbal ambiguities involved. And the fact that he, the potential bird, is the one trapped in the "sack" *by* the cat, suggests an important issue that Guerard fails to emphasize. The unconscious is unlimited; hence, a position from which certain unconscious elements become undistorted is the same position from which new unconscious elements come into view in their initial, more distorted form. This is what allows Hawkes to introduce new latent material into each novel; this is what allows each successive novel to probe deeper into the unconscious of mankind. It is not that all latent content becomes manifest in *Travesty* (or any other Hawkes novel), it is just that certain contents like Oedipal tensions which had been latent in earlier novels become manifest, at the same time that deeper material is being introduced into the latent level of this novel. Consider a passage from *Travesty* which does introduce distorted latent content. "Silence. The bird in flight. Silence falling between driver and passenger [Henri] who find themselves deadlocked on a lonely road,

deadlocked in their purposes, deadlocked between love and hatred. . . ."[19]
Certainly, the narrator is not aware of his own complex unconscious associations
between Monique and Henri, stressed here by the reappearance of "the bird in
flight," and, most certainly, he does not realize the transcendent, phallic
communion possible here if silence could become bird and bird could become
phallus.

Still, as we return to a consideration of Hawkes' "realism," even this brief
passage from *Travesty* should suggest that as Hawkes moves further into the
head, he moves further away from surface realism. As his first-person narrators
move into the unconscious, the first distortions to give way are the basic
ones—the extreme distortions which produced surface realism. Hence, as
Hawkes moves from *The Lime Twig* to *Second Skin* to *The Blood Oranges* to *Death,
Sleep and the Traveler* to *Travesty,* even the numbers of "individualized,"
realistic characters diminish. But as Hawkes moves from *The Lime Twig,* his
fictions become less realistic in another sense because the increasing awareness of
Hawkes' narrators allows more and more latent content to become manifest
content. Since later narrators can openly discuss obsessions that earlier narrators
were not conscious of, frequently even the manifest content in Hawkes' later
fictions concerns "unrealistic" material from the psychic cesspool. As old latent
content becomes new manifest content, however, we can see that it itself is the
distorted form of new latent content. Classical Oedipal concerns are, as Guerard
suggests, readily apparent in *Travesty,* but a close analysis of this novel shows
that these manifest concerns are in part a screen for both the narrator's latent
hatred of his wife and his own latent, incestuous love for his dead son."[20]

The Lime Twig, then, is the furthest Hawkes moves toward realism:
Hencher believes that he is concerned solely with surface reality, and he is
unaware that his surface reality is a distorted projection of his internal reality.
But by the time we come to Konrad Vost, the main character of *The Passion
Artist,* we have gradually come nearly a full circle because Vost realizes that "the
inner landscape [had] become externalized."[21] Indeed, with Konrad Vost,
Hawkes has once again moved his main character further into the unconscious.
Unlike the narrator of *Travesty,* Vost is aware of the implications of both the
bird *and* the cat. "The woman lying behind him [a projection of his mother
behind him in the past and behind his existence], reached over his hip and,
catching a handful of the trousers bunched between his legs, roughly shook him
like a cat with a bird."[22] This movement further into the unconscious is not
unexpected, but Hawkes' decision to use the third-person narration in *The
Passion Artist* might well seem surprising, surprising that is, until we realize
how the third-person narration in *The Passion Artist* differs from the more
conventional third-person narration of the earlier novels. Konrad Vost does not
directly tell his own story, but the above passage is typical since frequently the
ostensible third-person narration represents Vost's perspective. Indeed, the
point of view is always Konrad Vost's, but at times it is his conscious
perspective and at other times it is his unconscious perspective. With *The*

Passion Artist Hawkes has created a third-person narration which itself moves in and out of Vost's unconscious, so that in certain passages we are confronted with Vost's own distortions, while in other passages we are presented with his unconscious wishes in undistorted form.

> What sense could he make of the fact that he and Spapa, whom he had always disdained, no longer avoided each other's eyes and, without meaning to do so, achieved a curious unison in their paired assault. . . . (pp. 56–57)

> After all, the closing of the darkest gate is like a burst of light, and Konrad Vost found himself exactly where he had always wished to be without knowing it. . . . (p. 120)

In the second passage we are told what Vost is not consciously aware of: namely, that he has always longed to be in La Violaine—the prison for women, where his mother is an inmate. However, in the first passage we must discover what Vost is not conscious of: we must penetrate the distortion in "Spapa" to make sense of this latent union with one of the Papas.

Thus, we see that by making his main character more conscious of the inner self and by creating a narrative form that can present what even Vost himself is not conscious of, Hawkes takes us far into the unconscious. It is not surprising that parts of *The Passion Artist* would be compared to the hallucinatory visions of *The Cannibal* since Hawkes' movement inward has taken him a long way from surface realism. But it is important to stress that in *The Passion Artist* it is Vost's inner landscape that is externalized, not Hawkes'. Hawkes is now the controlled artist creating and exploring the inner depths of Konrad Vost. Hawkes has, for example, moved away from the realistic, "individualized" characters of *The Lime Twig, Second Skin,* and *The Blood Oranges,* but the characters of *The Passion Artist* are projections of Vost's unconscious, not Hawkes'.

> . . . now [Vost's] contradictory selves were more deeply opposed yet closer to reconciliation than ever. . . . (p. 153)

> For Konrad Vost, he told himself, the world was now in a constant state of metamorphosis, duplication, multiplication; figures deserving existence only within the limits of the dream now sprang alive; the object of least significance was inspired with its secret animation. . . . (pp. 90–91)

These passages suggest another important innovation in *The Passion Artist*: by moving Vost deeper into the unconscious and by creating his unique, fluctuating third-person narration, Hawkes is able to talk directly about the techniques of dream distortion. These passages introduce projection, bisexuality, the merging of characters, and the manifest de-emphasizing of crucial latent content; other passages direct our attention to suppression—

[Vost stood] creating a dream, escaping a dream, clinging as best he could to incomprehension (p. 34);

screen fantasies—

He awoke to the knowledge of a constellation of thoughts and perceptions so arranged in his mind as to conceal the most important fact of all (p. 68);

and over-determination—

Memory was an infinitely expanding structure of events recollected from life, events that had been imagined, imaginary events that had been recollected, dreams that had been recollected, recomposed, dreamt once again, remembered. Yes, he told himself, the storehouse of memory was like a railway terminal for trains of unlimited destination. (p. 22)

And as the manifest content deals with Freud's techniques of dream distortion—the very techniques used to create this manifest content—we become more aware of the importance of Freud to an understanding of Hawkes' fiction. Guerard frequently discusses Hawkes' work in Freudian terms,[23] and Hawkes himself encourages Freudian criticism of his work both through explicit references to Freud in his discussions of literature and implicit references to Freud in his fictions. In *The Passion Artist,* for example, we find: "[Vost] was in the hands of darkness . . . the external darkness of that interior world into which no light can shine and whose nomenclature can be found only in the formulations of the psychological function" (p. 58).

Freud's theories of the unconscious do not just show us how latent content is distorted into manifest content, but also since they provide the "nomenclature" we need to discuss Vost's inner darkness, they help us to explore the latent content of *The Passion Artist.* And this help is essential since the latent content of *The Passion Artist* is quite complex, despite the fact that Hawkes has moved us further into the unconscious. Even though we are told, for example, that Vost has always longed to be in La Violaine, we are never told why this is so. Indeed, the "whys" in *The Passion Artist* are quite challenging. Vost's unconscious motivations for his journey from the prison of the family to his mother imprisoned in La Violaine entail a complicated fusion of Oedipal longings, inverted Oedipal longings, castration fears, and homosexuality, which cannot be thoroughly understood without Freud's theory.

Consider an example which demonstrates not only the complexities of Vost's motivation and Hawkes' use of Freud, but also the depths of psychic material present in *The Passion Artist.* By connecting the patterns associated with Vost's silver hand, his silver twig, and the silver trumpet of his childhood, Guerard proves both that "masturbation was a source of anxiety and guilt" in Vost's childhood (p. 29) and that this fact is presented through the most transparent displacement. And, indeed, Guerard is correct, but awareness of Vost's childhood guilt only leads us to deeper issues. Why, for example, is Vost still obsessed with past guilt? But we can't understand the effect this guilt has on Vost's present life until we realize that Freud associated masturbation, bed-wetting, the punitive threats of the loss of the penis and the loss of a hand, and the resultant guilt and shame. Only then can we understand lines like: "in the midst of his shock and pleasure [during fellatio] he was now refusing what he knew was inevitable inside himself, fighting the greedy mouth as the child fights his bladder in the night" (p. 40). Only then can we see why for half the novel Vost believes he has lost his right hand. Only then can we see why Vost still fights against the "shameful wetness" of his phallus that "he had always attempted to disown" (p. 159). As we understand Hawkes's utilization of Freudian theory, we begin to understand that childhood guilt is both the screen for, and the source of, adult guilt and that Vost's adult life is merely a distorted reenactment of his childhood obsessions.

When Vost, for example, confronts a released prisoner from La Violaine —the mother-figure who has escaped from the prison of his own unconscious —he is obsessed with the woman's hat. "She was wearing a small red brimless hat perched on the top of her head. It was the hat, rather than the woman herself, that held his attention . . . he detested the small bright red hat and even more the fact that it was perched on top of the woman's head at a crooked angle" (p. 24). We must use both Freud's theories and Vost's past to explain this surprising obsession. To begin with, Freud suggests that hats are phallic[24] and, of course, this suggestion is emphasized here by the color and shape of the hat and, since birds are phallic, by the fact that it is "perched" on the woman's head. Now, the phallic connotation of hats helps us to see why Vost himself is "bareheaded" (p. 29) during this confrontation and why the *"revolting* inmates" of La Violaine wear the guard's kepis *"cocked* on their heads" (p. 52, respectively, my italics). However, even when we penetrate the distortion achieved here through symbols and verbal ambiguities, we are once again left with "whys": "Why do the women have the phallus?" "Why doesn't Vost?" "Why is Vost both attracted to and repulsed by the mother's phallus?" To understand Vost's unconscious motivations, we, like Vost himself, must turn to his past and to the prison of the family.

Vost pictures both his mother Eva Laubenstein and his "anti-mother" (p. 52) Anna Kossowski as domineering, aggressive, and masculine. Indeed, Eva, often called "the woman of the house" (p. 118), makes a "human pyre" (p. 119) of Vost's father who is never called "the man of the house"; Anna is "lightly bearded, heavy, passionate, with the thick large hands and feet of a man" (p. 134). At the most transparent level, Vost imagines such imposing women in order to protect himself from his own incestuous desires. These women are so intimidating that Vost cannot even look at them, let alone think of possessing them. "He had hardly dared look at [Eva] as a child, yet even now he loved the sight of her, though he averted his eyes" (p. 127). Yet, the love/fear duality is still there, so Vost must make Eva so aggressive that she is imprisoned and, hence, inaccessible; he must make Anna so masculine that he is forced to displace his desires onto "Anna Kossowski the horse"—itself a priapic animal.

Vost's phallic mothers are, then, the suppressive distortions of his own incestuous longings, but as Vost plunges into the unconscious, he gets beyond transparent suppressions; Eva escapes her cell in La Violaine (the rape/groin) and Anna exposes Konrad Vost to the vagina he has attempted to deny. Anna Kossowski, in fact, forces Konrad's head toward her own groin and thrusts the truth upon him. "*He opened his eyes:* he was overwhelmed with disappointment at the sight of the thick hair; then he was sickened as, behind the hair, he saw not at all what he had seen on the horse [the horse's anus] but instead the briefest glimpse of what to him was a small face beaten unrecognizable by the blows of a cruel fist. In terror he saw that from this hidden and ruined face between Anna Kossowski's legs there were streaming two long single files of black ants" (p. 151, my italics). As Konrad is forced to admit that women are vaginal, the intensity of his reaction implies that the concept of the phallic mother is a screen for more than his incestuous desires. And, indeed, Freud suggests that the phallic mother represents both dread of mother-incest and horror of the female genitals[25]; the mother's genitals are, of course, horrible to a boy because they imply that he too might lose his penis. If the mother is vaginal and not phallic, castration is a real possibility. Now, Vost sees the clitoris as "the nostril of a dead bird" (p. 67) and the notion that the vagina itself is the dead, castrated phallus is enforced in the above passage by the violence of the beating, the resultant loss of identity, Vost's extreme terror, the suggestion of blood "streaming" down the thighs, and the fact that "ant" and "circumcise" come from the same root in Hebrew.[26]

The threat of castration here is, in fact, so intense that Konrad Vost screams, crawls away from his anti-mother, showers himself with water and comes back "unable to look" (p. 152); he regresses by "crawling" back to the infantile screen of the phallic mother and by refusing to face up to the vagina and the possibility of castration. So, Vost is left with aggressive, masculine women and we're left trying to understand *why* Vost is so intimidated by the threat of castration. The fact that he crawls away to wash himself suggests Vost's guilt and his fear of retribution for his incestuous, masturbatory fantasies, which he considers dirty. However, the fact that after washing he comes right back to Anna Kossowski implies that the entire incest/threat/ guilt/purgation cycle is itself a screen for a deeper level of Vost's unconscious.

Indeed, throughout the novel Vost moves alternately from and toward castration; his imagined artificial hand itself is to him "emblematic of terrible loss, mysterious gain" (p. 71). And these dualities suggest that Vost's exaggerated dread of castration is, in fact, a distortion—the Freudian dream distortion of affect reversal. In the depths of his unconscious, Vost longs for castration. This is why he does not leave Anna Kossowski until he has "felt

[her] great hands crushing his hipbones" (p. 174). And this is why the phallic women Vost creates as a denial of castration themselves become the castrators. Vost ultimately craves the castration he superficially attempts to deny because he wants to play the female to the mother's male. Anna's "great hands" are "masculine"; the female who "cuts off" Vost's hand is the "tall and handsome woman of the transfiguring hatchet . . . [with a] butcher's apron . . . a choirboy's voice . . . [and] thighs . . . as large as a man's" (pp. 121, 127, 179 and 178 respectively). And this emphasizes the fact that Vost wants to be gloriously transformed ("transfigured") into a female so that he can be violated by the masculine, castrating female. He goes to La Violaine both to find the female locked in his unconscious and to be violated; in La Violaine he recognizes himself as "an imposter in the black pants of manhood" (p. 154) and he finds "the rich light of expiation. The light of dead birds" (p. 125). Castration, the dead bird, is the ultimate expiation; it takes one beyond the "black" phallic guilt of manhood to the "light" vaginal innocence of femininity. Vost believes that the passive victim cannot be guilty, and this is why he wants to be the violated rather than the violator. This is why he is completely passive during his sexual encounters with the woman of the transfiguring hatchet; this is why he plays the passive—and even masochistic—role throughout all of his sexual encounters.

Once we see that Vost longs to be the castrated female, we can understand not just Vost's passivity and masochism, but we can also understand his recurring emphasis on anality. When, for example, the child prostitute puts her phallic finger into his rectum (pp. 39–40), Vost becomes the female because for Vost the anus is the distorted representation of the vagina. Indeed, early in the novel as he projects his inner landscape onto a "toothless" dog with "nearly deformed short legs," we see that Vost equates the castrated phallus with the anus. "Something had misfired in the docking of the tail, which, curled briefly above the rump, was naked at the tip and revealed there a spot of wet pinkness very like the tiny anus that was always exposed. The customer most preferred by this shocking creature was the meticulous Konrad Vost" (p. 7). The docked tail is the castrated phallus and it is very like the tiny anus. And once we realize that water is a female symbol and pink signifies the birth of a girl, we can see that both are a "spot of wet pinkness" because both offer the anally "meticulous" Vost a chance to give birth to the female within. But pink also has ominous implications here because we have noted that for Vost the release of the female self is the way to innocence; to see why the white of innocence is sullied here by the red of passion, we must realize that Vost associates pink with the flesh of the father. When Vost recalls the stove in his childhood home, he sees it as "decorated with little flowers . . . [and] in the shape of a great white egg" when it is cold, but when he pictures it hot, it becomes "the dangerous pink color of scalded flesh" (p. 44, respectively). The implicit transformation from cold, white mother—egg-like and flowered—to the scalded pink father who was burned alive suggests the ultimate screen in Vost's unconscious projections.

The phallic mother is a screen for the father; the innocence of Vost's passive relationships with masculine women is a screen for the guilt of the one relationship Vost longs for—the homosexual union with the father. Vost associates the pinkness of his own castration and anality with the father because he wants to be the female that the father violates. Indeed, the "tip" of the father's "living cigar" is "pink" (p. 81), just like the "tip" of the dog's docked tail is pink, because in the depths of his unconscious Vost craves a union of father's "cigar" and his own docked tail.

Once again, Freud's theories are supportive since they suggest that males who picture themselves in a masochistic relationship to the mother, who themselves play the female role in their conscious fantasies and who endow their women with masculine attributes are trying to escape their homosexual feelings for the father.[27] Freud also notes that the desire for intercourse with the father lies in the deepest parts of the unconscious; this fact is enforced with respect to Konrad Vost through Hawkes' unique narrative form. "Laubenstein was his mother's maiden name. To allow it to consciousness was an ordeal he seldom undertook, assigning it, and the reasons she preferred that name to his own, to that interior place where he concealed the images of the man who had fathered him . . ." (p. 21). Konrad Vost the Son's tragedy is that he is unable to plunge far enough into his unconscious to reach Konrad Vost the Father. This passage, then, becomes a metaphor for the novel. Since the father is deeper in his unconscious than the mother, he should pass through the feminine realms to reach the masculine realms, but he is unable to do so. Vost realizes that "the journey . . . [takes] him . . . from woman to woman" (p. 44), but he never realizes that a man is at the end of the journey. So, at the end of the novel Vost remains what he was at the start—"a man who spent his life among women" (p. 1). And although Vost does see through many of the distortions associated with the feminine realms and, hence, is finally able to leave La Violaine, he never understands that the feminine realms themselves are a distortion of the masculine realms. Indeed, he is never able to see through the distortions directly associated with the father-figures; it is emblematic that, as we have seen, he is not even able to understand "Spapa." He never faces his true feelings for "the old man" Hermann Herzenbrecher—his boss, his authority figure, his father. He never understands why he is "oddly reluctant to part from *the old man* there on his *knees*" (p. 76, my italics). He never understands why the old man is the only one in *The Passion Artist* to use a first-person plural pronoun ("look what [the women] have done to us," p. 76). Hence, he misses the potential union here and Hermann Herzenbrecher remains her man and his heart breaker (Herzenbrecher). Vost never realizes his feelings for Gagnon, who yells, "Konrad don't go," as Vost heads off to La Violaine (p. 47). But Gagnon, who is "obsessive in his love of birds" (p. 19), is another father-figure; if Vost could have realized this, he would not have had to die. But because he cannot understand, when he leaves the feminine realms that he has come to terms with, he has nowhere to go. He is killed by Gagnon, by the male that he has failed to understand. As the depths of his unconscious finally burst forth, his very death becomes the last distortion of the sexual union he has struggled to suppress. "Through the smoke he saw that Gagnon's face and hands were covered with soot and that from his eyes, ears, mouth, nostrils, were streaming spurts and sudden clouds of feathers shining with all the colors of water thrown into the sun. Through the noise and smoke of the explosion he knew, as he fell, that the hole torn in his abdomen by Gagnon's shot was precisely the same as would have been opened in his flesh by the dog in the marsh" (p. 184).

We can see through the distortions. We can move beyond Vost as we come to terms with his death. The smoke here is the "white smoke" of his father's cigar (p. 81); "the dog in the marsh" is the dog with the wet pinkness of the docked tail (p. 7); and Gagnon himself, covered with feathers and soot, is the "dirty" phallus. Vost, then, is still obsessed with phallic threats, anality and castration, blacks and whites, guilt and expiation; indeed, his death is the ultimate expiation for the paternal phallic assault that Vost has never been able to face in undistorted form. But as we see through John Hawkes' subtle and ever so conscious distortions, we discover that Freud provides the "nomenclature" to illuminate *The Passion Artist* and that *The Passion Artist,* in turn, illuminates the darkest depths of mankind. And when we recall Guerard's claim that Hawkes' movement toward *Travesty* is a progression toward "a more conscious and a more suave psychology and art," we can see that *The Passion Artist* is most certainly a logical progression from *Travesty.*

Notes

1. Albert J. Guerard, "Introduction," *The Cannibal* by John Hawkes (New York: New Directions, 1949), p. x; Guerard, as quoted in "John Hawkes: A Longish View," *A John Hawkes Symposium,* ed. Anthony Santore and Michael Pocalyko (New York: New Directions, 1977), p. 3; Ibid.; Guerard, *"The Passion Artist* by John Hawkes," *The New Republic,* Vol. 181, No. 19 (Nov. 19, 1979), p. 29, respectively.

2. Ron Imhoff, "On *Second Skin," Mosaic,* 8, No. 1 (1974), p. 61.

3. Guerard, *The New Republic,* p. 29.

4. Thomas Le Clair, "The Novelists: John Hawkes," *The New Republic,* Vol. 181, No. 19 (Nov. 10, 1979), p. 28.

5. "Imagination, Fantasy, Dream," *The Personal Voice,* ed. John Hawkes et al. (Philadelphia: J. B. Lippincott, 1964), pp. 521–22.

6. Richard Yarborough, "Hawkes' *Second Skin," Mosaic,* 8, No. 1 (1974), p. 75.

7. "John Hawkes and Albert Guerard in Dialogue," *A John Hawkes Symposium,* ed. Anthony Santore and Michael Pocalyko (New York: New Directions, 1977), p. 23.

8. "The Landscape of the Imagination," transcript of a telediphone recording of BBC broadcast with John Hawkes and George Macbeth and others, November 2, 1966, p. 7.

9. Interview with John Enck, "John Hawkes: An Interview," *Wisconsin Studies in Comparative Literature,* 6, No. 2 (Summer 1964), p. 142; John Hawkes, *"The Floating Opera* and *Second Skin," Mosaic,* 8, No. 1 (1974), p. 20; Yarborough, p. 75; Interview with John Graham, "John Hawkes and His Novels," *The Massachusetts Review,* 7, No. 3 (Summer 1966), p. 452, respectively.

10. Sigmund Freud, *On Dreams,* trans. by James Strachey, The Norton Library Series (New York: W.W. Norton & Company, Inc., 1952), p. 44.

11. John Hawkes, "Charivari," *Lunar Landscapes* (New York: New Directions, 1969), p. 51.

12. Hawkes, *The Lime Twig* (New York: New Directions, 1961), p. 17.

13. John Kuehl, "An Interview with John Hawkes," *John Hawkes and the Craft of Conflict* (New Brunswick, Rutgers University Press, 1975), pp. 163–64.

14. Hawkes, *The Lime Twig,* p. 18.

15. Kuehl, p. 164 and Paul Emmett, "The Reader's Voyage Through Travesty," *Chicago Review,* 28, No. 2 (Fall 1976).

16. Guerard, *The New Republic,* p. 7.

17. Hawkes, *The Lime Twig,* p. 28.

18. Hawkes, *Travesty* (New York: New Directions, 1976), pp. 74 and 72 respectively.

19. Ibid., p. 102.

20. See Emmett, "The Reader's Voyage Through Travesty."

21. Hawkes, *The Passion Artist* (New York: Harper & Row, 1979), p. 84.

22. Ibid. Subsequent references to *The Passion Artist* are to the above edition and are cited by page numbers enclosed in parentheses.

23. For example, Guerard finds: "[Hawkes'] fictional world [to be one] in which violence, anxiety and regression are everyday norms, and our deepest fears and most anti-social impulses are dramatized fairly openly. Oral fantasies and castration fears, inversion, murder and mutilation, dread of impotence and dread of sex—these appear either manifestly or beneath thin disguises." ("The Prose Style of John Hawkes," *Critique,* 6 [Fall, 1963], p. 19.)

24. Freud, *The Standard Edition of the Complete Psychological Works of Sigmund Freud,* Vol. XV: *Introductory Lectures on Psychoanalysis I and II,* ed. and trans. by James Strachey (London: The Hogarth Press and The Institute of Psycho-Analysis, 1961), p. 155.

25. Ibid., Vol. XXII: *New Introductory Lectures on Psycho-Analysis and Other Works* (1964), p. 24.

26. Gertrude Jobes, *Dictionary of Mythology, Folklore, and Symbols* (New York: The Scarecrow Press, Inc., 1962), Part I, p. 101.

27. Freud, Vol. XVII: *An Infantile Neurosis and Other Works* (1955), pp. 198–200.

Stories My Father Never Told Me: On Hawkes's *Adventures in the Alaskan Skin Trade*

PATRICK O'DONNELL

For the reader used to John Hawkes's infamous eschewals of plot, character, and theme, the appearance of *Adventures in the Alaskan Skin Trade* in 1985 must have come as something of a shock. Even though Hawkes had been moving for years toward more traditional "story lines" in certain aspects of his work, the sprawling, loose-jointed collation of adventures, tall tales, dreams, and remembrances that comprise *Adventures in the Alaskan Skin Trade* seems unrecognizable. Gone, apparently, are the dense successions of surreal, erotic, or outlandishly parodic tableaux that characterize *Virginie: Her Two Lives* or *Death, Sleep, and the Traveler;* in their place, there is the domineering voice and the rambling, shaggy dog stories of "Uncle Jake" Deauville, adventurer and *raconteur extraordinaire.* One recognizes in the large canvas of Hawkes's Alaskan novel traces of Meville, Twain, Hemingway, and Faulkner, or more recently, Barth and Elkin; one hears echoes of Hawkes's previous novels, as if Hawkes were attempting to insert himself into the legendary traditions that these writers either effect or modify through parody. But where is the signature of Hawkes in this, his most clearly "autobiographical" fiction? As Christine Laniel has argued, *Adventures in the Alaskan Skin Trade* is "a reorchestration of [Hawkes's] previous texts, integrating the polar and the solar aspects of his work in a concentric motion, as well as the reinterpretation of these texts"; hence, the novel signifies "a return to the origin" of his own life (his childhood in Alaska) and his lifework.[1] Yet this "return" is also a divagation into the male traditions of the Great American Novel, into the discursively picaresque, as if John Hawkes wanted to separate himself from the original, distinct authorial presence he has inscribed and signed in contemporary American letters, as well as to reinscribe that presence, thus "intertextualizing" it. Negotiating this paradox will allow us to see how Hawkes, in this most "accessible" of his novels, limns authorial identity.

The review by Jack Beatty of *Adventures in the Alaskan Skin Trade,*

This essay was expressly written for this volume and is published here for the first time by permission of the author.

published in the *New York Times Book Review,* includes a photograph of the young John Hawkes with his father, John Clendennin Burne Hawkes, and his mother, Helen Ziefle Hawkes, on their boat in Alaska.[2] Led by the senior Hawkes who, in the wake of the depression, decided to go to Alaska "in order to speculate," the Hawkeses left the family home in Connecticut in search of wealth and adventure; the family remained together in Alaska for five years.[3] As Caryn James discovers in her interview with Hawkes that accompanies the review, the family triptych depicted in the photograph is repeated, with crucial differences, in the novel. Hawkes reveals to James that his father's nicknames were "Jack" (Hawkes's own nickname), and "Jake"; that John Hawkes, Sr., called Helen Hawkes "Chickie," just as Uncle Jake of *Adventures in the Alaskan Skin Trade* calls his wife "Sissy"; that the young Hawkes was often called "Jackie," close to the given name of Sunny (Jacqueline Burne Deauville) in the novel.

Hence, the fictional heroine bears the overdetermined name of the father/author in this translated genealogy: Jake, Jack, Jackie, Jacqueline, and the Hawkes family name of "Burne." Yet, as Hawkes explains, this is not a wholly "autobiographical" translation, for Sunny (whose male line of descent is proclaimed in *her* nickname) is female, and the Oedipal family triangle is thus skewed, displaced: "The novelist Jack Burne Hawkes became the autobiographical Jacqueline Burne Deauville—Sunny—because as a boy he had asthma, and his father 'treated me as one might treat a daughter . . . I couldn't use a male narrator because I'd get too close emotionally. I needed a narrator very different from myself. I tried to imagine the kind of woman I would want to be.' "[4] The gender switch in the translation of "life" into "art" is justified on the basis of the familiar Hawkesian criteria of detachment and the imagining of difference; the displacement of the father-son relation into a father-daughter relation, and the displacement of "father" into "uncle" is explained by Hawkes: "I put the 'Uncle' on to make it clear that the novel is about the absolute ruthless, unintended control a father exerts over a daughter. It's a simple Oedipal thing."[5] Thus, the genealogy of the novel itself—its origins in Hawkes's remembered and photographed life—is both overdetermined and displaced in relation to his life and, arguably, his art. These ruptures and detachments, I believe, are the sure signs of Hawkes's own artistry, in which the "Oedipal thing" both catalyzes and constrains the activity of the imagination that seeks to define its difference from or transcending of "life."

If we turn from autobiography to imaginative canon, we see that this novel, which seems so different from Hawkes's others, recapitulates them at several points. One might almost think of *Adventures in the Alaskan Skin Trade* as John Hawkes's LETTERS, the novel by John Barth in which all of Barth's other novels are, in some way, repeated and transformed. As in Barth's epistolary "meganovel," we can see in Hawkes's longest work a kind of parodic textual networking of his other fictions. For example, the entrance to Gamelands, Sunny's self-produced "male paradise," is a rough-hewn version of the entrance to the chateau (the "training school for women") of *Virginie:* "[the entrance is] an archway of two tall, thick cedar poles spanned by a fifteen-foot crescent of pine wood with Gamelands burned by a fiery iron in a large and flowery script across all the curving surface of that great slab of wood."[6] As much as this may "look" somewhat like an image from the previous novel, we are also compelled by this echoing to note the differences between them: Sunny's "chateau" is not in sunny France, but in frigid Alaska; its entrance is not made of iron, but of wood; and the person in charge of the women in this house of prostitution is, herself, a woman, not the lordly, chauvinistic Seigneur of *Virginie.* Smaller and more precarious authorial gestures and transpositions can be noted in the language of the description: the name of Sunny's establishment is inscribed by means of, if not with the name of, the removed autobiographical father ("burned," Burne); the flowery script made on the homely surface with a "fiery iron" reflects on the act of writing itself, which, characteristically for Hawkes, as seen in *The Passion Artist,* merges a controlled, ironic detachment with the expressions of passion and eroticism, and, in *Adventures in the Alaskan Skin Trade,* brings Hawkes's notorious exoticism (his "flowery script") home to roost in the rawness of Alaska and the unpolished form of the adventure novel.[7] In this single instance, writing and intertextual self-referencing are conflated with repetition and displacement in the description of the proscenium of Sunny's vocation, identity, and estate—an estate that is, here, written over with the variegated inscriptions of her author and his.

The intertextual process that lies behind the writing of *Adventures in the Alaskan Skin Trade* can be viewed as a form of self-consumption, in which Hawkes borrows from his own materials even as he "detaches" himself from them by writing a novel that mutates its origins, its textual "past," while speculating on the thematic issues of origins and the identity of the daughter in relation to the father. This involuted plagiarism or self-cannibalization takes recognizably comic turns in the novel, especially when we recall that, for Hawkes, as Donald J. Greiner argues, the comic arises out of a disjunction between external forms (which may bear superficial similarities to each other) and the monstrosities and grotesqueries—the utter heterogeneity—that those forms frame or conceal.[8] What are we to make of the heroine's nickname, Sunny, a homonym for Sonny, the name of Skipper's black sidekick in *Second Skin,* when we note the following distortions and lines of flight?: Sunny is not a son, but a daughter; she lives not in sunny but in polar regions; her father is not "Papa", but "Uncle"; Sonny plays Friday to a Crusoe-like Skipper whose alias (one of several) is "Papa Cue Ball"; between Sonny and Sunny (that is, between *Second Skin* and *Adventures in the Alaskan Skin Trade*) stands the "Papa" of *Travesty,* who annihilates himself, his daughter, and his son-in-law in a fiery crash.

In these examples, we have a genealogy of sorts, or a kinship system, which exists between novels as well as among characters, but in each case we see that the pattern of names and relations is overdetermined or slightly askew. The disparities reveal incongruities, psychic excesses, relational disorders. Within his utopian scheme, and despite Papa Cue Ball's egalitarian protestations, Skipper's Sonny must play Friday or Sambo to the tune of the master's fabulations; thus, the Papa-Sonny relation (in Hawkes, always an analogy for the creator-created relation) is shown up for its ruthlessness and mastery—a ruthlessness that turns "serious" in *Travesty*, where Papa, like Kronos destroys his own children. Analogously, in *Adventures in the Alaskan Skin Trade*, Sunny is dominated by a lugubrious father (her past, her identity *are* his stories) whose naming as "Uncle" suggests both the overdetermination (he is both father and uncle) and the diminution of the father's power (he is "only" an uncle). Paradoxically, the multiple father of *Adventures in the Alaskan Skin Trade*— multiple because he assimilates the roles of Skipper, Papa, father, uncle, and author—gains back with a vengeance what he loses in the displaced father-Sunny relation by virtue of his placement as "uncle" to "niece." In this movement, the ever-present threat or act of incest can be enacted under the guise of a slightly detached, uncle-like benevolence. Intertextuality and genealogical skewing in these three novels make possible both a "near" and "far" relation between author and work, and between father and progeny. Through these effects, we can observe a series of authorial homologies at work, where repetition (overdetermination of the same, narcissism, self-cannibalization, psychic incest) is posed against its opposite (installation of difference, distortion by means of textual echo, genealogical displacement, detachment). This is the dialectic of identity in Hawkes's fiction that *Adventures in the Alaskan Skin Trade* brings to the surface.

Identity, then—the quest for it, its nature, even its possibility—is the central concern of Hawkes's Alaskan novel. That this quest should take place in an "autobiographical" novel that tangles up (in the sense of, using Thomas Pynchon's phrase, a "knotting into") origins and genealogy, that intertwines the author's regress to his textual past with the return to his boyhood, that portrays the autobiographical subject of the male author as female, bears further scrutiny.

In his lengthy reflection on novelistic beginnings, Edward W. Said locates a "shift" in twentieth-century writing, where, he argues, we are compelled to "understand language as an intentional structure signifying a series of displacements. Words are the beginning sign of a method that replaces another method. The series being replaced is the set of relationships linked together by family analogy: father and son, the image, the process of genesis, a story. In their place stands: the brother, discontinuous concepts, paragenesis, construction. The first of these series is dynastic, bound to sources and origins, mimetic. The relationships holding in the second series are complementarity and adjacency; instead of a source we have the intentional beginning, instead of a story a construction."[9] We have already noted evidence of this movement or shift in *Adventures in the Alaskan Skin Trade:* the "dynastic" relation between father and son is doubly displaced in the relation between father and daughter, then in "uncle" and daughter; the mimeticism of the adventure novel is skewed by the discontinuities of intertextual distortion; autobiographical potential is converted to either a parody of autobiography or to the fabrication of an alternate identity (Hawkes: "I tried to imagine the kind of woman I would want to be"); Sunny's quest for the "source" (her father) results in what Said calls an "intentional beginning," the erection and maintenance of a constructed realm (Gamelands) or the projected Alaska, where she can say, "So here I am, an Alaskan woman feeling good in her skin in Alaska" (396). Borrowing from Said's terminology, *Adventures in the Alaskan Skin Trade* is a novel of "adjacency" in which "dynastic" or hierarchical relations between father and child, creator and created, prior and belated text are represented, transmuted, and questioned. In the type of conflation that marks all of Hawkes's fictions, text, author, and agency—always interrelated and, here, presented as part of a network of adjacent relations—become the vehicles for speculating upon the *constructed* nature of human identity.

In *Adventures in the Alaskan Skin Trade,* what might be called "identity-constructions" are cast in the form of the tall tale, which, of course, is an appropriate form for a novel of the Alaskan frontier; these are exactly the kinds of stories that the idealized father-adventurer is expected to tell to his enthralled progeny. In his illuminating book on autobiography and lying, Timothy Dow Adams argues that in autobiography "we have an imagined literary character, based on an actual person, who claims that his life is a metaphor for the author who created him in the first place"; hence (in a discussion of Gertrude Stein), "the fundamental device of her autobiography—pretending to be someone else writing about her own exploits—is a prime characteristic of the tall tale."[10] These qualities infest Uncle Jake's stories of his own exploits, eagerly awaited by his wife, daughter, and friends "back home." They are told as if the "real" father were a kind of cipher, a bystander who reacts with boyish amazement and enthusiasm to the adventures he recounts. In Hawkes's novel, these autobiographical tendencies are all the more entangled with the fictional foundations of identity, in that Uncle Jake, a literary stand-in for John Hawkes, Sr., tells his stories from the position of adjacency to his daughter (the daughter John Hawkes, Sr., never had) who is a literary stand-in for the author, John Hawkes. But of course the "real-life" author (now a palimpsest of tellers, tales, texts) is thoroughly displaced in this sequence. The autobiographical "truth" of the novel is established through the tales of the father, transmitted through so many removed, fictive screen-identities that "John Hawkes" becomes the signature attached to a text that projects unmoored facticity of a desired identity: "the kind of woman I would want to be."

What kind of woman is this? The answer lies partially in Sunny's retelling of the father's stories: a retelling that maintains the pretense that these stories come to us exactly as Uncle Jake related them. Many of them stand as parodic theatricalizations of what might be called stereotypical "gender stories." The stories range from Uncle Jake's rescuing of a group of lost hunters and killing a bear with his first shot to his performing *bricoleur* dental work on an Alaskan Indian chief in an isolated village. In all of these, Uncle Jake is the self-effacing male frontier hero who, like his American literary predecessors—Natty Bumpo, Ike McCaslin—paradoxically combines knowledge and experience of the wilderness with an assumed sexual innocence: "Uncle Jake was deaf to sexual messages, immune to emissions of sexual stimulation, and thought the Baranof Hotel [the rustic forerunner to Gamelands] was a place of comfort and good repute, a classic of northwest public lodgings comparable, in its way, to some small and highly recommended hotel resort town in France" (56–57). This sexual "deafness"—matched by the literal deafness of Robert McGinnis and his wife in the novel, and ironically commented on by Uncle Jake's origins in "Sound Beach, Connecticut" (156)—clearly delimits the father's power as oral storyteller, for if he turns a deaf ear to *this,* how can he hope to convey, in his tales, what Sunny figures as the very essence of voice, sound, life:

> Sex is my favorite word. It's a nice word, a cute word, a tiny green snake stiff in the mouth. It clips sibilance in the middle so that the little rush of air left to expire behind the teeth, in the pink pocket between plump tongue and shiny palate, becomes the most seductive sound there is, for those with an ear. It is anything but a mere hiss, since the air of it is regulated in pronunciation as by a valve, is a precise deposit and the same with every saying of the word. And yet it lingers, in that air, that little wind that could not flow were the tongue not engorged with shapeliness, bedded to the teeth, and its duration varies infinitely each time this word, my word, is voiced. . . . It's so short, the word, so small, with its vowel that hardly deserves the name, is so purely of the mouth that it cannot be said without invoking the ear. The smallness and closeness of the ear is drawn to that sound as to no other. No sooner does it say it—sex—than you want to put your ear to his mouth. Or hers. (27)

Here, Sunny articulates a form of orality patently absent from her father's adventure stories, stories that are legends, that are meant to be retold and passed on forever. Sunny's voicing of a word (an act) dies upon the lips as soon as it is spoken, but in its "variances," seductiveness, and endless incarnate "deposits," it bespeaks infinity and invites the ear of the other. The voiced word "sex" stands in stark contrast to the father's repeated stories, which are paternalistic and egotistical commemorations of pain and disaster. That Uncle Jake is innocent of or deaf to every principle of these stories—their origins in the sexed syllable, their "aboutness" as stories of the father's positioning as author— represents a shortcoming that belies their constructed and utterly denatured qualities: they are, in essence, as Sunny's dreams suggest, epitaphs, stories of the dead.

The story about her father that bears the most profound impact in the novel is the one that Sunny must tell herself, since Uncle Jake has disappeared —this time, forever—as the result of a partially failed quest for a mythic totem pole in the Alaskan wilderness. The totem pole, clearly a parodic and uproariously exaggerated version of the father's phallus (always virtual), is rumored to have been carved in the traditional manner save that at the top of the pole there is a bust of Abraham Lincoln, sculpted by the mysterious Suslota Indians in commemoration of, in Jake's words, "the freedom that had been granted to them and to all their kind in Alaska . . . to acknowledge their indebtedness to Mr. Lincoln" (367). Jake's fervent pursuit of what he conceives to be a national treasure is, of course, a transparently symbolic quest for his own male identity, as are all of his explorations, but he is disappointed, for the Lincoln totem pole turns out to be so corroded by time and the elements that it is on the verge of disintegration and impossible to move. The place where the fallen pole lies in Jake's "post-infernal paradise" (370) is a sacred grove of century-old totem poles, a characteristically Hawkesian scene of life and death commingling several elements. Lemmings, the suicidal animals whose lives typify the merging of sex and death, run over the fallen poles that seem half buried by the unexpectedly luxurious and colorful vegetation of the Suslotas' tribal home. Jake admires the vegetation in paradoxical terms. " 'All that mountain cranberry with its icy fruit, and the swarming of caribou-antler lichen,' " he notes with amazement of the new life grown up around the ruined totem-pole, and asks his companions, " 'Have you ever seen such a lovely bone-yellowish color . . . ?' " (369). Yet for Jake, the most remarkable thing about the Lincoln totem pole is the enduring quality of the black paint used to indicate Lincoln's clothing. In this scene of origins and ends, Jake (or rather, Sunny, telling Jake's story) discovers that this paternal totem, which figures the source of paternity, is corrupted and given over to temporality, that it incorporates death as well as life, and that, as something whose purpose is to stand out in the wilderness, to mark identity, freedom, nationhood, it is condemned by its own nature.

After this final adventure, Jake's disappearance as "father," or his commemoration in Sunny's dreams as the dead father on ice—like the Lincoln pole, preserved in his dilapidated state but immovable—is assured. With one last story to Sunny, the tale of his brother, Granny's, death as a pilot who crashed his plane into a French village cemetery during World War I, Jake (Sunny later discovers) jumps over the side of his ship with an anchor attached to his leg. This final tale of death and displacement (starring Sunny's dead uncle bearing the nickname of a grandmother) seals the fate of the dynastic impulse that has been so thoroughly undermined in this novel, just as the phallus, that rule of relation existing between fathers and sons and daughters, has been shown up for its impotency and decrepitude. And with this, one sees that the contents of Jake's stories, like the ends of his adventures, are deathly and phantasmic, more remarkable for what they elide in their "innocence" than anything else.

Yet Sunny's story, which may be said to be *Adventures in the Alaskan Skin Trade* itself—her father's stories retold and conflated with her own—preserves as well as deconstructs paternal origins and the rule of the phallus. In other terms, her father's voice, as well as the emblematization of paternal desire (comically, here, the preservation of the phallus as a "national monument") survive, but in a parodic or mutated form. They survive in Sunny's periodic nightmares in which she envisages her father, "the King of the North," both frozen and decomposing: "He rears back, throws back his head, looks up, and there before my eyes he freezes. One long pink cheek turns black, hangs down, the right hand blackens. He loses three black fingers from the right hand. . . . Slowly he lifts [his right arm] high above his head, and now the thick black hair is white with frost, the happy eyes are lit with pain, on the last black frozen finger of the right hand the Deauville family ring is a lump of gold" (18–19). We can hear the paternal desire for origins and order in the symmetrical intonations of Sunny's recollections: her grandfather is one of nine brothers who "rode to the hounds" at the ancestral home in Chantilly (throughout much of the novel, Sunny wishes to leave Alaska and return to France); Sunny employs nine women at Gamelands; there are 900 Indians in Juneau, Alaska; there are nine coats of lacquer on Sunny's jeep. Yet Sunny's jeep may be seen, in the mode of adjacency, as a "masculine" version of the fetishized Stutz Bearcats of her father's family in Connecticut; her "girls" are aggressive, erotically-charged redactions of the nine brothers whose sexual dynamism, diverted into fox hunts, has exhausted itself (along the male line) in Uncle Jake, a suicide without male heirs.

Above all, there is Sunny's own totem pole erected at the entrance to Gamelands, "carved to [her] design": "It rose a full thirty feet into the air, and except for the traditional winged creatures of Indian lore which divided it into quarters, and except for the greater-than-life figure surmounting it, the entire totem pole was entwined with the bodies of nude women. Around and around my totem pole they went, snaking their way upwards, climbing on each other's shoulders, hanging on to the wings of the sacramental birds, hugging the cruel beaks" (108–9). The larger-than-life figure at the top is, of course, a bust of Uncle Jake, pointing, with his wooden gun "north to adventure" (109). In this complex image, a narrative in itself emblematic of the whole of *Adventures in the Alaskan Skin Trade,* the father remains in the traditional dynastic position atop the pole, but the pole has been refigured (and brought back to life) by means of an ambivalent eroticism that can be read in a number of ways, or in terms of a number of adjacent, conflicting stories. Is Jake, who Sunny states "was afraid of women" (109), the source of eroticism in this image, or of impotency (the wooden gun) about to be overwhelmed by "feminine" desire? Is the potential for *jouissance* depicted here undermined by the fact that it is figured by a "Sunny" in a novel by John Hawkes where, clearly, the "male imagination" can only recast itself even as it is being limned? Does the representation of eroticism (what Uncle Jake fears)—its authorization via the emblem of the pole, its legitimation in Gamelands—rest upon the principle of pleasure, or pain (the women "hugging the cruel beaks" of the birds, conceivably hawks)? The answers to these questions are negotiated here and in Hawkes's canon in general; most pointedly in this novel, the mutation or deformation of the father's story into its alterities serves to sever them—but not completely—from their origins.

But *Adventures in the Alaskan Skin Trade* is also the story of the daughter's identity and desire, at least as it can be told in terms of the transformation of the story of paternal desire, though the daughter's story can never be totally "other," unsubjected to tone deafness: not here, not in Hawkes.[11] Hawkes's self-conscious rendering of this dilemma comes not just in the epicenic characterization of Sunny, but most vividly in the figure of Martha Washington, who Sunny comes to recognize as "my own father reincarnated in the form of a woman" (303). As her name comically indicates, Martha is a female variation of what Abraham Lincoln represents to Uncle Jake, but in dynastic terms, prior to Lincoln, she is "the mother of our country." She relates her own version of a hair-raising wilderness initiation rite told in a mocking parody of the Hemingway deadpan style (a parody made more explicit in Martha's retelling of one of Hemingway's Nick Adams stories, "Indian Camp"), and she claims that she is a feminist. In brief, Martha inserts herself into the stories of adventure and paternal desire as the incarnation of difference, which is, in truth, a repetition of the same. She provides what might be termed the literalized alternative to Uncle Jake, but in Hawkes's vision, paragenetic stories can only be related in the form of echo, mutation, deformation. Martha, then, is the mirror to Uncle Jake that reflects back the absurdities and distortions of his own image.

Sunny, the figure of the woman Hawkes would like to be, survives as an excess of voice her father's suicide, and Martha Washington's intrusions and departure. After the tellings and retellings of the paternal story and its parodic mimesis in the tales of Martha Washington, Sunny remains as a form of vocal residue, "comfortable in her skin" (for Hawkes, the characteristic image of the scene of inscription) in Alaska. We can note the presence of this figural residue or excess—that which escapes the autobiographical law of self-replication and self-preservation purveyed through the illusion of mirroring difference—in such passages as Sunny's meditations on the word "sex," or in the scenes in which she scandalously defiles the male totem. One startling instance of her defilement of origins takes place in an Indian burial ground, where Sunny incorporates into her own body and voice the deathly but attenuated relic of male identity: "Suddenly I ran the middle three fingers of my left hand lightly around the surface of one of the skull's eye sockets and, raising my eyes to Robert McGinnis's, stuffed my fingers into my mouth and licked them clean of the soot which was all that remained of the smoke that once had been the dead man's flesh" (214). In such scenes, male ancestry (or all that is left of it, smoke and ash) is transmitted, but figuratively, the paternal desire for replication through story or gender is changed, embodied as eroticized impulse and afterthought, even as the romantic grandeur of that desire is deflated. Sunny's decision not to leave Alaska for an imaginary sunny France (a place to which, autobiographically speaking, Hawkes has always been drawn) comes as the result of the discovery that her father's enslavement to "totemic desire" is so great that he is compelled to kill himself when it is not fulfilled: a conclusion to which all of his stories run. As the epicenic presence behind all of these stories, Sunny remains—though only as that which, like the word "sex," comes in the form of a paradox, escaping vocalization as it is being voiced. In her narrative, Sunny incorporates the father's remains and converts them into stories all too given over to or robbed of their diminished origins. For Hawkes this paradox, conveyed through the deformation of the paternal story—repeating it with parodic difference, intertextually skewing it, compounding it with its alternate, adjacent versions—marks the desire to abrogate the iron bond between identity and gender in a novel that is also an unauthorized life story bound to replicate its inheritance.

Notes

1. Christine Laniel, "John Hawkes's Return to the Origin," in *Facing Texts: Encounters between Contemporary Writers and Critics,* ed. Heide Ziegler (Durham: Duke University Press, 1988): 243, 222.

2. Jack Beatty, "Uncle Jake and the Mosquito-Crazed Prospector," *New York Times Book Review,* 29 September 1985, 9.

3. Patrick O'Donnell, "Life and Art: An Interview with John Hawkes," *Review of Contemporary Fiction,* 3, no. 3 (1983): 107.

4. Caryn James, sidebar to Jack Beatty, "Uncle Jake and the Mosquito-Crazed Prospector," 9.

5. Ibid. Laniel, too, notes the autobiographical overlay substantiated in James's interview, and defines the displacement of "uncle" to "father" as an example of "a slight difference within identity, by the dialectics of the Same and the Other" ("John Hawkes' Return to the Origin," 239). I quite agree; however, distinct from Laniel, I shall be concentrating on how this "difference within identity" is produced by gender roles and gender shifts in the novel, or between the novel and life.

6. John Hawkes, *Adventures in the Alaskan Skin Trade* (New York: Simon and Schuster, 1985), 25. All future references are to this edition and will be cited parenthetically in the text.

7. For an intricate discussion of the scenographies of writing in Hawkes's fiction, see Marc Chénetier, " 'The Pen and the Skin': Inscription and Cryptography in John Hawkes's *Second Skin,*" *Review of Contemporary Fiction,* 3, no. 3 (1983): 167–77.

8. See Donald J. Greiner, *Comic Terror: The Novels of John Hawkes* (Memphis: Memphis State University Press, 1978), especially pp. 1–28.

9. Edward W. Said, *Beginnings: Intention and Method* (Baltimore: Johns Hopkins University Press, 1975), 66.

10. Timothy Dow Adams, *Telling Lies in Modern American Autobiography* (Chapel Hill: University of North Carolina Press, 1990): 35, 37.

11. Nor, perhaps, can it be told anywhere. See Lynda Zwinger, *Fathers, Daughters, and the Novel* (Madison: University of Wisconsin Press, forthcoming) for important discussions of how the story of heterosexual desire is always a version of the father's desiring of the daughter, and of the daughter's being made to think that she desires him in a seemingly different version.

The Photographer's Sight and the Painter's Sign in *Whistlejacket*

Donald J. Greiner

Early in *Whistlejacket,* Michael, a self-assured fashion photographer and the primary narrator, indirectly describes himself as "an old Impressionist and his erotic flowers."[1] John Hawkes has long understood the connection between impressions and sexuality, and thus it should come as no surprise that a painting of a horse, the combination of strength and grace, dominates the erotic atmosphere of *Whistlejacket.* Initiated readers will recall Hawkes's earlier novel *The Lime Twig* (1961) in which the great racehorse Rock Castle personifies the dreamworld of forbidden sex and violent death. But whereas *The Lime Twig* is a sophisticated parody of the detective novel, *Whistlejacket* is a metaphysical thriller that probes both the unreliability of signs and the uncertainty of seeing.

Hawkes frames this most postmodern of themes in a technique of self-reflexivity in order to investigate the relationships among seer, sign, and meaning. The issue is announced on the first page when Michael confidently begins his narrative with a statement that the reader immediately questions: "Beauty is not in the eye of the beholder, as they say, but in the lens of the camera" (3). Confronted with this opinion, the reader may object that the eye directs the camera. Michael thinks otherwise. A man who loves not women but woman, he is a voyeur of the beautiful, a disturbed witness who sees himself as "innocent though not entirely pure" (3). In a sense, then, *Whistlejacket* is an arrangement of what Michael calls "photographic scenes," staged, created, and developed by his lens-pointing eye. His point of view, which controls the first section ("The Photographer") and the third section ("The Fox Hunter") of the novel, is the camera; except for the second section ("The Horse Painter"), *Whistlejacket* is the photograph album that Michael offers to the reader, who becomes, on finishing the novel, Michael's accomplice—another voyeur. Hawkes's refusal to supply transitions among the three sections is a primary sign of his intent to distinguish photographer from painter.

One need not stress that Hawkes has long been considered a master of American postmodernism, a writer who has consistently exposed the limitations of the realistic novel and the epistemological framework it expresses.

This essay was expressly written for this volume and is published here for the first time by permission of the author.

Aware of this point, then, one appreciates how, after a first reading, *Whistlejacket* may be discussed as Hawkes's intricately constructed contrast between Michael, the contemporary exemplar of postmodern art, and the painter George Stubbs, the eighteenth-century exemplar of representational art. In such a discussion, Michael would understand that there is no single reality but only signs, language, surface realities. In this sense *Whistlejacket* would seem to probe the mind of the postmodern artist who denigrates painters like Stubbs as being little more than semiotically retrograde draftsmen who struggled to make their lucid paintings represent the real.

Whistlejacket may indeed be read this way, but I want to propose the opposite because I believe that the tone of the book complicates such a reading. Despite one's appreciation of Michael's conflict with sight and sign, the novel encourages laughter at the photographer's pretensions and admiration for the painter's discipline. Stubbs is shown to be the true artist, because as a painter he understands that creation results more from seeing an object by first deconstructing and then reconstructing it than it does from striving for only accurate descriptions of surfaces. In *Whistlejacket* Hawkes may be taking a more conservative stance than one would expect from the innovative author of such postmodern classics as *Second Skin* (1964) and *Travesty* (1976). Postmodern difficulty with the nature of signs is one thing, but Campbell soup cans replicating Campbell soup cans, as it were, is quite another. Hawkes is not so cynical about the power of language and imagination.

I

The two words essential to Michael's life and art are "act and image," the tools of the photographer's trade. One suspects that Michael has compromised his life and art to the degree that he prefers artificial arrangement to living act.[2] Describing himself as "photographer, biographer, person," he unwittingly exposes the hierarchy of his commitments: being a person is last (6). Like a novelist determined to educate the reader of his text, however, he instructs his fellow voyeurs, his readers, that although a "procuress" supplies his female models, he never substitutes the word "shoot" for "to photograph." Violence is not his style, but peering is his obsession. He glories in the shadowed corridor, the furtive glance, and he boasts of his lack of culpability: "Natural light and dark secrets are in the realm of innocence, the beat of a horse's hooves, the sounds of a silent photographer curling himself about his subject" (7).

Proclaiming his virtue, insisting on the clarity of the voyeur's vision, Michael prepares his narrative—his album—to reveal to the reader the mystery of a violent death at the estate named Steepleton. Hal Van Fleet—owner of Steepleton, Master of Foxhounds, husband of Alexandra—is found dead at age sixty-two. How did he die? At Hal's slowly paced, all-but-choreographed funeral, Michael can think of nothing except how he would have staged the scene for the camera. The mourners are no more than models for the arrangement of his text: "The pursuit quickens when I find myself among those who do not wish to be seen. They are the ones I most want to see" (16). One all but hears the shutter click. The irony is that the reader watches Michael even while the photographer thinks he hides behind the camera to see others.

Hawkes's conceit in *Whistlejacket* is the contrast between photography and painting. Both are narratives, as Michael understands when he agrees to Alexandra's request that he "do" Hal Van Fleet's biography in snapshots while she plans a memorial fox hunt in her dead husband's honor. Can immortality be achieved through photographs? Do signs reveal essence? Such ambiguities concern Hawkes but not Michael: "I said that everything I saw was in a sense the same" (43). The text of his life is the arrangement of his models, and he luxuriates in descriptions of artificially produced light and mechanically staged poses. Preferring to glimpse life through a lens, to deflect the immediacy of experience in an effort to exert control, he even positions himself in restaurants so as to spy on other patrons via the mirror at the bar. Proud of his art, Michael claims the freedom of inspiration—"choice means variable, variable means discontinuity, discontinuity destroys hierarchy"—but only for the objects of his voyeurism (50). For himself, the master of narrative angle, logic has to lead to truth. His narcissism is clear. "It is the photographer who counts and not his models," he confides, because he is convinced that a photographer's vision peers far beyond the ordinary sight of the mundane viewer (57).

But does it? In the first section of *Whistlejacket,* one has no reason to doubt Michael except for the usual reservation about the reliability of first-person narrators. Hawkes knows this, of course, understands that narrative engages readers, and prepares the primary sign in the novel as he shifts focus in the second section from Michael the photographer to George Stubbs the painter. Hawkes's subject is the artist's urge to determine the essence beneath the surface, "the real horse beneath the false color," as signified by the presence of Stubbs's famous eighteenth-century painting of Whistlejacket, now housed at Steepleton (18). This sign points to the question that the reader has asked of Michael all through part one of his album: What happened to Hal?

Although this puzzle lurks at the center of the Van Fleets, the soul of the family is more aesthetic than mysterious. Paintings, including "copies more enticing than the originals," (71) have been the passion of past masters of Steepleton, but no painting dominates the scene more than Stubbs's portrait of Whistlejacket. Since the philosophical issue that frames *Whistlejacket* is the reliability of sight and signification, Hawkes turns in part two of the novel from Michael's languorous album to Stubbs's disciplined life. It is a daring strategy that first appeared in Hawkes's canon when he merged fictional character and historical personage in *The Cannibal* (1949). In the earlier novel, however, the connection between history and fiction is abstract; in *Whistlejacket* Hawkes devotes an entire section to Stubbs. One appreciates Hawkes's control of tone, sign, and language when he reveals that Stubbs vowed "never to paint what he saw outside unless he had seen the inside first." Stubbs's insistence on dissecting "dead horses for love of the living bodies he painted" is the metaphorical credo of all true artists—novelists or otherwise—who would be more than voyeurs (73).

II

Readers who desire a scholarly account of George Stubbs (1724–1806) to compare with Hawkes's fictionalization of the painter's career should examine the work of Basil Taylor.[3] Taylor's book includes a color plate of Whistlejacket that communicates the menace that Hawkes intends this imposing sign to convey. Painted in 1761–62, the portrait measures ten feet, eight inches by eight feet, six inches, so the horse in the picture is life-size. Stubbs painted Whistlejacket rearing on hind legs, eyes showing fear and rage. Other than the horse, the portrait has no details, no human or natural background. This curious feature may be explained by reference to Whistlejacket's first owner, Charles, second marquis of Rockingham. According to tradition, Rockingham's original intention was to commission other artists to fill in the setting with a figure of George III and a landscape, once Stubbs had completed his work. Apparently, however, Rockingham was so pleased with the painting —which *is* imposing and imperial—that he decided against the additions.

As Taylor concedes, biographical information and supporting documentation about George Stubbs are scarce and thus problematical.[4] What is certain is that Stubbs came to London from Lincolnshire in 1759 at age 35, that he lived at 24 Somerset Street, that he died there with little notice in 1806, and that he was buried in a now unidentifiable grave. His achievement fell into obscurity for the next two generations, and even today, reports Taylor, historians have difficulty placing him in their reconstructions of the age. The point that both Taylor and Hawkes stress is that Stubbs never fit neatly within the then prevailing artistic tastes and standards. Taylor's assessment is succinct: "Although his contemporary reputation irked him, Stubbs did not seek to acquire a greater prestige by any permanent or radical adjustment of his art to the most influential taste and opinion; he cannot be presented as a rebel or a romantic outsider. Simply, his identity as a painter and his intellectual purposes were too strong to be adapted or disguised" (Taylor, 7). Stubbs was neither visionary nor spiritually wounded artistic hero but was a straightforward man of determined will and clear sight. Taylor speaks of "resilience and integrity," and his essay documents that Stubbs's originality was not suggestiveness but meticulousness (Taylor, 8). Never a neutral observer, Stubbs was committed to the concept of reality. Michael, on the other hand, pretends to be a neutral seer, but the reader soon realizes that Hawkes's photographer longs for narrative closure, that he elects to be a prisoner in the house of signs, where each signification has an undisputed meaning.

Aware of the gaps in Stubbs's life story, Hawkes fills in the biographical blanks with imaginative details. Significantly, Hawkes's reconstruction of Stubbs indirectly links him to the eighteenth-century British novelist Laurence Sterne who, like Hawkes, deconstructed the realistic novel. For example, Stubbs's interest in anatomy resulted first in his tutoring medical students and later in a commission from Dr. John Burton to illustrate Burton's *Essay towards a Complete New System of Midwifery* (1751). Burton was Sterne's model for Dr. Slop in *Tristram Shandy* (1760–67). Thus Hawkes's experiments with narrative in *Whistlejacket* are placed in a historical context that reaches back to one of the first great innovators of the novel.

To prepare the illustrations for Dr. Burton's book, Stubbs secretly dissected the corpse of a woman who had died in childbirth. One needs to remember that many people in the eighteenth century would have judged etchings of a child in the womb to be close to witchcraft. Apparently Hawkes researched what little is known of Stubbs's life, for his account of the artist stealthily engaging in the anatomical investigation of humans and horses is corroborated by Taylor.[5] According to Taylor, the preliminary dissections and drawings for Stubbs's *The Anatomy of the Horse* (not published until 1766) took place in the isolated village of Horkstow so that Stubbs could escape the "vile renown" he had attracted with his previous inquiries.[6] In Horkstow he devised the necessary tackle for hoisting dead horses into lifelike positions, anatomized the carcasses for study, and put them back together in art.[7] His only reliable assistant was Mary Spencer, the woman he lived with until he died (and a companion far more trustworthy than Alexandra Van Fleet).

Stubbs's arrival in London generally coincided with the popularization of fox hunting and racing as the activities of wealthy young men, many of whom had political connections.[8] Such patrons as Rockingham, the duke of Richmond, and Sir Henry Bridgeman made Stubbs's reputation, for they recognized his genius in representational painting. Although he is generally unknown today, in the 1760s Stubbs was, says Taylor, "the most talented, responsive and versatile interpreter of such an iconography of rural life; his work should be seen in this context and not regarded—as it has been formerly—as one unusually refined and distinguished manifestation of sporting art" (Taylor, 12). His fortunes changed for the worse in the late 1770s and 1780s, for his subject matter and style did not conform to the popular taste as decreed by the Royal Academy.[9] Committed to, even obsessed by anatomical study, Stubbs insisted on an art of representation—on, in other words, the sign that the eye sees. But being intimate with the interior, he could portray the exterior with such precision that it seemed to be revealed from the inside out. Stubbs's dedication to anatomy signified his commitment to a reality that goes beyond complacent acceptance of the sign that one first sees when viewing an object. His paintings are lucid and vital, far more than mere photographic reporting, far beyond mechanical reproductions of fact, because he did not accept a single, empirical model of representation. His semiotically sophisticated re-presentations attempt to show the essence of his subjects, to the extent that his many paintings of horses may be viewed as an effort to see The Horse, an enterprise he likely accepted as impossible but necessary. Stubbs's genius was his ability to combine "scientific knowledge and artistic empathy," as he did in the portrait of Whistlejacket (Taylor, 24). Moral judgments and sentimental considerations were extraneous.

One understands Hawkes's sympathy with Stubbs's failure to be embraced by the mainstream. Henry Fuseli's contemporary comment is to the point: Stubbs's "skil in comparative anatomy never suggested to him the propriety of style in forms" (Taylor, 47). Fuseli wrote these words around 1810, four years after the horse painter's death, but they still describe the always conservative academy reaction to artists who break the mold, who reject the very concept of a "propriety of style." Stubbs and Hawkes are such artists.[10] Michael is not.

In the remarkable middle section of *Whistlejacket,* Hawkes peers beyond the signification of Stubbs's massive text of the horse to investigate context in a manner foreign to Michael. Describing both himself and the painter, Hawkes defines the true artist as a seer who moves from "bone and soul to finished figure" (82). To make his point, he re-creates four key moments from Stubbs's life: the dissection of the woman who died in childbirth; the painting of Lady Nelthorpe's seven-year-old son; the dissection of horses; and, most dramatic of all, Whistlejacket's panic at seeing his own portrait.[11]

Hawkes's own signification of Whistlejacket's violent reaction follows art historian Constance-Anne Parker's account and confirms her description of the stallion as "a difficult horse, and at times vicious, and almost unmanageable."[12] To illustrate, she reconstructs the extraordinary moment when Stubbs was completing the portrait. Left in the care of a stable boy while posing for the painter, the horse bolted when brought face-to-face with the canvas. He screamed, reared, and lashed out with his forelegs. Trying to control the enraged animal, the stable boy was lifted off his feet and was rescued only when Stubbs beat Whistlejacket with his palette and turned him away from the painting. The union of construction and destruction is clear to those who can read the signs. Michael can't read. What happened to Hal?

III

With an unremarked irony to signal the contrast, Hawkes shifts from Stubbs's paintings to Michael's photographs in the novel's final section. By this point in *Whistlejacket,* one suspects the truth about Hal's death, for one has seen the signs in the portrait of the rearing horse. Thus the careful reader joins Stubbs and Hawkes as artists who rework signs to reveal a reality. Michael must learn, on the other hand, to anatomize the text, and if he is to succeed he will have to see beyond the gloss of his immaculately arranged surfaces.

He has a hard time doing so. Selecting old photos of Hal for a pictorial narrative is one thing, but complying with Alexandra's additional request is quite another: She wants the signs of her dead husband to be Michael's own artwork. Hawkes's comic twist is that Michael must now take photographs of photographs. That is, rather than create new signs, he duplicates old ones. Such replication is surely postmodern, an act that one would expect Hawkes to applaud. But Hawkes understands what Michael misses. Instead of accepting these re-presentations as no more than additional signs, as perhaps truths but not Truth, Michael becomes convinced that the signs he constructs tell all. Stubbs's investigation of interiors in order to see exteriors illustrates an artistic power far beyond the photographer's studied voyeurism.

Placing Michael in the darkroom, Hawkes suggests his own intertextual links with Michelangelo Antonioni's classic film *Blow-Up* and the Julio Cortázar short story on which the film is based. In both movie and novel, a fashion photographer goes from negative to negative as he works his way toward a murder. But Antonioni's antihero dodges the implications of the signs, while Hawkes's narrator assembles the pieces of the text as best he can. Michael understands the position of the postmodern novelist, that the complexities of language are more important than the conventions of plot. In 1965, for example, Hawkes defined the "enemies" of the novel as plot, character, setting, and theme.[13] Michael claims agreement with Hawkes's provocative opinion: "The photograph for which the artist strives has no story. Story is the anathema of the true photographer. Narrative, dull narrative, of interest only to those who sit or stand at the frame's center or lurk at its edges trying to squeeze themselves into the picture, is what the chronicler of the family hopes to preserve" (106). In other words, conventional readers require traditional plot. Standing at the edge of the tale, they try to squeeze themselves into the text by personalizing the significations with story.

Yet for all his supposed sophistication about narrative, Michael succumbs to looking for coherent plot in fractured signs. As he rephotographs and enlarges Alexandra's scattered snapshots of Hal, he begins to justify interpretations of the symbols caught on film. Unlike Stubbs, who probed from the inside, Michael imposes from without. Thus a photograph—a sign—of teenage Hal at a formal dance with a girl whose corsage is not crushed becomes for Michael proof that Hal rejects his date by refusing to dance with her long enough to squeeze the gardenia. Michael's evidence convinces so long as one accepts his vision, but one always suspects his readings because of his disclaimer about narrative. Boasting that the true artist abjures plot, he undercuts his own words when he imposes a univocal reading on a multivocal text. Unlike Stubbs, he cannot paint the horse without the background.

What happened to Hal? Many things, but Michael insists on just one. His metaphysical need distorts his claim to postmodern art. Unable to rest easy with absence-as-presence, with what he sees in the context of what he does not see, he finds "wit and mystery despite banality" (109). Through his photographer-as-seer, Hawkes deconstructs readers who are so obsessed with deconstruction that they inadvertently see yet another definitive reading while trying to uncover the gaps in the text. Disparaging narrative on the one hand, Michael asks on the other, "Where is the narrative?" (111). Hawkes makes sure that Michael's plots for each text—each photograph—are exciting, exhilarating, and exuberant, the signs of mystery. Both novelist and photographer are skilled storytellers, but with this difference: Hawkes sees the interior whereas Michael merely invents it.

What happened to Hal? Hawkes finds ambiguities; Michael claims *the* truth. One can imagine the photographer's joy, then, when he finally connects Hal's unruly stallion, Marcabru, with the sign that has been in front of him all along, Stubbs's *Whistlejacket*. His need to photograph Marcabru directly instead of relying on photographs of photographs simultaneously brings him closer to the horse and farther from the painter. Stubbs knew all he could know about his subjects, but Michael resorts to taking pictures of the dead Hal's clothes and personal effects in an effort to see the depths beneath the skin. And so although the photographer is shocked, the reader is not surprised when an unknown intruder switches the negatives of Marcabru with Michael's while Michael wastes time on Hal's clothes. Not Michael's futile surface signs but someone else's snapshots hold the clue to the echoing question in *Whistlejacket:* What happened to Hal?

The answer is love and death. But Hawkes's interest all along has been in a different query: What happened to Michael? The answer to this question is more resonant: language and imagination. At the end of the novel, the photographer is as much a pawn of the erotic women at Steepleton as he is of his faith in the sight of the camera. Alexandra tells him "You can believe what you see," but she knows that she sees with more vision than he does (148). *Whistlejacket* ends with the words "Shall we look?," a question that both invites readers into the text and warns them about the ambiguity of signs.

John Hawkes has consistently advocated the primacy of verbal and psychological coherence over the conventions of plot. His mastery of this postmodern technique was evident as early as *The Cannibal,* in which the narrative structure illustrates his position that history is not linear and orderly but discontinuous and absurd. With *Second Skin,* however, he began more forcefully to unify technique and theme, with the result that the difficulties of sight and sign became the primary preoccupations of the fumbling narrator and his self-reflexive tale. *Whistlejacket* extends this interest in a daring new way. By including a fictional reconstruction of the historical figure George Stubbs, Hawkes simultaneously undercuts his confident narrator's text and deconstructs the narrative that relies on plot. Freeing the novel from conventions, he liberates the reader to see beyond the traditional staples of the genre and to dissect the possibilities of fiction itself.

Notes

1. John Hawkes, *Whistlejacket* (New York: Weidenfeld & Nicolson, 1988), 48. Subsequent references will be cited parenthetically in the text.

2. Another photographer, Hugh, has a similar problem in Hawkes's *The Blood Oranges* (1971).

3. Basil Taylor, *Stubbs* (London: Phaidon, 1971). Subsequent references will be cited parenthetically in the text.

4. The principal contemporary documents pertaining to Stubbs's life are the biographical notes compiled by Ozias Humphrey during conversations with the painter in the late eighteenth century. But Taylor warns that these recollections lack precision and that any account of Stubbs must remain "a speculative sketch" (Taylor, 8).

5. Stubbs's father was a tanner. One assumes that the painter grew up at ease with the sights, smells, and carcasses of the tannery.

6. "To conduct anatomical research involving dissection was then to invite criticism and distrust" (Taylor, 10).

7. See Constance-Anne Parker, *Mr. Stubbs the Horse Painter* (London: J. A. Allen, 1971), 19–20, for an account of how Stubbs dissected horses.

8. The Jockey Club, for example, was founded around 1750.

9. Stubbs was not elected to the Royal Academy until 1780, but he left the organization three years later following a dispute.

10. That Lord and Lady Nelthorpe, two of Stubbs's first patrons, were named John and Sophia (the names of Hawkes and his wife) symbolizes the affinity between Stubbs, the master of painting, and Hawkes, the master of words.

11. For a reproduction of the Whistlejacket Room at Wentworth Woodhouse (owned by Earl Fitzwilliam), see Parker, *Mr. Stubbs the Horse Painter,* 66. In the photograph of this huge (40-foot-square) room, Stubbs's painting of the horse dominates the perspective.

12. Parker, *Mr. Stubbs the Horse Painter,* 65.

13. John Enck, "John Hawkes: An Interview," *Wisconsin Studies in Contemporary Literature* 6 (1965): 141–55.

Index

♦